The American Discovery of Ancient Egypt: Essays

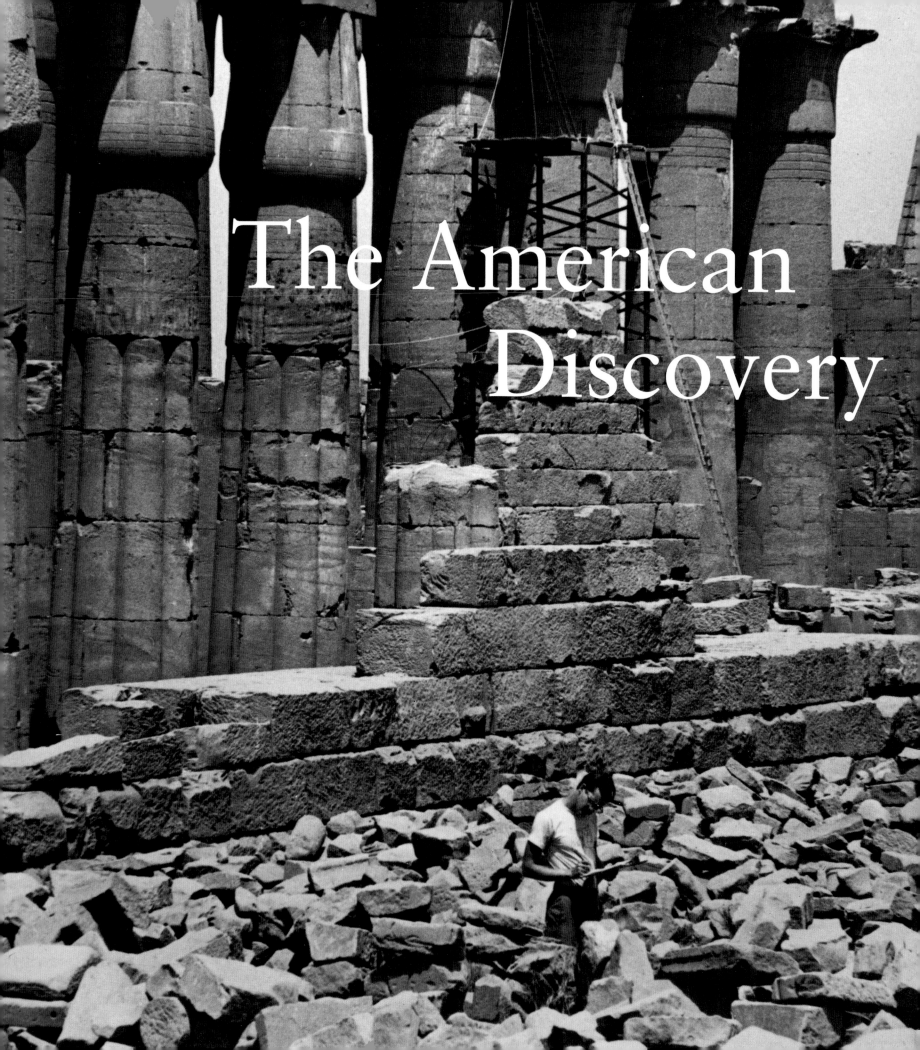

The American
Discovery

of Ancient Egypt
Essays

Edited by

Nancy Thomas

With essays by

James P. Allen, Dorothea Arnold, Lanny Bell,
Robert S. Bianchi, Edward Brovarski,
Richard A. Fazzini, Timothy Kendall, Peter Lacovara,
David O'Connor, Kent R. Weeks

LOS ANGELES COUNTY MUSEUM OF ART • AMERICAN RESEARCH CENTER IN EGYPT
Distributed by HARRY N. ABRAMS, INC., PUBLISHERS

Published by the
Los Angeles County Museum of Art
5905 Wilshire Boulevard
Los Angeles, California 90036

Distributed worldwide in 1996 by
Harry N. Abrams, Incorporated, New York,
A Times Mirror Company

Library of Congress Catalog Card Number:
95-079852

ISBN: 0-8109-6313-2 (cloth)

COVER: James Henry Breasted and team
surveying the temple of Ramesses II at Abu
Simbel during the University of Chicago's
first epigraphic survey, 1905–6.

TITLE PAGE: Raymond Johnson, staff member
of the Epigraphic Survey of the Oriental
Institute of the University of Chicago, collating
loose blocks at Luxor temple.

RIGHT: Staff member of the Epigraphic
Survey of the University of Chicago working
at Karnak temple.

*Printed in Hong Kong through
Global Interprint*

This book was published in conjunction
with the exhibition *The American Discovery
of Ancient Egypt*. A catalogue of the exhibition is included in a companion volume,
The American Discovery of Ancient Egypt,
published by the Los Angeles County
Museum of Art in 1995 and distributed by
Harry N. Abrams, Inc.

Exhibition Itinerary

LOS ANGELES COUNTY MUSEUM OF ART
November 5, 1995–January 21, 1996

THE SAINT LOUIS ART MUSEUM
February 29–May 27, 1996

THE INDIANAPOLIS MUSEUM OF ART
July 13–September 29, 1996

This exhibition was co-organized by the
Los Angeles County Museum of Art and the
American Research Center in Egypt.
Exclusive sponsorship for this exhibition has
been provided through a generous grant from
The May Department Stores Company and
its Robinsons-May division in Los Angeles,
its Famous-Barr and Lord & Taylor divisions
in St. Louis, and its L.S. Ayres stores in
Indianapolis. Additional funds were provided
by Gily AG, the National Endowment for
the Arts, the National Endowment for the
Humanities, and the City of Los Angeles
Cultural Affairs Department.

Contents

Foreword

mericans carry varied mental images of Egypt, images derived from sources as diverse as the Bible, Hollywood movies, and documentaries produced for public television. Though some Americans have been fortunate enough to travel to Egypt and experience its monuments firsthand, most of us had our first direct contact with the artifacts of this ancient civilization closer to home, in museum galleries. How those objects came to reside in American collections is a question that few museum-goers stop to consider, yet the story of the American discovery of ancient Egypt is a complex and fascinating one.

The first professionally trained American Egyptologists began working in Egypt only around the turn of the twentieth century, decades after their European counterparts. Within a short time, however, through numerous projects, they had a dramatic impact on the discipline, revolutionizing archaeological field techniques and reshaping our knowledge of this highly sophisticated ancient culture. By the 1920s American expeditions to Egypt were better equipped, more ambitious in their goals, and more generously financed than those sent by any other country to any area. The success of these expeditions sparked the founding of academic research centers and, thanks to the Egyptian Antiquities Department's generous policy for dividing finds, created rich repositories of Egyptian works of art in many major American museums.

The names of European Egyptologists Jean-François Champollion and Howard Carter are universally recognized because of their extraordinary contributions to the understanding of Egyptian culture—the former made the final step toward deciphering Egyptian hieroglyphs in 1822, and the latter, working a century later, discovered the tomb of Tutankhamun—yet American Egyptologists have also made remarkable discoveries. For example, George A. Reisner, working at the Giza Plateau, unearthed the mortuary temple of King Menkaure and cleared more than four hundred private tombs, creating a corpus of information on the Old Kingdom, a seminal period of Egyptian history. In addition, spectacular finds in Nubia allowed Reisner to piece together not only the succession of Nubian and Meroitic kings but also the history of their monuments. Likewise, Herbert E. Winlock of the Metropolitan Museum of Art worked tirelessly on the museum's excavations at sites such as Deir el-Bahri in order to illuminate the history of the pivotal 11th Dynasty (the first dynasty of the Middle Kingdom) and the enigmatic kingship of the 18th Dynasty female pharaoh Hatshepsut. Clarence Fisher, sponsored by the University of Pennsylvania Museum, brought to light one of the few extant ancient royal palaces in Egypt, belonging to King Merneptah of the 19th Dynasty.

Other crucial American contributions to Egyptology have been in the area of epigraphy, the copying and study of ancient wall scenes and hieroglyphic texts. Modern environmental conditions are causing the rapid deterioration of many of Egypt's monuments, and the efforts of American epigraphers such as James Henry Breasted, founder of the University of Chicago's Oriental Institute, have helped to document records that will soon be irretrievably lost.

Following its peak in the 1920s, the scope of American fieldwork in Egypt gradually declined during the 1930s and 1940s, due to the Great Depression and World War II. With the unearthing of the intact tomb of Tutankhamun in 1922, the Egyptian government began to take steps to ensure that most excavated finds remain in Egypt, curtailing the growth of American collections. Nevertheless, in the early 1960s, with UNESCO's international call to rescue the soon-to-be-submerged monuments of Nubia, Americans returned to the region and initiated a new wave of archaeological projects. This renewed effort continues to the present, although current projects focus on the conservation of monuments and on smaller-scale, multidisciplinary excavations.

As a companion to the exhibition catalogue *The American Discovery of Ancient Egypt*, this volume includes ten essays evaluating projects from the 1890s to the present and examining their relevance to various periods of ancient Egyptian history. For example, Richard A. Fazzini, writing about the Third Intermediate and Late Periods (c. 1100–305 B.C.), weighs the merits of various North American projects and their contribution to the understanding of this complex era. American Egyptologists extended their activities to Nubia, a culturally related region to the south of Egypt, in present-day Sudan; essays by Peter Lacovara and Timothy Kendall evaluate the highly important achievements of American projects in this region.

Preliminary versions of these essays were presented at a symposium organized by the American Research Center in Egypt, held with generous funding from the National Endowment for the Humanities at New York University, October 24–25, 1992. This conference served to promote scholarly discussion and exploration of the subject and to jump-start both the writing process and the organization of the exhibition.

We are hopeful that American archaeological projects in Egypt will continue through the 1990s and into the next century and that the richness of this fascinating ancient culture will continue to unfold. We are very grateful to the co-organizer of this ambitious exhibition and publication project, the American Research Center in Egypt. We continue to be appreciative of our hosts in Egypt, as represented by the Supreme Council of Antiquities. We would also like to thank our many collaborators on this project: the thirty authors who contributed to this two-volume catalogue and the curators, archivists, and researchers from numerous institutions who aided in this joint effort. Without the support of staffs of the Los Angeles County Museum of Art, the Saint Louis Art Museum, the Indianapolis Museum of Art, and the lending institutions, this substantial exhibition could not have been undertaken. I applaud the efforts of the exhibition curators, Nancy Thomas and Gerry Scott III, and of David O'Connor and Peter Lacovara, who assisted them with this enormous task. I take particular pleasure in launching this exciting project, inaugurating my tenure at the Los Angeles County Museum of Art.

ANDREA RICH
President and chief executive officer,
Los Angeles County Museum of Art

Note to the Reader

ABBREVIATIONS

AJA   *American Journal of Archaeology*

ARCE   American Research Center in Egypt

ASAE   *Annales du Service des antiquités de l'Egypte*

BES   *Bulletin of the Egyptological Seminar*

BIFAO   *Bulletin de l'Institut français d'archéologie orientale du Caire*

BMB   *The Brooklyn Museum Bulletin*

BMFA   *Bulletin of the Museum of Fine Arts (Boston)*

BMMA   *Bulletin of the Metropolitan Museum of Art*

BSFE   *Bulletin de la Société française d'égyptologie*

CdE   *Chronique d'Egypte*

CG   Catalogue général des antiquités égyptiennes du Musée du Caire

IFAO   Institut français d'archéologie orientale du Caire

JARCE   *Journal of the American Research Center in Egypt*

JEA   *Journal of Egyptian Archaeology*

JNES   *Journal of Near Eastern Studies*

JSSEA   *Journal of the Society for the Study of Egyptian Antiquities*

KUSH   *Kush: Journal of the Sudan Antiquities Service*

LÄ   *Lexikon der Ägyptologie*, 6 vols., ed. H. W. Helck and W. Westendorf (Wiesbaden: Harrassowitz, 1975–86)

MDAIK   *Mitteilungen des Deutschen archäologischen Instituts, Abteilung Kairo*

MFA   Museum of Fine Arts, Boston

MMA   Metropolitan Museum of Art

NARCE   *Newsletter of the American Research Center in Egypt*

OIC   Oriental Institute Communications

OINE   Oriental Institute Nubian Expedition

OIP   Oriental Institute Publications

PAHMA   Phoebe A. Hearst Museum of Anthropology

PM   B. Porter and R. Moss, *Topographical Bibliography of Ancient Egyptian Hieroglyphic Texts, Reliefs, and Paintings*, 7 vols. (Oxford: Griffith Institute, Ashmolean Museum, 1934–81). The second, revised edition is cited for vols. 1 (pts. 1, 2), 2, and 3 (fascs. 1–3).

RdE   *Revue d'égyptologie*

SAK   *Studien zur altägyptischen Kultur*

ZÄS   *Zeitschrift für ägyptische Sprache und Altertumskunde*

Dates

The dates given for the major periods of Egyptian history, dynasties, and reigns of individual rulers are based upon those used in John Baines and Jaromír Málek, *Atlas of Ancient Egypt* (New York: Facts on File, 1994). A somewhat revised version of this chronology can be found in the article "Egypt," in the *Encyclopaedia Britannica*, 15th ed. (beginning with the 1988 printing).

Place Names

The orthography of place names also follows the usage in Baines and Málek, *Atlas of Ancient Egypt*. Frequently used modern names for ancient sites are provided in parentheses, such as Mit Rahina for Memphis or Tell Umm el-Breigat for Tebtunis.

Spelling of Egyptian Names

The spelling of royal and private Egyptian personal names in this catalogue is based upon Bruce G. Trigger et al., *Ancient Egypt: A Social History* (Cambridge: Cambridge University Press, 1983). Exceptions have been made for key historical figures based on institutional preference (for example, the Metropolitan Museum of Art's use of "Senwosret," rather than "Senusret," for the second king of the 12th Dynasty). Other exceptions have been made to allow for more consistent spellings of the names of two Egyptian gods—Amun and Re—whose names are incorporated into many Egyptian royal and private names, such as Tutankhamun and Menkaure.

Catalogue Numbers

The catalogue numbers cited in the text refer to the exhibition catalogue *The American Discovery of Ancient Egypt* (Los Angeles: Los Angeles County Museum of Art; New York: ARCE, 1995).

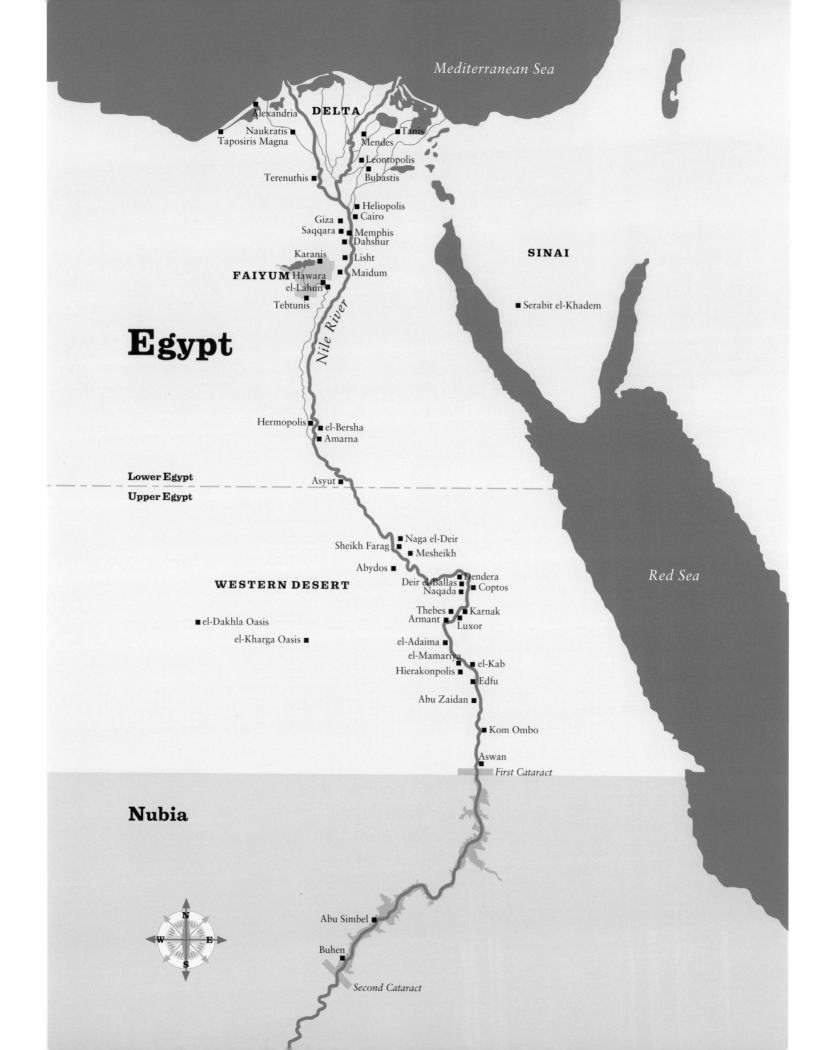

Mediterranean Sea

DELTA

Alexandria
Naukratis
Taposiris Magna

Tanis
Mendes
Leontopolis
Bubastis

Terenuthis

Heliopolis
Giza
Saqqara
Memphis
Dahshur
Karanis
Lisht
FAIYUM Hawara
el-Lahun
Maidum

Tebtunis

SINAI

Serabit el-Khadem

Egypt

Nile River

Hermopolis
el-Bersha
Amarna

Lower Egypt

Upper Egypt

Asyut

Naga el-Deir
Sheikh Farag
Mesheikh

Abydos

Dendera
WESTERN DESERT
Deir el-Ballas
Naqada
Coptos

Thebes
Armant
Karnak
Luxor

el-Dakhla Oasis

el-Kharga Oasis

el-Adaima
el-Mamariya
el-Kab
Hierakonpolis
Edfu

Abu Zaidan

Red Sea

Kom Ombo

Aswan
First Cataract

Nubia

N
W **E**
S

Abu Simbel

Buhen

Second Cataract

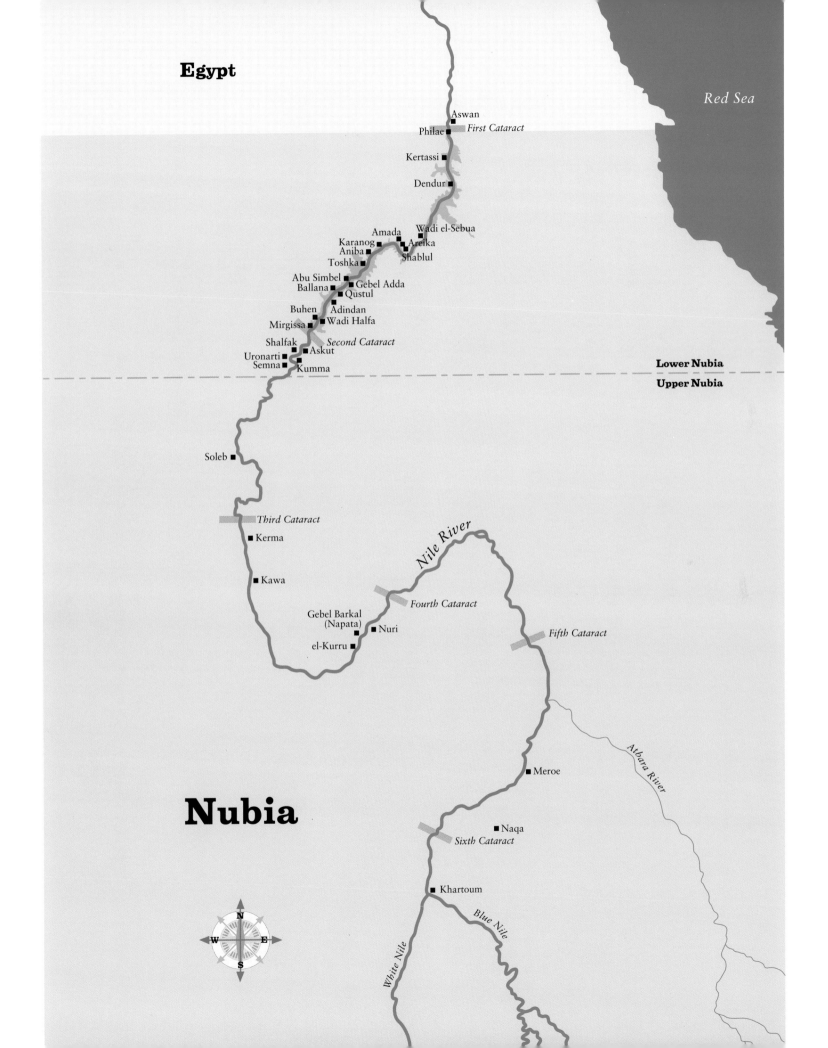

Egypt

Red Sea

Aswan ■
Philae ■   *First Cataract*
Kertassi ■
Dendur ■

Wadi el-Sebua ■
Amada ■
Karanog ■   Areika ■
Aniba ■   Shablul ■
Toshka ■
Abu Simbel ■   Gebel Adda ■
Ballana ■   Qustul ■
Buhen ■   Adindan ■
Mirgissa ■   Wadi Halfa ■
   Second Cataract
Shalfak ■
Uronarti ■   Askut ■
Semna ■   Kumma ■

Lower Nubia
- - - - - - - - - - - - - - - - - - -
Upper Nubia

Soleb ■

Third Cataract

Kerma ■

Nile River

Kawa ■

Fourth Cataract

Gebel Barkal
(Napata) ■   Nuri ■
el-Kurru ■

Fifth Cataract

Meroe ■

Atbara River

Nubia

Naqa ■
Sixth Cataract

Khartoum ■

Blue Nile

White Nile

N
W   E
S

The American Contribution to an Understanding of Prehistoric Egypt

Kent R. Weeks

At the end of the American Civil War the khedive of Egypt employed Union general Charles P. Stone to train Egyptian soldiers and to develop Egypt's coastal fortifications. Stone lived and worked in Egypt for thirteen years. When he returned to the United States in 1883, he was hired to supervise the building of the foundation and pedestal for the Statue of Liberty. As costs mounted and construction funds proved inadequate, he volunteered to raise money by conducting a lecture tour throughout the United States. Surprisingly he did not lecture about the Statue of Liberty. Instead he talked about Egypt and particularly about the origin of its people and their ancient culture.[1]

Clearly Stone knew the interests of his audiences. Ancient Egypt was a popular subject in nineteenth-century America, and people would pay to hear about it. Egypt's great antiquity stood in profound contrast to America's youth, and its monuments spoke of dignity, power, and permanence, attributes Americans greatly admired. By 1823 American museums were regularly exhibiting Egyptian artifacts, and these objects influenced American art, architecture, and interior design. The Statue of Liberty itself was posed and dressed as a romanticized Egyptian figure.[2]

If ancient Egypt fascinated Americans, it was not simply because they admired her monuments. Americans saw similarities between their idealized notion of the noble savage, particularly the American Indian, and their concept of Egyptian culture. Nineteenth-century America was deeply interested in origins—of races, of cultures, of ideas, of humankind itself. These interests significantly affected some of America's early religious movements. Joseph Smith, for example, founder of the Mormon Church, maintained that long before Europeans visited the New World, one of the lost tribes of Israel had migrated to America, bringing with it many traces of Egyptian culture. Scores of nineteenth-century writers maintained that bands of "pre-Cheops Egyptians" had journeyed across Asia to North America, finally settling along the Mississippi—"America's Nile." Thus many cities founded

FIGURE 1
Examination of house floor at site E-75-6 at Nabta Playa, dated c. 6000 B.C., by members of the Combined Prehistoric Expedition, sponsored by Southern Methodist University.

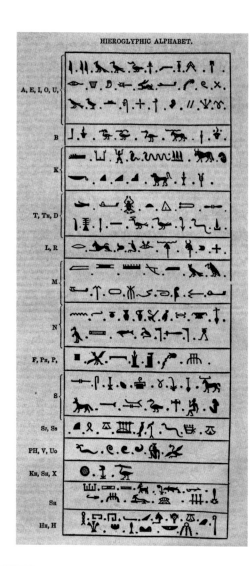

FIGURE 2
Hieroglyphic alphabet
from George R.
Gliddon's *Ancient
Egypt* (1848), 21.

FIGURE 3
Image of the god
Khnum from George R.
Gliddon's *Ancient
Egypt*, 28

along the Mississippi during the 1800s bear names like
Memphis, Cairo, and Karnak.[3] From this American Nile,
Egyptian migrants were believed to have fanned out and
founded the various Indian nations of the Americas.[4]

Racial Origins and Chronology

The belief that New World Indians were descendants of the
Egyptians raised an inevitable question: to which race did
the ancient Egyptians and America's Indians belong? Race
and slavery were serious concerns in nineteenth-century
America, and the answer could determine how Indians were
to be treated.

The first "serious" examination of the racial question
appeared in the early 1840s. George R. Gliddon (1809–57;
see figs. 2, 3), who had served as American vice consul in
Egypt, returned to the United States in the early 1840s and
delivered a series of lectures—later successfully published—
in which he argued, citing biblical sources, that the Egyptians
were members of the Caucasian race.[5] The Philadelphia
physician Samuel George Morton (1799–1851) also believed
this, and from Gliddon he accepted a collection of more than
one hundred Egyptian crania, whose study, he hoped, would
scientifically prove his racial theory. Morton published the
skulls in *Crania Aegyptiaca* (1844; see fig. 4), and based on
cranial measurements, he argued that the earliest Egyptians
lay midway between the Caucasian race's Semitic and Indo-
European branches. Comparison with American Indian
skulls showed the Egyptians to be more "advanced," he said,
and comparison of Indians with African-American slaves
proved the Indians to be more "intelligent."[6] Implicit in these
conclusions was the idea that, if Egyptians and Indians and
Negroes lay at different points on a continuum of intelligence,
society must treat each group differently. (These racist views
have since been shown to be utterly without foundation.[7])

Morton advocated a theory of polygenesis positing that
God separately created each race as a distinct species. As
part of his proof he pointed to depictions on Egyptian monuments of both Caucasians (the Egyptians) and Negroes
(their southern neighbors). The seventeenth-century Irish

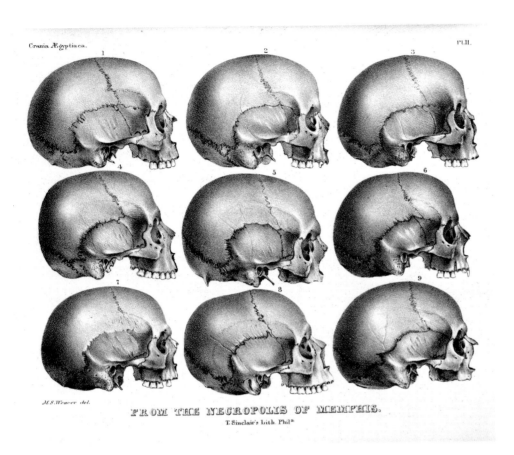

Crania Ægyptiaca.   PL.II.

M.S. Weaver del.

FROM THE NECROPOLIS OF MEMPHIS.

T. Sinclair's Lith. Phil*.

FIGURE 4
Illustration from Samuel
George Morton's *Crania
Aegyptiaca* (1844), pl. 2.

archbishop James Ussher, working
from biblical genealogies, had calcu-
lated that Adam was created in 4004
B.C. and that the Flood occurred
in 2349 B.C. Given Ussher's widely
accepted dates, ancient Egypt could
not be more than about three thousand
years old.[8] The short time separating
God's creation of Adam from the date
of the ancient paintings made it seemingly impossible for both races to have
evolved gradually from a single source.

Other nineteenth-century scholars,
however, citing the work of archaeologists and geologists, were beginning to
argue that Egyptian civilization had
arisen at least five thousand years earlier. Paleolithic hand axes discovered in
Egypt in 1865 were the first Stone Age
artifacts to be found in Africa. By
the 1890s a score of Paleolithic and
Neolithic sites had been identified along the Nile, and a complete reappraisal
of Egypt's origins seemed essential.[9] A few scholars rejected this new data. Some
would not abandon Ussher's chronology; others were concerned about the data's
broader implications. In the mid-nineteenth century adherents of diffusionism, the
most widely accepted explanation of origins, argued that civilization had developed only once, and it was inconceivable that it could have originated in Africa.
But the discovery of Paleolithic and Neolithic sites in Egypt implied that Egyptian
civilization was indigenous, and its origins had to be sought in Egypt's prehistory.

This was not a popular idea. Some scholars, trying to soften the import of
these archaeological discoveries, suggested that any prehistoric occupants of the
Nile Valley certainly would have been brutish beings incapable of sophisticated
cultural development. These savages, they argued, must have been conquered by
an intellectually superior people, a so-called dynastic race (perhaps originating in
the present-day Republic of Georgia), which had invaded the Nile Valley at the
beginning of the 1st Dynasty and introduced civilization to Egypt. The idea of
a dynastic race, long since abandoned by Egyptologists, was very appealing a century ago; it tied cultural development to racial attributes and provided American
society with a rationale for maintaining racial inequalities.[10]

After the Civil War American scholars rarely returned to the subject of the
racial composition of Egyptians. More recent American studies in physical anthropology and human paleontology have dealt with other questions. For example,
researchers from Duke University, focusing on early primate development, found
the earliest known primate, thirty-million-year-old *Aegyptopithecus*, north of
the Faiyum.[11] Anthropologists from the University of Illinois discovered a thirty-
three-thousand-year-old *Homo sapiens sapiens* in the Sinai. Southern Methodist
University, working with the Polish Academy of Sciences, found Upper Paleolithic
human remains dating to about twenty thousand years ago at Wadi Kubbaniya
in the Western Desert (see fig. 5). American expeditions in Nubia have studied
the dentition, skeletal growth, and paleopathology of human remains between
one and six thousand years old found between the first and second cataracts of
the Nile. A number of projects are working on prehistoric demography, diet, and
health. Others are applying such nontraditional tests as blood typing or DNA
studies (so far unsuccessfully) to tissue samples from mummified human remains.[12]

Much of the chronological framework for the prehistory of Egypt has come
from geological work conducted by Americans or American institutions. George
Sandys (1578–1644), an early treasurer of the Virginia Company, visited Egypt
in 1610 and correctly explained the origins of limestone strata at Giza.[13] An
American army lieutenant, Oscar Fechet, conducted the first geological survey
of the Nile Valley in 1873, from Cairo to Khartoum, and recommended the site
for the Aswan Dam.[14]

James Henry Breasted (1865–1935), founder of the Oriental Institute at the
University of Chicago, was very much aware of geology's importance to the study
of ancient chronology and human history. From 1926 to 1938 he directed Kenneth

S. Sandford and William J. Arkell's detailed survey of Pleistocene geology from the second cataract northward. Their work was the first to place the prehistoric chronology of northeast Africa on a reasonable footing. Sandford and Arkell (both Englishmen) identified a series of geological terraces along the river whose study allowed them to reconstruct the Nile Valley's history and to suggest dates for the prehistoric artifacts lying along it.[15]

More recent work, such as that by scholars at the University of Pennsylvania, Boston University, and Southern Methodist University, has substantially improved the Sandford-Arkell system and made Egypt's prehistoric chronology more reliable. It has also provided important information about the environmental history of Egypt from Paleolithic times onward. The picture these scientists offer of Nile River hydrology and African climatic change has been essential in reconstructing the complex history of the transition from hunting-gathering to agriculture in Egypt.[16]

Archaeological Excavations before 1910

Not until the end of the nineteenth century did archaeologists uncover evidence of the Neolithic period and the crucial era between about 3300 and 3000 B.C., when dynastic Egyptian civilization took form. W. M. Flinders Petrie and James E.

FIGURE 6
Excavated tombs at the Predynastic cemetery 7000 at Naga el-Deir.

Quibell's excavations of Naqada and Deir el-Ballas were perhaps the first (1892); they were soon followed by Emile Amélineau at Abydos (1895), Henri de Morgan and Petrie at Naqada (1896), and Quibell and Frederick W. Green at Hierakonpolis (1899). With the exception of de Morgan and Amélineau, these first excavators were British, but a fair portion of their money came from American contributions to their sponsor, the Egypt Exploration Fund, a relationship that resulted in the transfer of a number of prehistoric objects to American museums.[17] De Morgan (1854–1909), a French prehistorian, undertook significant excavations at several Predynastic Period sites in southern Upper Egypt for the Brooklyn Museum between 1906 and 1908 (see cat. nos. 18–22, 25–26).

The most important American archaeologist to work in Egypt at this time was George Andrew Reisner (1867–1942). Reisner worked with the University of California at Berkeley from 1899 to 1904 (after which time he moved to Harvard University and the Museum of Fine Arts, Boston). With funding from Phoebe Apperson Hearst, he led a number of expeditions to Egypt and spent several seasons working in the prehistoric cemeteries at Naga el-Deir (see fig. 6) and el-

Ahaiwa. The thousands of objects he uncovered there went to what became the Robert H. Lowie Museum of Anthropology at Berkeley (since 1992 called the Phoebe A. Hearst Museum of Anthropology). They constitute the largest collection of prehistoric Egyptian antiquities outside Egypt. Reisner went on to record a number of prehistoric sites during his directorship of the Archaeological Survey of Nubia from 1906 to 1910. His major work was at Giza, however, and his masterful study, *The Development of the Egyptian Tomb down to the Accession of Cheops* (1936), traced the development of mortuary architecture from earliest prehistoric times through the Early Dynastic Period. That book, and Reisner's detailed studies of pottery, together with the seriation analyses of Petrie, helped form the basis of a valid chronology for Neolithic and Early Dynastic Egypt.[18] More recent typological studies by Germany's Werner Kaiser and, from North America, Walter Federn, Helene Kantor, and Winifred Needler, have further refined that chronology.[19]

The Development of Theory, 1910–60

Because of the Depression and World Wars I and II—and because some benefactors insisted that the projects they funded dig for museum-quality objects— American archaeologists undertook no significant prehistoric excavations or surveys in Egypt from about 1910 until 1960.[20] Excavators concentrated instead on dynastic mortuary sites. Nevertheless, during the first half of this century, Americans did make important theoretical contributions to an understanding of prehistoric Egypt and the origin of civilization. Several anthropological theories of cultural development, the appearance of agriculture, and the origins of civilization gave focus to archaeological work and greatly influenced American scholars who returned to prehistoric Egyptian and Nubian sites in the 1960s.

More often than not, American approaches to prehistoric Egypt have been anthropologically oriented in theory and interpretation and more closely allied in methodology to New World archaeology than to traditional Egyptology. American scholars have been using Egyptian materials to formulate general theories of cultural development since the late nineteenth century, when anthropologist Lewis Henry Morgan (1818–81) offered his explanation of the progressive stages of civilization. Such work continued in the twentieth century with Alfred Kroeber's definitions of such terms as *culture* and *civilization*, Robert Redfield's folk-urban continuum, Julian Steward's multilineal scheme of cultural evolution, Karl Wittfogel's emphasis on the role of irrigation in the creation of complex cultures, and Leslie White's studies of "culturology."[21]

In the 1950s and 1960s American scholars with wide-ranging backgrounds tackled the question of civilization's origins and brought many new approaches

FIGURE 7
The Oriental Institute Nubian Expedition at Qustul, April–May 1963. *Seated, left to right*: expedition director Keith Seele, Fuad Yakub, Louis Zabkar, Mr. Murad, James Knudstad; *standing*: Otto Schaden, Alfred Hoerth, Labib Habachi, and four Sudanese assistants.

to the study of Early Dynastic Egypt. For example, Talcott Parsons and Lawrence Krader, social scientists concerned with broad theoretical issues, delved into Egyptian data.[22] Comparative approaches to civilization have had an increasing impact on studies of Egypt's dynastic origins: Kent Flannery and Robert Braidwood, among others, introduced Mesopotamian data into these discussions.[23] American archaeologists working in Peru and Mesoamerica have developed theories of civilization's origins that draw extensively upon New World data. Some Egyptologists, including William Edgerton and John A. Wilson of the University of Chicago, have rightly questioned the validity of some anthropological incursions into Egyptology,[24] but there is no doubt that several recent studies—such as those of anthropologist Bruce G. Trigger; geographer Karl Butzer; and prehistorians Michael Hoffman, Fekri Hassan, Fred Wendorf, and their colleagues—have made significant and long-lasting interdisciplinary contributions.[25] Among other things, they have confirmed that the development of civilization in Egypt must be seen not as a sudden, revolutionary event, but as a process driven, to a large degree, by an indigenous Nilotic culture.

Archaeological Work since 1960

American work on prehistoric Egypt flourished in the 1960s. The UNESCO Nubian Salvage Campaign issued a plea in 1959–60 for trained archaeologists to help save monuments south of the Nile's first cataract from flooding caused by the building of the Aswan High Dam. Several expeditions came from America, most of them staffed by anthropologically oriented excavators trained in the methodology of New World prehistory (see fig. 7). Many participants came in answer to appeals from William Y. Adams, the American archaeologist in charge of UNESCO's Sudanese Nubian work, and his interests gave to their selection a degree of theoretical and methodological cohesiveness that would prove to be of great value. Participating institutions included the University of Colorado, Columbia University, the University of Kentucky, and the Museum of New Mexico. (Wendorf's Combined Prehistoric Expedition and Yale University worked farther north.)

The impact of these projects on our picture of prehistoric Nile Valley cultures was profound. To cite but one example, the University of Chicago's work near Qustul, on sites of the A-Group, found evidence of a culture more sophisticated than anything suspected to have existed along the Nile prior to Egypt's 1st Dynasty. In addition the 1960s saw syntheses of prehistoric data, most notably in William C. Hayes's *Most Ancient Egypt* (1968) (which, because of Hayes's death, unfortunately ended with the beginning of the Neolithic) and in Trigger's *Beyond History* (1968).[26]

Since the early 1970s, when the Nubian Salvage Campaign came to an end, many prehistoric surveys have continued to work in other areas of Egypt. Investigations by Wendorf and the Combined Prehistoric Expedition into Paleolithic sites in the Western Desert, sponsored by Southern Methodist University, have dramatically changed our understanding of northeast Africa twenty thousand years ago and earlier (see fig. 1). Smaller-scale projects, in both the field and the laboratory, offered meaningful information on cultural activities through the study of seemingly unimportant bits of data.[27] Douglas Brewer's study, for example, of Nile catfish remains in the Neolithic Faiyum demonstrates the seasonal pattern of fishing there,[28] and the interdisciplinary approach taken by excavators at Hierakonpolis has yielded new data on the complex origins of dynastic Egyptian society.[29]

At least half a dozen American expeditions are presently working on Neolithic sites in Egypt. Eager to test anthropologists' theories of development, these highly sophisticated, interdisciplinary, problem-oriented studies are seeking answers to specific questions about the appearance of agriculture, complex culture, and civilization in the Nile Valley. Walter A. Fairservis, Michael A. Hoffman, Jay Mills, and others have worked on Neolithic and Early Dynastic settlements at Hierakonpolis (see figs. 8, 9); Fekri Hassan and Wilma Wetterstrom have worked at the important Neolithic site of Naqada; Robert Wenke has worked in the Faiyum and the Egyptian Delta. Their data has already contributed to recent syntheses and theoretical studies.[30]

FIGURE 8
View of Predynastic house site excavated by Michael A. Hoffman at Hierakonpolis.

IF THE SUCCESS OF *The First Egyptians*, an exhibition organized in 1988 which traveled to museums across the country, is any indication, America's interest in prehistoric Egypt is as great today as it was 130 years ago.[31] One hopes this interest will continue and will encourage the valuable—and often unique—approaches American scholars have taken to prehistoric Egypt. American prehistorians and anthropologists have shown themselves willing to test prehistoric Egyptian data against the theories of other disciplines. At their best, American studies have

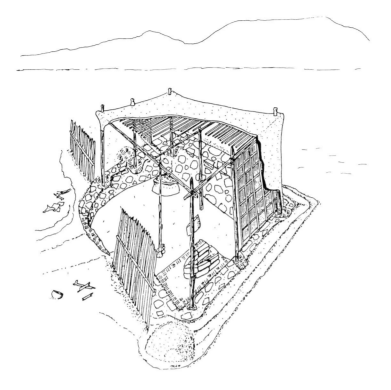

treated Egypt's cultural development not as an isolated occurrence but within the broader context of anthropological and archaeological theory.

If the American approach has a weakness, it is the prehistorian's reluctance to accept as valid traditional Egyptology's interpretations of Predynastic and Early Dynastic data. Philological, historical, and religious studies of dynastic materials have been called irrelevant and their interpretations too subjective to be of value in understanding preliterate Egypt. But both approaches—the anthropological and the Egyptological—should be recognized as eminently compatible and complementary. By going a step further and deriving from the two approaches a single synthesis, it may be possible to develop theories that explain, more clearly and completely than ever before, the complex processes that led to the emergence of one of humankind's greatest achievements—the civilization of ancient Egypt.

Notes

1 John Luter, "Stone of Egypt," *Aramco World Magazine* (January–February 1972); Pierre Crabites, *Americans in the Egyptian Army* (London: Routledge and Sons, 1938); William B. Hesseltine and Hazel C. Wolf, *The Blue and the Gray on the Nile* (Chicago: University of Chicago Press, 1961).

2 John T. Irwin, *American Hieroglyphs: Symbolism of the Egyptian Hieroglyphs in the American Renaissance* (New Haven: Yale University Press, 1980).

3 Richard G. Carrott, *The Egyptian Revival: Its Sources, Monuments, and Meanings, 1808–1858* (Berkeley: University of California Press, 1978), 50.

4 Ibid.

5 George R. Gliddon, *Ancient Egypt: A Series of Lectures on Early Egyptian History,* 12th ed. (Philadelphia: Peterson, 1848).

6 See, e.g., Samuel George Morton, "On the Form of the Head, and Other Ethnographic Characters of the Ancient Egyptians," *Proceedings of the American Philosophical Society* 2 (1842): 239–41; idem, "Observations on a Second Series of Egyptian Crania," *Proceedings of the Academy of Natural Sciences, Philadelphia* 2 (1844): 122–36; idem, "Observations on Egyptian Ethnography, Derived from Anatomy, History, and the Monuments," *Transactions of the American Philosophical Society* 9 (1846): 93–159; idem, "Account of a Craniological Collection with Remarks on the Clarification of Some Families of the Human Race," *Transactions of the American Ethnological Society* 2 (1848): 215–22; Josiah C. Nott and George R. Gliddon, *Types of Mankind; or, Ethnological Researches Based upon the Ancient Monuments, Paintings, Sculptures Illustrated by Selections from the Inedited Papers of Samuel George Morton, M.D.* (Philadelphia, 1855).

7 Stephen Jay Gould, *The Mismeasure of Man* (New York: W. W. Norton, 1981).

8 Bruce G. Trigger, *A History of Archaeological Thought* (Cambridge: Cambridge University Press, 1989); Stephen Toulmin and June Goodfield, *The Discovery of Time* (Chicago: University of Chicago Press, 1965).

9 A bibliographical note on the history of these first discoveries can be found in Kent R. Weeks, *An Historical Bibliography of Egyptian Prehistory,* ARCE, Catalogs 6 (Winona Lake, Ind.: Eisenbrauns, 1985). This bibliography and its brief essays provide an introduction to much of the literature relevant to the study of Egyptian prehistory.

10 Wyatt MacGaffey, "Concepts of Race in the Historiography of Northeast Africa," *Journal of African History* 7 (1966): 1–17; reprinted in *Papers in African Prehistory,* ed. J. D. Fage and R. A. Oliver (Cambridge: Cambridge University Press, 1970), 99–116.

11 Earlier work is summarized in the articles "Fayum" and "Propliopithecus," in Ian Tattersall, Eric Delson, and John van Couvering, eds., *Encyclopedia of Human Evolution and Prehistory* (New York: Garland, 1988).

12 There is a large body of literature on these and other, related discoveries. See, e.g., the references in Weeks, *Historical Bibliography,* esp. xiv–xvi; Torgny Säve-Söderbergh, *Temples and Tombs of Ancient Nubia: The International Rescue Campaign of Abu Simbel, Philae, and Other Sites* (London: Thames and Hudson, 1987); W. Vivian Davies and Roxie Walker, eds., *Biological Anthropology and the Study of Ancient Egypt* (London: British Museum Press, 1994). Among Fekri Hassan's works are "Diet, Nutrition, and Agricultural Origins in the Near East," in *Origine de l'élevage et de la domestication,* ed. Eric Higgs (Paris: Centre national de la recherche scientifique, 1976), 227–47; and *Demographic Archaeology* (New York: Academic Press, 1981). See also Mark N. Cohen, *Health and the Rise of Civilization* (New Haven: Yale University Press, 1989); Dennis Vangerven, David Carlson, and George Armelagos, "Racial History and Biocultural Adaptation of Nubian Archaeological Populations," *Journal of African History* 14 (1973): 555–64.

13 George Sandys, *A Relation of a Journey Begun Anno Domini 1610* (London: Cotes-Allot, 1627).

14 John A. Wilson, *Signs and Wonders upon Pharaoh: A History of American Egyptology* (Chicago: University of Chicago Press, 1964), 64.

15 Sandford and Arkell published their findings in the University of Chicago's Oriental Institute Publications series, nos. 10 (1929), 17 (1933), 18 (1934), and 46 (1939).

16 See, e.g., Karl W. Butzer, *Environment and Archaeology: An Ecological Approach to Prehistory,* 2d ed. (Chicago: Aldine-Atherton, 1971); idem, "Klima," *LÄ,* vol. 2, 455–57; M. A. J. Williams and H. Faure, eds., *The Sahara and the Nile: Quaternary Environments and Prehistoric Occupation in Northern Africa* (Rotterdam: Balkema, 1980), esp. the article by Fred Wendorf and Fekri Hassan, "Holocene Ecology and Prehistory in the Egyptian Sahara," 407–19. For works on Neolithic chronology, see n. 19.

17 Among many sources for the study of this period, see Leslie Greener, *The Discovery of Egypt* (London: Cassell, 1966); Wilson, *Signs and Wonders;* John D. Wortham, *The Genesis of British Egyptology* (Norman: University of Oklahoma Press, 1971).

18 Weeks, *Historical Bibliography;* G. Ernest Wright, "The Phenomenon of American Archaeology in the Near East," in *Near Eastern Archaeology in the Twentieth Century,* ed. James A. Sanders (Garden City, N.Y.: Doubleday, 1970); Dows Dunham, *The Egyptian Department and Its Excavations* (Boston: MFA, 1958); Albert B. Elsasser and Vera-Mae Fredrickson, *Ancient Egypt: An Exhibition at the Robert H. Lowie Museum of Anthropology of the University of California, Berkeley* (Berkeley: Robert H. Lowie Museum of Anthropology, University of California, 1966); Richard A. Fazzini, *Images for Eternity: Egyptian Art from Berkeley and Brooklyn,* exh. cat. (San Francisco: Fine Arts Museums of San Francisco; Brooklyn: Brooklyn Museum, 1975).

19 Fekri Hassan, "Chronology of the Khartoum 'Mesolithic' and 'Neolithic' and Related Sites in the Sudan: Statistical Analysis and Comparisons with Egypt," *African Archaeological Review* 4 (1986): 83–102; idem, "Radiocarbon Chronology of Neolithic and Predynastic Sites in Upper Egypt and the Delta," *African Archaeological Review* 3 (1985): 95–116; idem, "Radiocarbon Chronology of Predynastic Naqada Settlements, Upper Egypt," in *Origin and Early Development of Food-Producing Cultures in North-Eastern Africa,* ed. Lech Krzyzaniak and Michael Kobusiewicz (Poznan: Polish Academy of Sciences, 1984), 681–83; Angela Close, "Current Research and Recent Radiocarbon Dates from Northern Africa, II," *Journal of African History* 25 (1984): 1–24; Winifred Needler, *Predynastic and Archaic Egypt in the Brooklyn Museum,* Wilbour Monographs 9 (Brooklyn: Brooklyn Museum, 1984); idem, "Federn's Revision of Petrie's Predynastic Pottery Classification," *JSSEA* 11 (1981): 69–74; T. R. Hays, "A Reappraisal of the Egyptian Predynastic," in *The Causes and Consequences of Food Production in Africa,* ed. J. Desmond Clark and S. A. Brandt (Berkeley: University of California Press, 1984):

65–73; Werner Kaiser, "Zur inneren Chronologie der Naqadakultur," *Archaeologia Geographica* 6 (1957): 69–77; Helene Kantor, "The Relative Chronology of Egypt and Its Foreign Correlations before the Late Bronze Age," in *Relative Chronologies in Old World Archaeology*, 2d ed. (Chicago: University of Chicago Press, 1965), 1–46.

20 About the only American excavation of an early site during this period was on the Mediterranean coast: see Oric Bates, "Archaic Burials at Marsa Matrûh," *Ancient Egypt* (1915): 158–65; idem, "Excavations at Marsa Matrûh," in *Varia Africana*, vol. 4, Harvard African Studies 8 (Cambridge: Peabody Museum, Harvard University, 1927), 123–97.

21 Lewis H. Morgan, *Ancient Society* (1877; reprint, Cambridge: Belknap Press of Harvard University Press, 1964); Alfred Kroeber, *The Nature of Culture* (Chicago: University of Chicago Press, 1952); idem, *A Roster of Civilization and Cultures* (Chicago: University of Chicago Press, 1962); Robert Redfield, "The Folk Society," *American Journal of Sociology* 52 (1947): 293–308; Julian Steward, *Theory of Culture Change: The Methodology of Multilinear Evolution* (Urbana: University of

Illinois Press, 1955); Karl Wittfogel, *Oriental Despotism: A Comparative Study of Total Power* (New Haven: Yale University Press, 1957); Leslie A. White, *The Evolution of Culture* (New York: McGraw Hill, 1959).

22 Talcott Parsons, *Societies: Evolutionary and Comparative Perspectives* (Englewood Cliffs, N.J.: Prentice Hall, 1966); Lawrence Krader, *Formation of the State* (Englewood Cliffs, N.J.: Prentice Hall, 1968).

23 Robert Braidwood, *The Near East and the Foundations for Civilization: An Essay in the Appraisal of the General Evidence* (Eugene: Oregon State System of Higher Education, 1952); Kent Flannery, "The Cultural Evolution of Civilizations," *Annual Review of Ecology and Systematics* 3 (1972): 399–426.

24 John A. Wilson, *The Burden of Egypt* (Chicago: University of Chicago Press, 1951); Leslie A. White, "Ikhnaton: The Great Man vs. the Culture Process," *Journal of the American Oriental Society* 68 (1948): 91ff.; William F. Edgerton, "'The Great Man': A Note on Methods," *Journal of the American Oriental Society* 68 (1948): 192–93.

25 Weeks, *Historical Bibliography*; Bruce Trigger, *Beyond History: The Methods of Prehistory* (New York: Harcourt Brace, 1968); idem, *Early Civilizations: Ancient Egypt in Context* (Cairo: American University in Cairo Press, 1993); Michael Hoffman, *Egypt before the Pharaohs: The Prehistoric Foundations of Egyptian Civilization* (New York: Knopf, 1979); idem, *The Predynastic of Hierakonpolis: An Interim Report*, Egyptian Studies Association 1 (Macomb: Department of Sociology and Anthropology, Western Illinois University, 1982); idem, "Predynastic Cultural Ecology and Patterns of Settlement in Upper Egypt as Viewed from Hierakonpolis," in Krzyzaniak and Kobusiewicz, eds., *Origin and Early Development of Food-Producing Cultures*, 235–45; Fekri Hassan, "Origin of Civilization in Predynastic Egypt: Toward an Evolutionary Model," *L'Egypte avant l'histoire* 1 (1980): 16–23; idem, "Environment and Subsistence in Predynastic Egypt," in Clark and Brandt, eds., *Causes and Consequences*; idem, "Toward a Model of Agricultural Development in Predynastic Egypt," in Krzyzaniak and Kobusiewicz, eds., *Origin and Early Development of Food-Producing Cultures*, 221–24; Karl Butzer,

Early Hydraulic Civilization in Egypt: A Study in Cultural Ecology (Chicago: University of Chicago Press, 1976).

26 See Säve-Söderbergh, *Temples and Tombs of Ancient Nubia*; and Fred Wendorf, Angela Close, and Romuald Schild, "Prehistoric Settlements in the Nubian Desert," *American Scientist* 73 (1985): 132–41.

27 William McHugh, "Late Prehistoric Cultural Adaptation in the Southwestern Libyan Desert" (Ph.D. diss., University of Wisconsin, 1971); T. R. Hays, "The Sudanese Neolithic: A Critical Analysis" (Ph.D. diss., Southern Methodist University, 1971); Fred Wendorf and Romuald Schild, "The Emergence of Food Production in the Egyptian Sahara," in Clark and Brandt, eds., *Causes and Consequences*; T. R. Hays, "A Reappraisal of the Egyptian Predynastic," in ibid.; idem, "Predynastic Development in Upper Egypt," in Krzyzaniak and Kobusiewicz, eds., *Origin and Early Development of Food-Producing Cultures*. See also Whitney Davis, *The Canonical Tradition in Ancient Egyptian Art* (Cambridge: Harvard University Press, 1989), esp. chap. 4, and his "Representation and Knowledge in the Prehistoric Rock Art of Africa," *African Archaeological Review* 2 (1984): 7–35.

28 Douglas Brewer, "Seasonality in the Prehistoric Faiyum Based on the Incremental Growth Structures of Nile Catfish (Pisces: *Clarias*)," *Journal of Archaeological Science* 14 (1987): 459–72.

29 Renée Friedman and Barbara Adams, eds., *The Followers of Horus: Studies Dedicated to Michael Allen Hoffman*, Egyptian Studies Association 2, Oxbow Monograph 20 (Oxford: Oxbow Books; Bloomington, Ind.: David Brown, 1992).

30 Robert Wenke and Mary Ellen Lane, "Fayum Expedition, 1981," *NARCE*, no. 116 (1981–82): 22–25; Hassan, "Origin of Civilization in Predynastic Egypt"; Wilma Wetterstrom, "Early Agriculture in Upper Egypt: A Note on Palaeoethnobotanical Studies at Predynastic Sites in the Nagada Area," *L'Egypte avant l'histoire* 1 (1980): 20–32. See also Fekri Hassan, "Desert Environment and Origins of Agriculture in Egypt," *Norwegian Archaeological Review* 19 (1986): 63–76; J. F. Harlan III, "Predynastic Settlement Patterns: A View from Hierakonpolis" (Ph.D. diss., Washington University, 1985); Elizabeth Finkenstadt, "Cognitive vs. Ecological Niches in Prehistoric Egypt," *JARCE* 22 (1985): 143–47; Kathryn A. Bard,

"The Geography of Excavated Predynastic Sites and the Rise of Complex Society," *JARCE* 24 (1987): 81–93; idem, "Toward an Interpretation of the Role of Ideology in the Evolution of Complex Society in Egypt," *Journal of Anthropological Archaeology* 11 (1992): 1–24; Bruce G. Trigger, "Egypt: A Fledgling Nation," *JSSEA* 17 (1987): 58–66; Fred Wendorf, Romuald Schild, and Angela Close, *Egypt during the Last Interglacial: The Middle Palaeolithic of Bir Tarfawi and Bir Sahara East* (New York: Plenum Press, 1993).

31 Michael A. Hoffman, *The First Egyptians*, exh. cat. (Columbia: McKissick Museum and the Earth Sciences and Resources Institute, University of South Carolina, 1988).

Epigraphic and Archaeological Documentation of Old Kingdom Tombs and Monuments at Giza and Saqqara

Edward Brovarski

The mastaba tombs of Egypt's Old Kingdom, or Pyramid Age—from about 2649 to 2134 B.C.—fell into ruin during the troubled times of the succeeding First Intermediate Period. By the 10th Dynasty, a hundred years or so after the end of the Old Kingdom, stones from the mastabas of the Teti pyramid cemetery at Saqqara, for example, were being utilized for the construction of neighboring tombs. Thus, a block with relief decoration from the chapel of Watetkhethor, wife of the vizier Mereruka, was reused as an altar in the stela chapel of Satinteti, a contemporary of one of the last Heracleopolitan sovereigns at the end of the First Intermediate Period.[1] The destruction of the pyramid cemeteries was continued by Egyptians of later dynasties and, in their turn, by the Romans, Byzantines, Copts, and Muslims. Ultimately the tombs were covered by the shifting desert sands. As the famous American Egyptologist James Henry Breasted well observed: "Far from being a destroyer of the tombs, the sand was on the contrary the sole protection which the tombs enjoyed."[2]

Blocks projecting above the sand were plundered by a flourishing antiquities trade, quarried for building stone, or reduced in lime kilns for use in mortar or plaster. An interesting illustration of the plundering of stone exists in the tombs of the Senedjemib complex at Giza, located at the northwest corner of the Great Pyramid. When the German Egyptologist Karl Richard Lepsius investigated the mastaba of the vizier Senedjemib Inti in 1842–43, the right (northern) half of the rear wall in one of the chambers was preserved nearly to its full height, with six registers of agricultural scenes.[3] Later all but the lowest register in the exposed portion was removed, presumably by the villagers of Kafr el-Haram, who made illicit excavations in the complex and removed some stones in or about 1901.[4] When George A. Reisner, on behalf of the Harvard University–Museum of Fine Arts, Boston, Expedition, cleared the entire chamber down to floor level in 1912, he found the blocks from the collapsed left (southern) part of the wall hidden

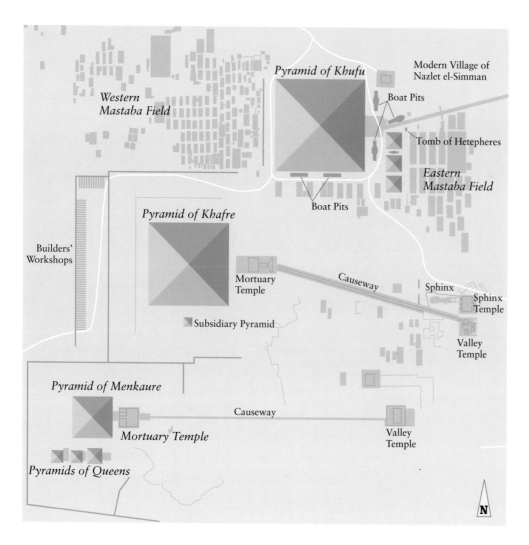

Labels on figure:
Western Mastaba Field
Pyramid of Khufu
Modern Village of Nazlet el-Simman
Boat Pits
Tomb of Hetepheres
Eastern Mastaba Field
Boat Pits
Pyramid of Khafre
Builders' Workshops
Mortuary Temple
Causeway
Sphinx
Sphinx Temple
Subsidiary Pyramid
Valley Temple
Pyramid of Menkaure
Causeway
Mortuary Temple
Valley Temple
Pyramids of Queens
N

FIGURE 11
Giza necropolis.

under the accumulated sand and debris and reconstructed the fallen portion. With the aid of Lepsius's published plate, virtually the entire wall can be restored, at least on paper. Lepsius also copied the reliefs in the neighboring tomb of Senedjemib's son, Mehi, including a table scene on the north wall of the offering room. It was presumably once again the enterprising villagers of Kafr el-Haram who removed the stones from the left end of the wall, which eventually made their way to the Field Museum of Natural History in Chicago.[5]

Unhappily, industrial pollution and vandalism are hastening the deterioration and destruction of ancient monuments at an alarming pace. This is especially so at Giza, where modern urban sprawl extends right to the edge of the pyramid plateau (see fig. 11).

The great cities of ancient Egypt, including its capital of Memphis, have been destroyed by later quarrying or have disappeared below modern towns and cities. The scenes and inscriptions that survive on tomb walls at Giza, Saqqara, and the less important Memphite cemeteries of Abu Rawash, Dahshur, and Maidum, as well as those in rock-cut tombs in the cliffs that border the Nile Valley as far south as Aswan, are therefore a critical source for much of what we know about the politics, economy, religious life, art, and society of Egypt's Old Kingdom, and the task of recording them has become one of considerable urgency.

The first concerted attempt to record the major monuments of the Nile Valley was made by the French engineers and architects who accompanied Napoleon Bonaparte's expeditionary force to Egypt in 1798. The extraordinary results of the scientific and artistic commission attached to the French expedition appeared between 1809 and 1828 in the monumental *Description de l'Egypte*, published in ten folio volumes of lithographed plates, many in color, and nine text volumes.[6] The admirable drawings of the *Description* by Dominique-Vivant Denon and other members of the expedition, made over a period of three years, represented for the first time, with great accuracy, the temples and tombs of the Nile together with the sculptures on their walls. This magnificent accomplishment was defective in one regard, however. The copies were made before Jean-François Champollion's decipherment of hieroglyphs in 1822, and "for scholarly purposes [recordings of] the inscriptions were a mishmash."[7]

In 1828 a joint French-Tuscan mission visited Egypt, headed by Champollion and his Italian pupil and friend, Ippolito Rosellini. For ten months they and their staff of architects and draftsmen copied and made notes from Alexandria to the second cataract.[8] The results of their efforts appeared in two sumptuous sets of volumes, Champollion's *Monuments* and Rosellini's *Monumenti*.[9] John A. Wilson offered this assessment of the publications: "It is easy to criticize their copies today: sometimes they are inexact for modern use; frequently they restored line or color; repetitive elements—such as a line of marching men—were apparently completed at home. Yet they were pioneers, and their volumes are still highly useful because there has been so much destruction since their day."[10]

In Champollion's time the most logical way to copy a scene or an inscription was to make a freehand drawing. Modern epigraphy, however, is more than the copying of texts and representations on temple and tombs walls for the purpose of publication;[11] it aims at rendering the actual appearance of a wall. Historically, many different recording methods have been used in the pursuit of that goal—the camera lucida, freehand copying, paper squeezes, latex or liquid rubber molds, rubbings, photography, direct tracings, drawing on photographs. The camera lucida has largely passed out of use, and squeezes, impressions, and rubbings in particular have fallen out of favor because of the damage they can inflict on friable surfaces and paint.[12] Freehand copies are infrequently used, since even a keen eye and steady hand are often insufficient to prevent distortions. The other recording methods—photography, direct tracings, and drawing on photographs—will be discussed below.

Epigraphers are frequently asked, "Why not just take a photograph?" But photographs alone rarely, if ever, constitute an adequate record of a sculptured wall surface. No single photograph can capture all the lines carved on the face of a stone wall, even if the wall surface is well preserved. The sculptured lines adequately recorded in a photograph are those that lie transversely in the path of the rays of light falling on the wall. The illumination throws a highlight on one side of the transverse line and a shadow on the other, producing contrasts that emphasize and sharply define the line. Lines that receive no such light and cast no shadows tend to disappear.[13] Breasted once observed that it would be necessary to take at least eight negatives of every inscription, each with a different illumination coming from top, bottom, right, left, and diagonally from each of the four corners to secure all the camera might record. Even then the photographs would not record all the wall discloses to the eye of a trained and experienced epigrapher.[14]

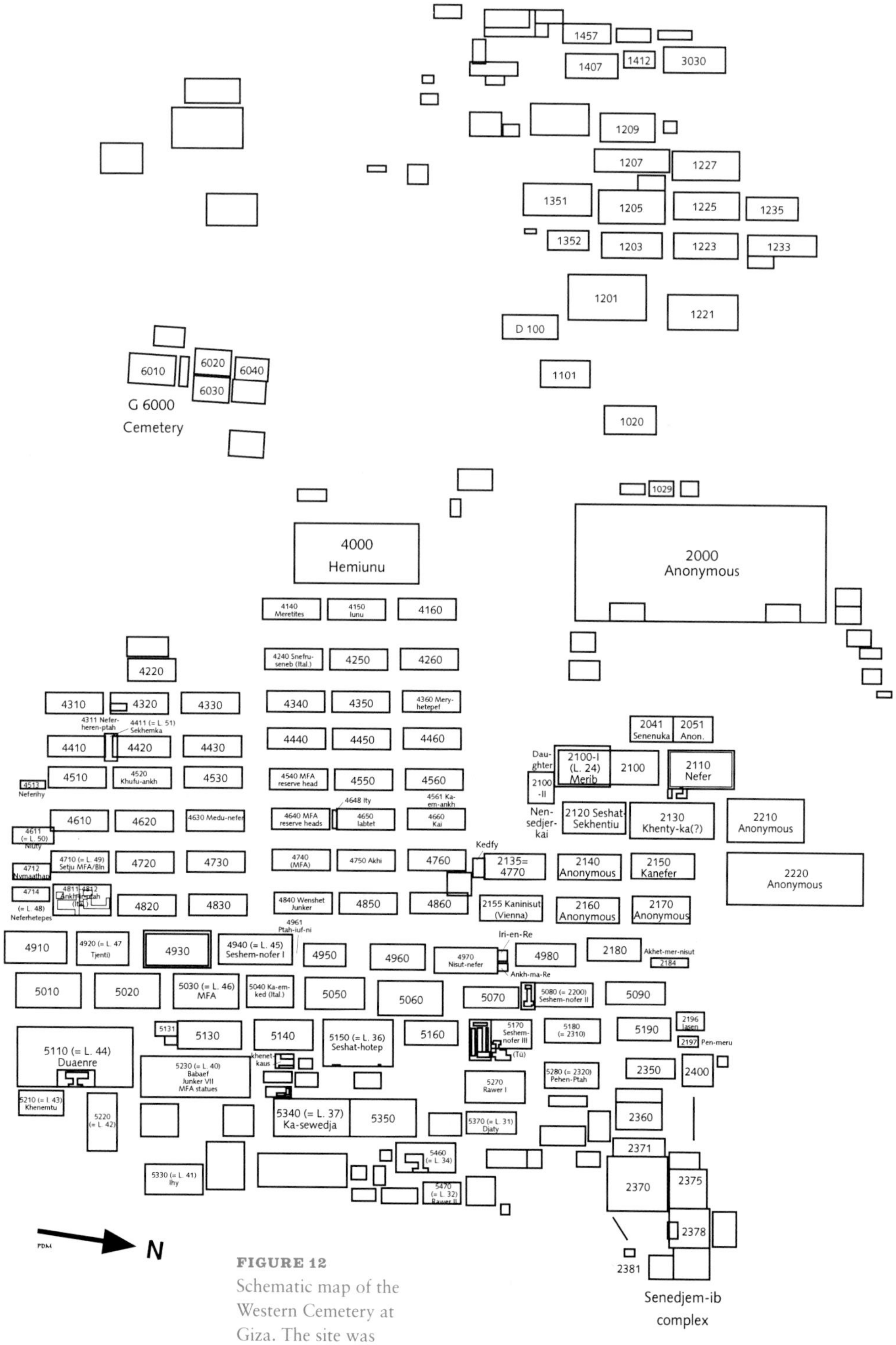

1457
1407 1412 3030

1209
1207 1227
1351 1205 1225 1235
1352 1203 1223 1233
1201 1221
D 100
1101
1020

6010 6020 6040
6030
G 6000
Cemetery

1029

4000
Hemiunu

2000
Anonymous

4140 Meretites | 4150 Iunu | 4160

4220

4240 Snefru-semeb (Ital.) | 4250 | 4260

4310 | 4320 | 4330 | 4340 | 4350 | 4360 Mery-hetepet
4311 Nefer-heren-ptah | 4411 (= L. 51) Sekhemka
4410 | 4420 | 4430 | 4440 | 4450 | 4460
4520 Khufu-ankh
4513 Neferihy | 4510 | 4530 | 4540 MFA reserve head | 4550 | 4560

2041 Senenuka | 2051 Anon.

4648 Ity | 4561 Ka-em-ankh
Daughter | 2100-I (L. 24) Merib | 2100 | 2110 Nefer
4610 | 4620 | 4630 Medu-nefer | 4640 MFA reserve heads | 4650 Iabtet | 4660 Kai
2100-II

4611 (= L. 50) Nizfy | Nen-sedjer-kai | 2120 Seshat-Sekhentiu | 2130 Khenty-ka(?) | 2210 Anonymous
4712 Setju MFA/Bln | 4710 (= L. 49) | 4720 | 4730 | 4740 (MFA) | 4750 Akhi | 4760 | Kedfy
4714 (= L. 48) Neferhetepes | 4811 4812 Ankh-haf-ptah | 4820 | 4830 | 4840 Wenshet Junker | 4850 | 4860 | 2135= 4770 | 2140 Anonymous | 2150 Kanefer | 2220 Anonymous
4961 Ptah-iuf-ni | 2155 Kaninisut (Vienna) | 2160 Anonymous | 2170 Anonymous
Iri-en-Re
4910 | 4920 (= L. 47 Tjenti) | 4930 | 4940 (= L. 45) Seshem-nofer I | 4950 | 4960 | 4970 Nisut-nefer | 4980 | 2180 | Akhet-mer-nisut 2184
Ankh-ma-Re
5010 | 5020 | 5030 (= L. 46) MFA | 5040 Ka-em-ked (Ital.) | 5050 | 5060 | 5070 | 5080 (= 2200) Seshem-nofer II | 5090
5131 | 5130 | 5140 | 5150 (= L. 36) Seshat-hotep | 5160 | 5170 Seshem-nofer III | 5180 (= 2310) | 5190 | 2196 Jasen | 2197 Peni-meru
Khenet-kaus | (Tji)
5110 (= L. 44) Duaenre | 5230 (= L. 40) Babaef Junker VIII MFA statues | 5280 (= 2320) Pehen-Ptah | 2350 | 2400
5210 (= L. 43) Khenemtu | 5270 Rawer I
5220 (= L. 42) | 5340 (= L. 37) Ka-sewedja | 5350 | 5370 (= L. 31) Djaty | 2360
5460 (= L. 34) | 2371
5330 (= L. 41) Ihy | 5470 (= L. 32) Rawer I | 2370 | 2375
2378
PDM → N | 2381

Senedjem-ib complex

FIGURE 12
Schematic map of the Western Cemetery at Giza. The site was divided into three vertical sections. George A. Reisner was initially assigned the northern third but ended up with excavation rights to two-thirds of the area when Italian excavators relinquished their section to the American expedition in 1905.

American Epigraphy at Giza

While the Saqqara cemeteries remained largely the preserve of European excavators or archaeologists from the Egyptian Antiquities Service, American archaeologists played a significantly greater role in the unearthing of the mastaba cemeteries surrounding the pyramids at Giza (see fig. 12). Indeed, the systematic excavation and recording of the Giza necropolis began with the concession granted in 1902 to an American and two European expeditions.[15]

In 1902 diplomatic pressure brought to bear by the British consul general in Egypt, Lord Cromer, forced Gaston Maspero, then director general of the Antiquities Service, to grant a concession to a Mr. Ballard, a member of the British Parliament.[16] In Reisner's opinion the Ballard expedition was a "mere looting operation."[17] Nevertheless this opened Giza to foreign concessionaires, and three foreign missions applied for and received permission to excavate at Giza. The Hearst Egyptian expedition of the University of California was represented by Reisner, the Egyptian Museum of Turin by Ernesto Schiaparelli, and the Sieglen expedition of the University of Leipzig by Georg Steindorff.[18]

As it happened, the Italian concession was given up in 1905 and assigned to Reisner. The German concession was transferred in 1911 to Hermann Junker, representing the Vienna Academy of Science and the Roemer- und Pelizaeus-Museum, Hildesheim. In 1929 Egyptian Egyptologist Selim Hassan, who later became director of the Egyptian Antiquities Department after the 1952 revolution, began excavating some rock-cut tombs in the Menkaure quarry cemetery east of the

Third Pyramid at Giza and went on to clear hundreds of tombs in the central field at Giza, on the far side of the causeway of Khafre's pyramid and the Sphinx.[19] Reisner worked at Giza between 1902 and 1941 (see fig. 10), Schiaparelli from 1903 to 1905, Steindorff from 1903 to 1907, Junker from 1912 to 1914 and 1926 to 1929, and Hassan from 1929 to 1937. Schiaparelli's excavations appeared in print only in 1963,[20] and Steindorff's work remains largely unpublished.[21] Junker's report, however, came out in twelve volumes between 1929 and 1955.[22] Hassan's excavations were the subject of ten volumes published between 1932 and 1960.[23] Both Junker and Hassan included drawings and photographs of the wall scenes they discovered, as well as lengthy commentaries, analyses, and excursuses. In addition, the English archaeologist W. M. Flinders Petrie; two Egyptians, Ahmed Fakhry and Abdel-Moneim Abu-Bakr;[24] and an American, Clarence S. Fisher (1876–1941),[25] excavated smaller areas at Giza.

Fisher conducted his excavations on behalf of the Eckley B. Coxe Jr. Expedition for the University Museum of the University of Pennsylvania from January to March 1915 and published his results in *The Minor Cemetery at Giza* (1924). The sector of the great Giza cemetery cleared by him (cemetery G3000) proved to be one of the areas set aside for tombs of lower-level bureaucrats, members of the armed forces and constabulary, sailors and dockyard staff, clergy of various mortuary cults, and the like. Most of the tombs were constructed of brick with stone fittings. A surprising number had stone casings, however, usually stepped, but this seems to have exhausted the resources of the owners, since few inscribed objects were found in the stone-cased mastabas. The only mastaba in the cemetery with significant preserved decoration belonged to an inspector of ordinary priests of the cult of King Sneferu, named Sneferuhotep after his deceased master. The offering room of this mastaba tomb had painted offering and agricultural scenes on stucco.[26]

Fisher graduated as an architect from the University of Pennsylvania and learned professional field techniques from Reisner. As a result, *The Minor Cemetery at Giza* is an excellent record of archaeological data and architectural interpretation. Fisher had never received formal Egyptological training,[27] however, and he entrusted the publication of the inscriptions, reproduced in photographs and typeset alone, to Alan Rowe, who made only an adequate job of it. The paintings of Sneferuhotep were reproduced in poor-quality aquarelles by a W. G. Kemp. Nonetheless, Fisher's excavations provide important insights into the personal circumstances and wherewithal of those on the lower rungs of the social ladder in Egypt's Old Kingdom, a class frequently ignored in Egyptological literature.

The lion's share of the Giza necropolis fell to Reisner, who turned his attention to the pyramid cemeteries in 1902. In addition to the tombs of royal family members and high state officials in the western field, Reisner cleared the great princely mastabas of the sons and daughters of Khufu in the eastern field and excavated the queen's pyramids and temples associated with the pyramid of Menkaure.[28] In 1904 Phoebe Apperson Hearst, Reisner's benefactor, notified him that "owing to a fault in the gold bearing stratum of the Homestake Mine, a large part of her income had been cut off and she was obliged to retrench her expenditures."[29] Thus she could not continue to support the expedition beyond 1905. Fortunately in that year the American concession at Giza was transferred to Harvard University and the Museum of Fine Arts, Boston.

According to Dows Dunham, Reisner's disciple and successor as curator of Egyptian art in Boston,

[Reisner] was a dedicated man devoted utterly to the service of scholarship, for which he made many sacrifices both of his own comfort and that of his family. He was largely indifferent to the amenities of life as he was to its financial rewards, and to him money was simply a necessary means to furthering the work of the Expedition. His natural bent as well as his thorough training in scholarly methods under the great German archaeologists in his early days, made him a leader in the application of scientific methods to excavation, and he trained many of the leading Egyptologists of [succeeding generations].[30]

When in the field, Reisner spent the winter excavating in the Sudan and the summer months working at Giza. Unlike many excavators of the day, he had a high regard for his Egyptian workmen and trained individuals to function as assistant draftsman, assistant publication secretary, and photographer for the expedition.[31] While at Giza Reisner lived at Harvard Camp, and there he died on June 6, 1942. His grave in the Mari Gigris cemetery in Cairo is marked by a simple tombstone of red Aswan granite bearing this inscription:

Erected in memory of George Andrew Reisner by his family by the Trustees of the Museum of Fine Arts, Boston, in honor to the archaeologist and by his Egyptian workmen in memory of their mudir and friend.

Reisner published his excavations on the Giza Plateau in his awesome *A History of the Giza Necropolis* (1942).[32] The tombs he discovered are discussed in minute detail and from almost every conceivable archaeological and architectural perspective. Reisner was interested in the typology of the wall scenes appearing in the tombs and their distribution, but only a limited number of the representations and texts were copied by the Harvard-Boston expedition. In 1905–6 Norman de

Garis Davies (1865–1941), who had earlier published the reliefs of the chapels of Ptahhotep and Akhethotep at Saqqara for the Archaeological Survey of the Egypt Exploration Fund, recorded the reliefs in a number of mastabas (G1029, G1151, G1234, G2001, etc.) for Reisner.[33] Davies and his wife, Anna (Nina) Macpherson Davies (1881–1965), later gained fame through the publication of their extraordinary facsimile copies in color of New Kingdom tombs at Thebes.[34] Winifred Firth also copied reliefs for the Harvard-Boston expedition in the chapels of the Menkaure quarry and G2184 in 1906–7.[35] Other individuals also recorded wall scenes in mastabas uncovered by Reisner at Giza, and Elizabeth Eaton copied the wall reliefs from Giza in the Museum of Fine Arts, Boston.[36]

Another member of the Harvard-Boston expedition was Joseph Lindon Smith (1863–1950), an American artist whose reproductions of Egyptian reliefs aimed at realism and three-dimensional illusion (see fig. 13). Smith had the good fortune to attract the attention of several eminent patrons, including Isabella Stuart Gardner, Phoebe Apperson Hearst, and Reisner. From 1910 Smith painted in oil many of the Giza reliefs in the Harvard-Boston concession.[37] Ultimately he became honorary curator of the Egyptian department of the Museum of Fine Arts, Boston.[38] Smith's work leaves something to be desired from the paleographical point of view, as he could not read Egyptian hieroglyphs, yet his canvases are still to be valued because of the subsequent damage and paint degradation suffered by many of the scenes he copied.

William Stevenson Smith (1907–69), a student of Reisner's and his second successor as curator of Egyptian art in Boston, incorporated numerous details of the wall reliefs found by the Harvard-Boston expedition into his fundamental study *A History of Egyptian Sculpture and Painting in the Old Kingdom* (1946), and he himself made a number of sensitive aquarelles from tombs in the Boston concession.[39] The systematic publication of the reliefs and inscriptions of the individual tomb chapels, however, was initiated only in 1974 with the appearance of *The Mastaba of Queen Mersyankh III, G7530–7540*, by Dows Dunham and William Kelly Simpson, the first volume in a series entitled Giza Mastabas and published by the Museum of Fine Arts, Boston. In the series facsimile line drawings of each scene are presented with accompanying photographs for purposes of control and comparison (see figs. 14, 15). The ability

FIGURE 13
Joseph Lindon Smith producing a facsimile painting in the tomb of Mereruka at Saqqara, 1907; from Joseph L. Smith, *Tombs, Temples, and Ancient Art* (1956), facing p. 16.

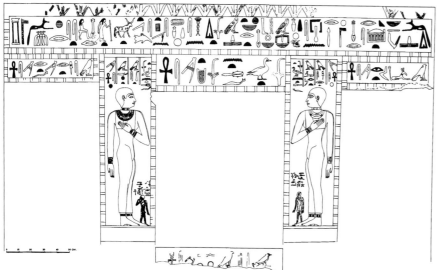

to compare is important, for in many tomb publications only a few photographs are reproduced. In the Giza Mastaba volumes the scholarly reader is able in most instances to check the accuracy of the facsimile drawings against a photograph. At the same time all the hieroglyphic texts are translated, and the scenes are described.

Subsequent volumes in the Giza Mastaba series incorporate nearly sixty other tombs, not counting subsidiary burials.[40] Reisner excavated hundreds of tombs at Giza; of these, 180 or so tombs are inscribed or decorated. Thus, approximately one hundred tombs still remain to be copied and published.

American Epigraphy at Saqqara

As already noted, the Saqqara cemeteries remained largely the preserve of archaeologists from the Egyptian Antiquities Department, either European or Egyptian. An exception, however, was the Sakkarah Expedition of the University of Chicago. Between 1931 and 1937 this expedition busied itself copying the extensive and important relief sculptures of the vizier Mereruka, a high official of King Teti, the first ruler of the 6th Dynasty.

The sumptuous two volumes of *The Mastaba of Mereruka*, published by the Oriental Institute of the University of Chicago in 1938,[41] utilized photographs, paintings, and line drawings to great advantage in reproducing the tomb's wall scenes (see figs. 16–18). As in most modern tomb publications, facsimile line drawings are accompanied by photographs for purposes of comparison and control. The volumes are unique, however, in their use of collotype, a gelatin photographic plate that yields a very rich effect (see fig. 17).

In a 1939 review of *The Mastaba of Mereruka*, Norman de Garis Davies suggested that the "two volumes could have been reduced to one of the same size and have lost little or nothing by compression," and added that the pages "cannot be rapidly run over without considerable physical fatigue."[42] He presumably was referring to the fact that the folio volumes measure nineteen by fifteen inches and weigh fifteen pounds apiece. Davies could not deny, however, that they set a new standard of publication.

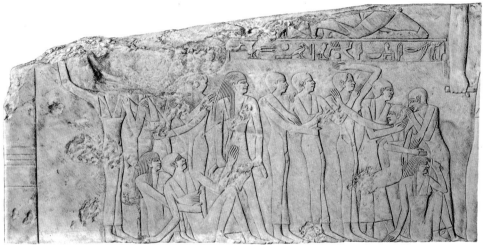

FIGURE 16
Line drawing of a scene
of mourning women
from chamber A13,
tomb of Mereruka;
from *The Mastaba of
Mereruka* (1938), vol.
2, pl. 130A (left).

FIGURE 18
Facsimile drawing of
scene of mourning
women from chamber
A13, tomb of Mereruka;
from *The Mastaba of
Mereruka* (1938), vol.
2, pl. 131.

FIGURE 17
Collotype plate of
Mereruka as repre-
sented on pier 3, west
side, chamber A13;
original painting by
expedition artist
Vcevold Strekalovsky,
from *The Mastaba of
Mereruka* (1938), vol.
2, pl. 183.

A more realistic criticism would be that no attempt was made to translate the texts or to discuss the scenes, both of which are standard practice at present. In addition, not every line drawing is accompanied by a photograph by which to check its accuracy. The absence of photographs is particularly regrettable in instances where recutting has taken place.

The famous mastabas of Princess Idut, Kagemni, Ptahhetep, and Ti were included in the Oriental Institute's original plans to salvage and publish ancient Egyptian painting in the Saqqara necropolis, but the program was abandoned and the subsidiary chapels of Mereruka's wife and son were not copied. Nearly half a century later, however, in 1986–87, Ann Macy Roth went to Saqqara as a National Endowment for the Humanities postdoctoral fellow at the American Research Center in Egypt (ARCE) to copy the tomb chapel of Watetkhethor, Mereruka's wife.[43] In 1992 and 1994 an expedition of the Museum of Fine Arts, Boston, and the University Museum, University of Pennsylvania, copied the reliefs in the chapel of the couple's son, Meriteti.[44]

Mastaba Chapels in American Institutions

Another aspect of American involvement with the Saqqara necropolis is the relocation and study of a number of mastaba chapels. These were removed from their original locations at Saqqara and presented or sold by the Egyptian government to various museums abroad, including a number of American institutions. Many of the mastabas, which Auguste Mariette had discovered and then reburied for their own protection in the 1860s,[45] had suffered severely from the depredations of dealers who paid locals to dig out the tombs by night and carry away decorated blocks for sale to museums.[46] After the turn of the century, to discourage this clandestine trade, the Egyptian Antiquities Service decided to offer complete mastaba chambers at a low price to the principal European and American museums, in the hope that the authorities of these museums would thenceforth refuse to buy detached and obviously stolen blocks.[47] Through this arrangement the Leiden museum acquired the chapel of Hetepherakhty in 1902; the Louvre purchased the chapel of Akhethotep in 1903, the surviving parts of the chapel of Werirenptah went to the British Museum in 1904; the Museum of Fine Arts, Boston, acquired the chapels of Sekhemankhptah and Kayemnofret in 1904; and Brussels received the chapel of Neferirtenef as a gift from the Egyptian government in 1905.[48] The offering chamber of Kapure, sent by the Egyptian government to America for exhibition at the Louisiana Purchase Exposition at Saint Louis in 1904, was purchased for the University Museum of the University of Pennsylvania.[49]

In 1907–8, in search of mastabas suitable for sale to museums that applied for them, James Edward Quibell, chief inspector at Saqqara, uncovered a series of tombs, most of them known since Mariette's day, in a long strip alongside the northern enclosure wall of the Step Pyramid, as well as a few tombs outside this area.[50] Copenhagen's Ny Carlsberg Glyptotek purchased most of the chapel of Kaemrehu in 1909,[51] but American museums benefited the most from Quibell's efforts. The mastaba of Perneb and the offering chamber of the tomb of Raemka, along with a wall from the tomb of Nykauhor, were taken down and sold in 1913 to the Metropolitan Museum of Art, New York.[52] Two mastaba chambers from Quibell's excavations, those of Netjeruser and Unisankh, went to the Field Museum of Natural History in Chicago.[53] Finally, in 1926, the west wall of the chapel of Kaemsenu, which had been excavated by Cecil M. Firth at Saqqara in 1921–22, was purchased by the Metropolitan Museum of Art.[54]

James Henry Breasted and T. George Allen reported on the progress made in the publication of the Saqqara mastabas removed to European and American museums in 1936.[55] There is no need to go over ground covered by them here, other than to note that in general the publication of the mastaba chapels in American museums has lagged well behind that of their European counterparts.

While the tomb chapels in European museums were often acquired with state funds, chapels in American collections were frequently purchased by wealthy benefactors. For example, Edward S. Harkness, a trustee of the Metropolitan Museum of Art, met all the expenses incurred in the purchase of the mastaba of Perneb, as well as its excavation, dismantling, and transportation to New York.[56] When the mastaba was reerected in the Egyptian galleries in 1916, a popular preliminary account was published, in which Albert M. Lythgoe detailed the tomb's removal and the principal features of its construction, and Caroline L. Ransom Williams (1872–1952) made a study of its decorative and inscriptional features.[57] Williams published a detailed study of the tomb's decoration in 1932. The volume is a signal contribution to our knowledge of the techniques used by the craftsmen who produced tomb reliefs and contains a fascinating account of the use of color in Egyptian art.[58]

Of the other mastaba sculptures from Saqqara in New York, a selection of scenes from Nykauhor's chapel was published by Quibell in line drawings.[59] Details from the carved relief scenes on the west wall of the chapel have appeared in various publications, especially the scene of a game of draughts and a group of musicians at a banquet.[60] The reliefs from the chapel of Kaemsenu were published in line drawings with commentary and translations shortly after their discovery,[61] and William C. Hayes published a photograph of the west wall, which conveys an impression of the quality of its relief.[62] No complete description of the offering room of Raemka has yet appeared, although Hayes reproduced several of the more interesting scenes, accompanied by an abbreviated commentary and translations of the texts.[63]

John Wanamaker, owner of the well-known Philadelphia department store, purchased the mastaba of Kapure for the University Museum of the University of Pennsylvania (at that time the Free Museum of Science and Art). For some years it was temporarily set up in the basement of the museum, where it might be seen, on application, by anyone who knew of its existence.[64] The chapel was permanently installed in 1926 in the museum's newly opened Eckley B. Coxe Jr. wing.[65] A publication on the tomb is being prepared by David P. Silverman.

Of the two mastaba chambers in Chicago, that of Netjeruser was among the six smaller and lesser-known tombs originally excavated by Mariette which were reexcavated and copied in 1903–4. Facsimile copies of its reliefs made by the Egyptologist Margaret Murray and two English artists, Miss F. Hansard and Miss Jessie Mothersole, were published in 1904.[66] The reliefs in the tomb of Unisankh are essentially unpublished.[67]

Except for a brief notice at the time of their accession to the museum,[68] two later articles on specific aspects of their sculptures,[69] and the illustration of certain scenes,[70] the tomb chapels of Sekhemankhptah and Kayemnofret in Boston long remained unpublished. In 1975 William Kelly Simpson presented the first complete edition of the chapel of Sekhemankhptah, followed in 1992 by a publication on the other chapel.[71]

Modern Epigraphic Technique

Two principal methods of copying wall scenes are in wide use today. The first of these is the Chicago House drawn-on photograph technique, which Prentice Duell and his colleagues used in their publication of the mastaba of Mereruka.[72] After the tomb or temple wall has been photographed, an enlarged photographic print is made. Standing before the actual wall, with the enlargement fastened to his or her drawing board, the artist adds in pencil all that can be seen, especially lines visible to the experienced eye but missed by the camera. Back in the drafting room, the artist traces in waterproof India ink the original photographic outlines and the additions made in pencil. The photographic print is then submerged in a chemical solution which bleaches out the photograph, leaving only the inked lines on a white background. A blueprint of the original is then made, and an Egyptologist-epigrapher compares it with the wall itself and makes any necessary additions or corrections. The technical term for this exhaustive process is "collation."

Before taking the drawing to the wall, the epigrapher intensively studies the inscription, including any earlier published or unpublished photographs or drawings, and searches for parallels to the scene elsewhere. At least two epigraphers, sometimes more, make corrections on the collation sheets in front of the wall. An artist then enters the epigraphers' alterations and additions on the original India ink drawing, which is checked at least once more by the epigraphers before the drawing goes to the photoengraver and printer. The drawing thus becomes a facsimile of the scene, reproducing the figures and characters carved on the wall "as accurately as may be done by inked lines on a flat surface" (see figs. 71–74).[73]

A second method is used by the Giza Pyramids Mastaba Project of the University of Pennsylvania, Yale University, and the Museum of Fine Arts, Boston, and by other expeditions currently working in Egypt. Sheets of high-transparency drafting paper with one dull surface are spread over the wall surface. An artist or Egyptologist-epigrapher traces the scene directly in pencil on the dull surface of the paper (fig. 19).[74] As with the Chicago House method, before taking the drawing to the wall, the epigrapher studies the inscription, including any earlier published or unpublished photographs or drawings, and searches for parallels to the scene. The Giza Mastabas Project is fortunate to possess the extensive archive of photographs taken by Reisner and a succession of Egyptian photographers during the course

FIGURE 19
Artist Nicholas Thayer tracing a broken lintel of Prince Minkhaf, eastern pyramid field, Giza.

of Reisner's Giza excavations.[75] The wall surfaces, particularly those outside and exposed to wind-driven sand or gratuitous vandalism, have undergone considerable deterioration in the intervening years, so these photographs, taken when the walls were freshly uncovered, are frequently consulted. After the tracing is collated by a second Egyptologist, the copies are retraced on standard drawing paper, the final tracing inked, and the resulting drawing reduced photographically to one-fifth the original size for publication.[76]

Both methods have advantages and disadvantages. The direct tracing method cannot be used when the wall surface is fragile, the paper is completely transparent only when perfectly smooth, and the wind often makes it difficult to keep the tracing against the wall.[77] The Chicago House method, by contrast, requires an elaborate infrastructure, support staff, and a substantial amount of time. Neither technique adequately accounts for the use of color in the original scene, a shortcoming that is exacerbated by the prohibitive cost of color plates.[78]

There are other methods of recording, however. Ann Macy Roth used 35mm slides to copy all reliefs in the chapel of Watetkhethor at Saqqara in 1986–87. The scenes were first photographed and measured to establish reference points; the resulting slides were then projected onto sheets of drawing paper, and the decoration recorded by tracing the projected images. Subsequently the drawings were collated on site, and the final inked drawings were made on tracing paper, incorporating the corrections.[79]

A relatively new method that holds considerable potential for the future is digital epigraphy. Photographs are scanned into the computer and traced on-screen using a vector drawing program. The drawing files can be edited, scaled, cropped, colorized, shaded, and so forth. Peter der Manuelian of the Museum of Fine Arts, Boston, has been experimenting with digital epigraphy in his publication of cemetery G2100 at Giza with excellent results.

Recent Explorations on the Giza Plateau

A number of recent and current American archaeological projects at Giza should be noted. In a series of related projects, Mark Lehner of the University of Chicago's Oriental Institute has aimed to clarify a variety of issues involving the necropolis and the people who labored and were buried there. From 1980 to 1984, under the auspices of ARCE and with the encouragement of the Egyptian Antiquities Organization, Lehner and James P. Allen (working 1978–81) carried out an architectural, archaeological, and geo-archaeological study of the Giza Sphinx.[80] The Sphinx Project resulted in a set of true-to-scale contoured drawings of the monument, achieved with the help of photogrammetry (the use of aerial photographs to obtain reliable measurements), conventional surveying techniques, and computer-

FIGURE 20
Computer-generated
isometric rendering of
the Sphinx.

generated models of the Sphinx, both as originally carved in the 4th Dynasty and as renovated during the 18th Dynasty (see fig. 20).[81] Of considerable import was Lehner's demonstration that the solar temple below the paws of the Sphinx definitely dated to the Old Kingdom: as the sedimentary bedrock of the Sphinx was cut from the top down, it was used to raise the walls of the temple.[82]

Since 1983 the Giza Plateau Mapping Project, also under Lehner's direction, has addressed many questions about the origins of the pyramids. Lehner has followed a contextual approach to the Giza Plateau which recognizes its overall spatial patterning and attempts to understand how that patterning relates to the shape and characteristics of the landforms that host the pyramids.[83] The main objective of the project is the production of a large-scale (1:1,000) contoured map that ties together the plans of the major pyramids, temples, and cemeteries with the topography of the site. Other goals include larger-scale archaeological studies of poorly documented structures in the necropolis; a geological study of the limestone formation of the Giza Plateau and the quarried stone forming the pyramids, temples, and tombs at the site to determine the source of the stone and the sequence of quarrying and construction; an examination of rock-cut features left in the floors around the Khufu and Khafre pyramids in an analysis of how stone was used in the layout and orientation of the pyramids;[84] and, to clarify the patterning of areas of various activities, a sedimentological study and spatial analysis to determine deposits resulting from quarrying, masonry, construction ramps, and settlements.[85] One result of the mapping project has been an extraordinary isometric rendering of the Giza Plateau showing how the landscape affected the manner in which the 4th Dynasty Egyptians mobilized to build the Great Pyramid of Khufu, the first major construction project on the plateau (see fig. 21).[86]

FIGURE 21
Isometric reconstruction
of the Giza Plateau by
Mark Lehner, 1995.

In 1988–89 the Giza Plateau Mapping Project shifted its focus to the whereabouts of workers' accommodations. Petrie had dug two of the one hundred or so long, narrow galleries contained within a great rectangular enclosure (four hundred by eighty meters) west of the Second Pyramid, and he concluded that they were the barracks of workmen. Lehner and his team found no evidence that people had once lived there and concluded from the remaining evidence that the galleries were utilized for royal craft work and storage activities only.[87] But in three areas of low desert to the south of the great stone wall south of the Sphinx, Lehner's excavation teams found impressive evidence of food storage and production for pyramid workers.[88]

Lehner and his team work in close collaboration with Zahi Hawass, general director of antiquities of the Giza pyramids and Saqqara. Immediately to the west of the food production complex uncovered by the American expedition, Hawass discovered the cemetery of the workmen who built the pyramids. Unique to the cemetery are beehive-shaped tombs of mud brick that mark the graves of many workers. Thirty large tombs and some six hundred small tombs have been found to date.[89]

Temple Reliefs

Americans have not played a large role in the publication of Old Kingdom royal temple reliefs. An exception is Hans Goedicke's study of Old Kingdom royal reliefs reused in the pyramid at Lisht of Amenemhat I, founder of the 12th Dynasty.[90] Publication of the reused blocks established beyond reasonable doubt that the pyramid temples and causeways of the 4th Dynasty sovereigns Khufu and Khafre were indeed decorated with relief carvings.

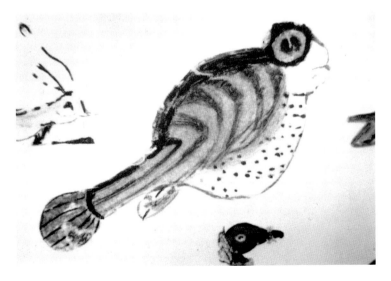

FIGURE 22
Watercolor rendering by William Stevenson Smith of the blowfish hieroglyph from the tomb of Kakherptah at Giza.

Old Kingdom Paleography

Although at present no comprehensive hieroglyphic paleography of the Old Kingdom, dealing with the origin and development of signs and their uses and values, exists,[91] American contributions to the field include William Stevenson Smith's tabulation of the coloring of Old Kingdom hieroglyphs, published along with two color plates of fifty or so complicated signs painted in watercolor in *A History of Egyptian Sculpture and Painting in the Old Kingdom*.[92] Extensive color notes by Smith together with a large number of his original watercolor renderings of hieroglyphic signs are conserved in Boston. The individual signs are frequently minor artworks in themselves (see fig. 22). Also on file in Boston are unpublished color notes by Caroline Ransom Williams on tombs in the Harvard-Boston concession at Giza.

No living Egyptologist has done more than Henry G. Fischer (b. 1923) to sensitize colleagues to the form and context of hieroglyphs. In a series of articles and books he has devoted considerable thought to the origin and development of individual hieroglyphic signs.[93] In "Archaeological Aspects of Epigraphy and Palaeography," he observed that "it is not sufficient only to examine the paleographic development of the signs; one must simultaneously take into account such epigraphic considerations as their location, orientation, layout and spacing. In short, it is not only the form that counts, but the context."[94] In the same essay Fischer reviewed various contexts, and in a later volume he examined in depth changes in orientation of hieroglyphs within the same inscription.[95]

Fischer has likewise pointed out that the paleographic development of signs, as well as such epigraphic considerations as their location, orientation, layout, and spacing, can be an important aid in dating and establishing the provenance of archaeological material. In periods when few conventional historical documents were produced, such as the late Old Kingdom and the Heracleopolitan period, the signs tended to develop local peculiarities that can even suggest the extent of contact and alliance between various towns and provinces.[96] Expanding on the earlier work of German scholars H. J. Polotsky[97] and Wolfgang Schenkel,[98] Fischer has analyzed some of these idiosyncrasies and has demonstrated how they can aid the scholar in writing the history of these dimly understood epochs.[99] Fischer's research has underlined the loss of information resulting from standardization of hieroglyphic signs and line drawings by many early epigraphers.[100]

CHAMPOLLION BEGAN THE COLOSSAL TASK of recording the monuments of ancient Egypt in 1829. In the following 150 years, to quote Darwin in another context, "progress has been much more general than retrogression."[101] But a great deal remains to be done, and it is devoutly hoped that Americans will continue to play a prominent role in the recording and publication of texts and representations from the great mastaba cemeteries of the Pyramid Age.

Notes

I would like to thank my wife, Del Nord, and an old friend and colleague, Cynthia May Sheikolislami, for a number of helpful suggestions that have been incorporated in the text.

1 Cecil M. Firth and Battiscombe Gunn, *Teti Pyramid Cemeteries*, Excavations at Saqqara 7 (Cairo: IFAO, 1926), vol. 1, 38, 142 [20], vol. 2, pl. 20 C (chapel of Satinteti in situ), D (reused block of Watetkhethor). For a second reused block from Watetkhethor's chapel, see vol. 2, 142 [19], 208 [9] (sidepiece of Nes[et]userti).

2 The Sakkarah Expedition, *The Mastaba of Mereruka*, vol. 1, OIP 31 (Chicago: University of Chicago Press, 1938), xii.

3 Karl Richard Lepsius, *Denkmäler aus Ägypten und Äthiopien: Ergänzungsband* (Leipzig: J. C. Hinrichs, 1913), xxii [b].

4 George A. Reisner, "A Family of Builders of the Sixth Dynasty, about 2600 B.C.," *BMFA* 11 (November 1913): 53.

5 Chicago, Field Museum 31705; Lepsius, *Ergänzungsband*, xvi.

6 See Sergio Donadoni et al., *Egypt from Myth to Egyptology* (Milan: Fabbri Editori, 1990), 110.

7 John A. Wilson, *Signs and Wonders upon Pharaoh: A History of American Egyptology* (Chicago: University of Chicago Press, 1964), 30.

8 Ibid.

9 Jean-François Champollion, *Monuments de l'Egypte et de la Nubie*, 4 vols. (Paris: Firmin Didot Frères, 1835–45); idem, *Notices descriptives*, 2 vols. (Paris: Firmin Didot Frères, 1844–89); Ippolito Rosellini, *I monumenti dell'Egitto e della Nubia*, 11 vols. (Pisa: Capurro, 1832–44).

10 Wilson, *Signs and Wonders*, 30.

11 See Ricardo Caminos and Henry G. Fischer, *Ancient Egyptian Epigraphy and Palaeography* (New York: MMA, 1976), 3.

12 Ibid., 15–16.

13 James H. Breasted, *The Oriental Institute*, University of Chicago Survey 12 (Chicago: University of Chicago Press, 1933), 203–4.

14 Ibid.

15 George A. Reisner, *A History of the Giza Necropolis*, vol. 1 (Cambridge: Harvard University Press, 1942), 22. Reisner provides a list of scholars who have copied reliefs and inscriptions in the Giza mastabas, beginning with the French expedition of 1798–1801.

16 For the Ballard excavations, see William Stevenson Smith, *A History of Egyptian Sculpture and Painting in the Old Kingdom*, 2d ed. (London: Oxford University Press, 1949), 67–68; PM, 2d ed., vol. 3, 175–76.

17 George A. Reisner, autobiographical ms., Department of Ancient Egyptian, Nubian, and Near Eastern Art, MFA, Boston, 4–5. All references to this manuscript have been cited with the kind permission of Rita E. Freed, curator of ancient Egyptian, Nubian, and ancient Near Eastern art.

18 See Reisner, *Giza Necropolis*, vol. 1, 22–23.

19 Ibid., 23.

20 Silvio Curto, *Gli scavi italiani a el-Ghiza (1903)*, Centro per le antichità e la storio dell'arte del Vicino Oriente, Monografie di archeologia e d'arte 1 (Rome: Aziende Tipografiche eredi Dotti G. Bardi, 1963).

21 See Georg Steindorff and Uvo Hölscher, *Die Mastabas westlich der Cheopspyramide nach den Ergebnissen der in den Jahren 1903–1907 im Auftrag der Universität Leipzig und des Hildesheimer Pelizaeus-Museums unternommenen Grabungen in Giza*, 2 vols., ed. and rev. by Alfred Grimm (Frankfurt am Main: Peter Lang, 1991). For texts and objects from the excavations, see PM, 2d ed., vol. 3, 108–18, 177.

22 Hermann Junker, *Giza: Bericht über die von der Akademie der Wissenschaften in Wien auf gemeinsame Kosten mit Dr. Wilhelm Pelizaeus unternommenen Grabungen auf Friedhof des Alten Reich bei den Pyramiden von Giza*, 12 vols. (Vienna: Hölder-Pichler-Tempsky and Rudolf M. Rohrer, 1929–55).

23 Selim Hassan, *Excavations at Giza*, 10 vols. (Oxford: Faculty of Arts of the Egyptian University; Cairo: Government Press, 1936–60); Warren R. Dawson and Eric P. Uphill, *Who Was Who in Egyptology*, 2d rev. ed. (London: Egypt Exploration Society, 1972), 134.

24 See W. M. Flinders Petrie, *Gizeh and Rifeh*, Publications of the Egyptian Research Account 13 (London: Bernard Quaritch, 1907), 8–9, pls. 7A–D; Ahmed Fakhry, *Sept tombeaux à l'est de la grande pyramide de Guizeh* (Cairo: IFAO, 1935); and Abdel-Moneim Abu Bakr, *Excavations at Giza, 1949–1950* (Cairo: Government Press, 1953).

25 For Fisher's achievements as an excavator, see David O'Connor and David Silverman, "The Museum in the Field," *Expedition* 21 (Winter 1979): 22–26.

26 Clarence S. Fisher, *The Minor Cemetery at Giza*, Eckley B. Coxe Jr. Foundation, n.s., 1 (Philadelphia: University Museum, 1924), pls. 53–55.

27 For Fisher's career, see O'Connor and Silverman, "Museum in the Field," 23.

28 In both the western and eastern fields the tombs of lesser officials and descendants or funerary priests of the original owners filled the streets and any available spaces.

29 Reisner, autobiographical ms., 5–6.

30 Dows Dunham, *The Egyptian Department and Its Excavations* (Boston: MFA, 1958), 23.

31 Reisner, *Giza Necropolis*, vol. 1, viii–ix.

32 The second part of *History of the Giza Necropolis*, vol. 1, chaps. 9–14, on the service equipment of the chapels and the funerary equipment found in the burial chambers, is presently being edited for publication by Edward Brovarski.

33 See Reisner, *Giza Necropolis*, vol. 1, vii. A watercolor reconstruction of the portico of Tjetu I (G2001) and two more details from the portico by Davies are published in William Kelly Simpson, *Mastabas of the Western Cemetery*, pt. 1 (Boston: MFA, 1980), frontispiece and color plates A and B. Davies also copied and published the reliefs in a number of Old Kingdom tombs for the Egypt Exploration Fund; see Norman de Garis Davies, *The Mastaba of Ptahhetep and Akhethetep at Saqqarah*, 2 vols., Memoirs of the Archaeological Survey of Egypt 8, 9 (London: Egypt Exploration Fund, 1900–1901); idem, *The Rock Tombs of Sheikh Said*, Memoirs of the Archaeological Survey of Egypt 10 (London: Egypt Exploration Fund, 1901); idem, *The Rock Tombs of Deir el Gebrâwi*, 2 vols., Memoirs of the Archaeological Survey of Egypt 11, 12 (London: Egypt Exploration Fund, 1902–3).

34 Nina Davies included four copies of Old Kingdom scenes in the first of two folio volumes of idem, *Ancient Egyptian Paintings* (Chicago: University of Chicago Press, 1936).

35 See Reisner, *Giza Necropolis*, vol. 1, vii. On G2184, see Sue D'Auria, Peter Lacovara, and Catharine H. Roehrig, *Mummies and Magic: The Funerary Arts of Ancient Egypt*, exh. cat. (Boston: MFA, 1988), no. 14.

36 Reisner, *Giza Necropolis*, vol. 1, vii, no. 14.

37 Ibid., vii.

38 For an eminently readable account of Smith's life, see Joseph L. Smith, *Tombs, Temples, and Ancient Art*, ed. Corinna L. Smith (Norman: University of Oklahoma Press, 1956).

39 See, e.g., Kent R. Weeks, *Mastabas of Cemetery G 6000, Including G6010 (Neferbauptah), G6020 (Iymery), G6030 (Ity), G6040 (Shepseskaf-ankh)*, Giza Mastabas 5 (Boston: MFA, 1995), color plates 6B, 7A–B, 8.

40 Simpson produced three more volumes in the series: *The Mastabas of Qar and Idu, G 7101 and 7102*, Giza Mastabas 2 (Boston: MFA, 1976); *The Mastabas of Kawab: Khafkhufu I and II, G 7110–20, 7130–40, and 7150 and Subsidiary Mastabas of Street G 7100*, Giza Mastabas 3 (Boston: MFA, 1978); *Mastabas of the Western Cemetery*, pt. 1, *Sekhemka (G 1029); Tjetu I (G 2001); Iasen (G 2196); Penmeru (G 2197); Hagy, Nefertjentet, and Herunefer (G 2352/53); Djaty, Tjetu II, and Nimesti (G 2337 X, 2343, 2366)*, Giza Mastabas 4 (Boston: MFA, 1980). In 1995, after a long hiatus, a fifth volume in the series appeared, *Mastabas of Cemetery G 6000*, authored by Kent R. Weeks, professor of Egyptology at the American University in Cairo. At present six additional volumes are well advanced or projected: Ann Macy Roth, *A Cemetery of Palace Attendants (Hntyw-š)*; Edward Brovarski, *The Senedjemib Complex*, pt. 1; William K. Simpson, *The Mastabas of the Seshemnofer I and II*; Peter der Manuelian, *Mastabas of Nucleus Cemetery G 2100*;

Edward Brovarski, *The Senedjemib Complex*, pt. 2; idem, *The Princely Mastabas of the Eastern Cemetery*.

41 The Sakkarah Expedition, *The Mastaba of Mereruka*, 2 vols., OIP 31, 39 (Chicago: University of Chicago Press, 1938).

42 Norman de Garis Davies, review of *The Mastaba of Mereruka*, *JEA* 25 (1939): 223–24.

43 Ann Macy Roth, "The Test of an Epigraphic Method," *NARCE*, no. 141 (Spring 1988): 7–13.

44 The codirectors of the project were Rita Freed and Edward Brovarski, Museum of Fine Arts, Boston, and David Silverman, University of Pennsylvania. This was one aspect of the work in the Teti pyramid cemetery, which also included the two Middle Kingdom chapels of Ihy and Hetep.

45 Auguste Mariette, *Les mastabas de l'ancien empire: Fragment du dernier ouvrage de A. Mariette* (Paris: F. Vieweg, 1889).

46 As James H. Breasted and T. G. H. Allen noted (foreword, *Mastaba of Mereruka*, vol. 1, xiv), the reexcavation and full publication of the Saqqara tombs discovered by Mariette remain a responsibility for the future.

47 James E. Quibell, *Excavations at Saqqara (1907–1908)*, Excavations at Saqqara 3 (Cairo: IFAO, 1909), 22–23.

48 Breasted and Allen, in *Mastaba of Mereruka*, vol. 1, xvi–xvii.

49 Ibid., xvii.

50 Quibell, *Excavations at Saqqara, 1907–1908*, 22–23.

51 As Breasted and Allen noted (*Mastaba of Mereruka*, vol. 1, xvii), the east wall of the chapel had been removed by Mariette and remained in Cairo (CG 1534).

52 Quibell, *Excavations at Saqqara, 1907–1908*, 24, 25; MMA, *The Tomb of Perneb* (New York: [Gilliss Press], 1916), 26–29.

53 Quibell, *Excavations at Saqqara, 1907–1908*, 23.

54 William C. Hayes, *The Scepter of Egypt: A Background for the Study of Egyptian Antiquities in the Metropolitan Museum of Art*, vol. 1 (New York: MMA, 1953), 104.

55 In *Mastaba of Mereruka*, vol. 1, xvi–xvii. The surviving parts of the chapel of Werirenptah in the British Museum have been republished in modern line drawings with a brief descriptive text, in T. G. H. James, *Hieroglyphic Texts from Egyptian Stelae, etc., in the British Museum*, 2d ed.

(London: British Museum, 1961), vol. 1, pls. 28–30. A definitive publication of the chapel of Neferirtenef in Brussels has appeared in Baudouin van de Walle, *La chapelle funéraire de Neferirtenef* (Brussels: Musées royaux d'art et d'histoire, 1978). The first complete edition and commentary on the Louvre mastaba appeared in Christiane Ziegler, *Le mastaba d'Akhethetep: Une chapelle funéraire de l'Ancien Empire* (Paris: Réunion des Musées Nationaux, 1993).

56 MMA, *The Tomb of Perneb*, 28–29.

57 Caroline Ransom Williams, *The Decoration of the Tomb of Per-neb*, Publications of the Department of Egyptian Art 3 (New York: MMA, 1932).

58 See Breasted and Allen, in *Mereruka*, vol. 1, xvii.

59 Quibell, *Excavations at Saqqara, 1907–1908*, pls. 62–66.

60 PM, 2d ed., vol. 3, 498.

61 Firth and Gunn, *Teti Pyramid Cemetery*, vol. 1, 32, 157–64, vol. 2, pls. 62–63.

62 Hayes, *Scepter of Egypt*, vol. 1, 105, fig. 60.

63 Ibid., 94–102, figs. 54–57.

64 David P. Silverman, "The Title *wr bzt* in the Tomb Chapel of *K3.(j)-pw-R(TM)*," in *For His Ka: Essays Offered in Memory of Klaus Baer*, ed. David P. Silverman, Studies in Ancient Oriental Civilization 55 (Chicago: Oriental Institute, University of Chicago, 1993) 245, and the following article.

65 See Cornelia H. Dam, "The Tomb Chapel of Ra-Ka-Pou," *Museum Journal* 18 (1927): 188–200, for a brief description of the scenes and small-scale photographs. For the conversation of the workmen depicted on the mastaba walls, see [C.] P[hillipus] M[iller], "Conversations and Calls Recorded on the Walls of the Tomb of Kapuire," *University Museum Bulletin* 7 (April 1937): 26–30. The author's name and this article were brought to my attention by David P. Silverman, curator of the Egyptian Section, University of Pennsylvania Museum of Archaeology and Anthropology.

66 Margaret A. Murray, *Saqqara Mastabas*, pt. 1, Memoirs of the Egyptian Research Account 10 (London: Bernard Quaritch, 1904), 19–24, pls. 20–23, 32.

67 See PM, 2d ed., vol. 2, 616–17.

68 L. E. Rowe, "Two Mastaba Chambers," *BMFA* 8 (1910): 19–20.

69 Dows Dunham, "A 'Palimpsest' on an Egyptian Mastaba Wall," *AJA* 39 (1935): 300–309; Emily Teeter, "Techniques and Terminology of Rope-Making in Ancient Egypt," *JEA* 73 (1987): 71–77.

70 For specific references, see PM, 2d ed., vol. 3, 454–55, 467–68.

71 William Kelly Simpson, *The Offering Chapel of Sekhem-ankh-ptah in the Museum of Fine Arts, Boston* (Boston: MFA, 1976); idem, *The Offering Chapel of Kayemnofret in the Museum of Fine Arts, Boston* (Boston: MFA, 1992). Both folio volumes include a concise commentary and translations of the hieroglyphic texts coupled with facsimile drawings and photographs of the chapels. The drawings are presented at a usable scale (1:5) that communicates the artistry of the ancient sculptor, and details are provided at larger scales. The numerous photographs provide a standard for verifying the accuracy of the drawings.

72 This summary of the Chicago House method closely follows Breasted, *The Oriental Institute*, 205–12.

73 Ibid., 209–12.

74 The Egypt Exploration Society in its work in the New Kingdom necropolis south of the Unas causeway at Saqqara utilizes an allied method, except that tracings are made with a fine-tipped marker on clear plastic film; once the facsimile tracings have been transferred to paper or photographically reproduced, the tracings can be washed off and the film used again.

75 See Reisner, *Giza Necropolis*, vol. 1, viii; and Peter der Manuelian, ed., "George Andrew Reisner on Archaeoogical Photography," *JARCE* 29 (1992): 1–34.

76 See William Kelly Simpson, "The Pennsylvania-Yale Giza Project," *Expedition* 21 (Winter 1979): 61–62.

77 Ibid.

78 As Ricardo Caminos has noted: "Paint is inseparable from the inscriptions and figures on which it is laid, and no record is either satisfactory or complete that fails to give an adequate account of it, no matter how large or small the amount of color still extant may be" (*Ancient Egyptian Epigraphy and Palaeography*, 22).

79 Roth, "The Test of an Epigraphic Method," 8–9.

80 For a concise summary of the work, see Mark Lehner, "Reconstructing the Sphinx," *Cambridge Archaeological Journal* 2 (1992): 3–26. The Sphinx Project actually began in 1980, with James P. Allen, then Cairo director of ARCE and now associate curator of Egyptian art at the Metropolitan Museum of Art, as project director and Mark Lehner as field director.

81 Ibid., 8–24, figs. 3–11.

82 Mark Lehner, "The ARCE Sphinx Project: A Preliminary Report," *NARCE*, no. 112 (Fall 1980): 14–15.

83 Ibid., 23–24.

84 See Mark Lehner, "Some Observations on the Layout of the Khufu and Khafre Pyramids," *JARCE* 20 (1983): 7–25.

85 Ibid., 26–27.

86 Mark Lehner, "Excavations at Giza, 1988–1991: The Location and Importance of the Pyramid Settlement," *The Oriental Institute: News and Notes*, no. 135 (Fall 1992): 1.

87 Ibid., 2.

88 Ibid., 6–7.

89 Zahi Hawass, personal communication.

90 Hans Goedicke, *Re-used Blocks from the Pyramid of Amenemhat I at Lisht*, MMA Egyptian Expedition 20 (New York: MMA, 1971). Modern facsimile drawings by Lindsley Hall in the volume are very fine.

91 Nathalie Beaux has embarked on just such a study, beginning with the hieroglyphic signs inscribed on the walls of the tomb chapels of the Harvard-Boston concession at Giza.

92 Smith, *Egyptian Sculpture and Painting*, 366–82, pls. A, B. In *Saqqara Mastabas*, vol. 1, pls. 41–45, Murray gives a list in tabular form of the colors of the hieroglyphs found in the tombs published in the volume.

93 See esp. Henry G. Fischer, *Varia*, Egyptian Studies 1 (New York: MMA, 1977); and idem, *Ancient Egyptian Calligraphy: A Beginner's Guide to Writing Hieroglyphs*, 3d ed. (New York: MMA, 1988). Fischer, in the latter volume, encouraged a better standard in writing Egyptian hieroglyphs and contributed numerous insightful remarks on the origin and development of hieroglyphic script. He has published in his articles and books numerous Old Kingdom monuments in line drawings and photographs.

94 Caminos and Fischer, *Ancient Egyptian Epigraphy and Palaeography*, 29.

95 Henry G. Fischer, *The Orientation of Hieroglyphs*, pt. 1, *Reversals*, Egyptian Studies 2 (New York: MMA, 1977).

96 Caminos and Fischer, *Ancient Egyptian Epigraphy and Palaeography*, 30.

97 H. J. Polotsky, *Zu den Inschriften der 11. Dynastie*, Untersuchungen zur Geschichte und Altertumskunde Ägyptens 11 (Leipzig: J. C. Hinrichs, 1929).

98 Wolfgang Schenkel, *Frühmittelägyptische Studien* (Bonn: Bonn University Press, 1962).

99 E.g., Henry G. Fischer, *Inscriptions from the Coptite Nome, Dynasties VI–XI*, Analecta Orientalia 40 (Rome: Pontificum Institutum Biblicum, 1964); idem, *Dendera in the Third Millennium B.C. down to the Theban Domination of Upper Egypt* (Locust Valley, N.Y.: J. J. Augustin, 1968).

100 See, e.g., the instances of the practice cited by Caminos, *Ancient Egyptian Epigraphy and Palaeography*, 4–6.

101 Charles Darwin, *The Descent of Man and Selection in Relation to Sex* (1871), chap. 4.

The American Discovery of Middle Kingdom Texts

James P. Allen

American scholars have expanded our knowledge of ancient Egypt not only through the archaeological discovery of its artifacts but also by recovering its texts through epigraphy. American contributions to epigraphy extend from the copying and preservation of textual sources to the larger area of translation, interpretation, and publication. This kind of study is generally classified as philology. As used by most Egyptologists, the term *philology* means the attempt to understand all aspects of an ancient text: its words and sentences (lexicography and grammar), how it was written down (epigraphy and paleography), and how it fits into the culture and history of its time.

The earliest publication by an American to address any of these aspects appeared in 1887 under the title "The Language of the Ancient Egyptians and Its Monumental Records."[1] Its author, Charles Moldenke (1860–1935), was a Lutheran minister who had studied at Columbia University and in Germany. Moldenke is otherwise remembered, if at all, for a small book on the New York obelisk (Cleopatra's Needle).[2] Despite its philological title, his article is mostly a useful survey of Egyptian collections in the United States.

Two of Moldenke's senior contemporaries better deserve to be honored as the first American philologists of ancient Egyptian, and they would, in fact, be so remembered except that neither ever published, a critical failing in a field where "reputation is more likely to be established not by what you accomplish but by what you publish."[3]

Edwin Smith (1822–1906) was born in Bridgeport, Connecticut, in the year that Jean-François Champollion first deciphered hieroglyphs. He studied Egyptian in London and Paris "when the science was only a quarter of a century old, and was probably the first American to learn scientifically the little then known about the Egyptian language."[4] Smith not only learned to read hieroglyphs, but he also specialized in hieratic, the handwritten form of hieroglyphs, about which even less was

FIGURE 23
James H. Breasted at his desk in the Haskell Museum.

known. He is recognized today for the medical papyrus that bears his name, one of two he bought in 1862 (the other he sold to the German Egyptologist Georg Ebers, who published it in 1874). Although Smith studied his papyrus extensively, he never published his findings, perhaps because there was little American interest in Egyptology.[5] In the years following the Civil War, America was looking west, toward the frontier and the future, and had little time for the past that lay behind to the east. In a sense the legacy of this orientation—or occidentalization—is still with us: most of America's major universities still do not support the study of Egyptology.

Smith's papyrus was presented to the New-York Historical Society at his death (it is now in the New York Academy of Medicine) and was finally published by James Henry Breasted in 1930. Breasted was surprised to find in Smith's notes "a remarkable attempt...at a complete translation" of the Middle Egyptian language of the text: "When we recall how scanty was the knowledge of hieratic in the sixties of the last century...not to mention the very limited knowledge of the Egyptian language itself available at so early a stage of Egyptian studies, it is extraordinary how much of the document Mr. Smith has understood."[6]

Smith's philological abilities were equaled, if not surpassed, by those of his contemporary Charles Edwin Wilbour (1833–96; see fig. 24).[7] From 1880 to 1896 Wilbour spent the winter months in Egypt, much of that time on his famous boat, the *Seven Hathors*, a *dahabiya* which was equipped with a full Egyptological library. His primary interest was in copying inscriptions. He was America's first epigrapher, driven to record the ancient texts he saw even then disappearing year by year. He wrote in 1883: "At Kom Ombos, I broke my neck copying the astronomical inscriptions on the ceiling til five...but I found when I went over to the little birth-temple on the brink [of the river] that one of its three remaining walls had fallen [into the river] and an interesting invocation to the Elder Horus, which I noted for copying just fourteen months ago, is lost to Egyptian literature as it will be known to us."[8]

John A. Wilson has cited the same letter, which tells how Wilbour then spent the night copying the remaining texts while his companions played chess in the *dahabiya*'s salon: "The servants were in terror of the ghost that haunted the temple, but [Wilbour] finally persuaded two of them to accompany him. 'And so with fear and trembling, a lantern and a chair, they went to the temple. It was much better than the cigars in the salon; the air was soft and warm, and I did not need my old cloak.' And so he copied on and on in happiness."[9]

The generation following Smith and Wilbour gave America its first professional Egyptologists. Two of these younger scholars, George Andrew Reisner and James Henry Breasted (see fig. 25), founded academic Egyptology in the United States, the first as the father of Egyptian archaeology, the other as the father of

Egyptian philology. Both men made significant contributions not only to the field in general but also to our knowledge of Middle Kingdom texts.

Reisner is best known for his work on the Old Kingdom cemetery in Giza and the Meroitic monuments of the Sudan, but his name is also associated with several major Middle Kingdom sources. Among these, the most significant are the First Intermediate Period and Middle Kingdom stelae, coffins, and papyri—including "perhaps the earliest inscribed and painted coffin with Coffin Texts"[10]—found by Reisner during excavations for the University of California, Harvard University, and the Museum of Fine Arts, Boston, at the sites of el-Bersha, Deir el-Ballas, and Naga el-Deir. Most of these finds have been studied and published by his successors in the Egyptian department at the Museum of Fine Arts, in particular Dows Dunham, William Kelly Simpson, and Edward J. Brovarski. Reisner himself published the Hearst Medical Papyrus, a Middle Egyptian text acquired during his work at Deir el-Ballas and named for the expedition's patron, Phoebe Apperson Hearst.

Breasted was appointed in 1894 to the first American teaching position in Egyptology, at the new University of Chicago.[11] In the same year he married and spent his honeymoon in Egypt recording ancient texts. In the tradition of Wilbour, Breasted too "never lost a moment copying inscriptions—and on one night at Karnak [even] by moonlight."[12] At Aswan he lamented, "Oh, for the time to copy and publish these inscriptions!"[13] These two themes would occupy his life. Rather than find new monuments, Breasted wanted to record and, unlike Wilbour, to publish the texts already visible: "Excavation seemed to him eminently worth-while but of secondary importance.... Egypt's *buried* antiquities were reasonably safe and could wait. But the inscribed records on her ancient monuments were exposed to weathering and vandalism, and even since the days of...Napoleon and Lepsius, had very perceptibly suffered."[14]

To accomplish these goals, Breasted established the Epigraphic Survey in 1924 under the auspices of the Oriental Institute, which he had founded at the University of Chicago in 1919. The work of the Epigraphic Survey has concentrated mostly on the New Kingdom tombs and temples of Thebes (see fig. 26), but Breasted himself had decided as early as 1922 that "the first project of the Oriental Institute in Egypt should be the formidable task of copying the thousands of surviving lines of Coffin Texts"—by his own count, actually 29,432 lines—"and preparing them for publication."[15]

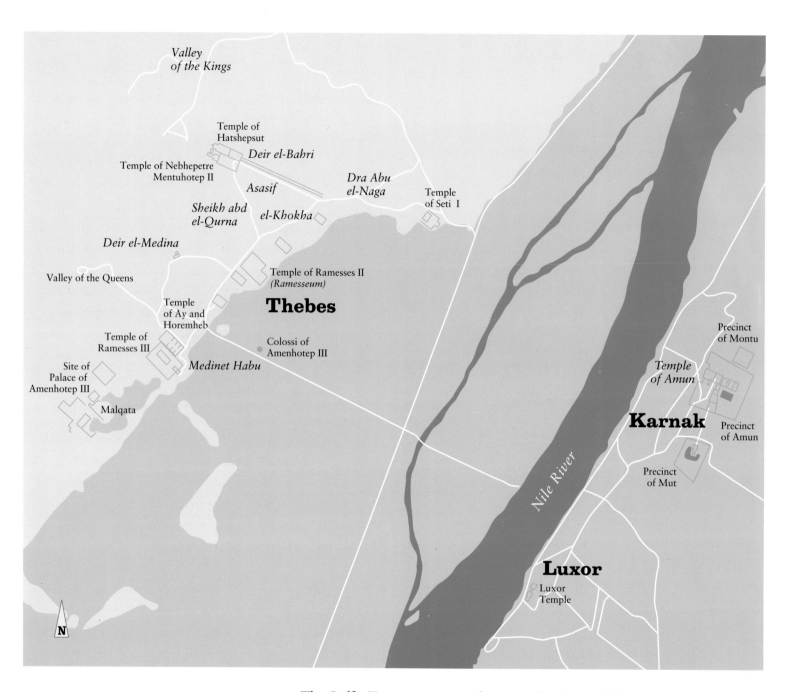

FIGURE 26
Thebes.

The Coffin Texts are a series of some twelve hundred funerary spells, inscribed for the most part on the inner walls of wood coffins of the First Intermediate Period and Middle Kingdom. They are the direct descendant of the royal Pyramid Texts of the Old Kingdom and the ancestor of the more famous Book of the Dead of the New Kingdom and later. Besides being an invaluable source for much of early Egyptian religion, they are one of the major bodies of Middle Kingdom language and literature. The French Egyptologist Pierre Lacau began recording and analyzing these texts in 1904, with his publication of the coffins in Cairo,[16] but Breasted's project was far more ambitious. It was to include all known coffins in museums throughout the world, with the texts photographed and published in facsimile transcription, with all copies of the same spell published side by side. In addition,

"no text should be regarded as properly copied until it had been collated by at least two persons"[17]—a practice that the Epigraphic Survey follows to this day (see figs. 27, 28).

Breasted and the British philologist Alan H. Gardiner (1874–1963) began the project in 1922, with the cooperation of Lacau, who by then was occupied full-time with his duties as director of the Antiquities Service. Breasted called it "the most formidable task I have ever undertaken," and Gardiner had to admit that even he became "intensely bored" with it.[18] Breasted was forced to withdraw from active copying after 1923 because of his commitments to the Oriental Institute and to his epigraphic work on the newly discovered tomb of Tutankhamun, but Gardiner noted that he had taken "an active part in our first season's work, and I marveled how accurately this many-sided scholar accomplished his copying."[19]

The Oriental Institute remained committed to the Coffin Texts project, eventually led by the Dutch Egyptologist Adriaan de Buck (1892–1959), who had signed on as Gardiner's assistant in 1924. Breasted's, Gardiner's, and de Buck's copies ultimately filled thirty-seven looseleaf notebooks, now housed together with the photographs in the archives of the Oriental Institute. The texts themselves—published by de Buck in seven volumes between 1935 and 1961—are an indispensable part of any Egyptological library. Complementing these are several related studies by American scholars, including Richard A. Parker's publication of the astronomical texts on Middle Kingdom coffin lids and Leonard Lesko's study of the Book of Two Ways on the bottom of Bersha coffins.[20] The Coffin Texts project also recorded most of the copies of Old Kingdom Pyramid Texts interspersed among the newer texts on the coffins; these were indexed by the Oriental Institute's T. George Allen and by Lesko and are now being prepared for publication in the same format as the Coffin Texts volumes.[21]

Breasted is remembered as a scholar primarily for his interpretive works: *A History of Egypt* (1905), now largely out of date but still the best general history of ancient Egypt ever written; *Ancient Times* (1916), a popular history that educated generations of American high-school students; and *Development of Religion and Thought in Ancient Egypt* (1912) and his last book, *The Dawn of Conscience* (1933), both brilliant interpretations of ancient Egyptian thought, though colored by Breasted's own firmly Christian perspective. He also produced scores of philological studies still useful to Egyptology, among them his five-volume *Ancient Records of Egypt* (1906), the first comprehensive collection of Egyptian historical texts in translation. For philologists, however, his masterwork

FIGURE 27
John Hartman of the University of Chicago's Coffin Texts project, working at the Egyptian Museum, Cairo, 1922–23.

FIGURE 28
Collated epigrapher's hand copy of Coffin Texts; from the Coffin Texts notebooks, Oriental Institute Archives, University of Chicago Survey 12, fig. 69.

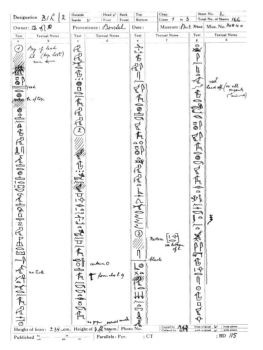

FIGURE 29
Arthur C. Mace
descending shaft
during the Metropolitan
Museum of Art's
excavations at Lisht.

remains his transcription, translation, and commentary of the Edwin Smith Surgical Papyrus (1930), a brilliant tour de force that remains a standard in the field.[22]

The University of Chicago's Oriental Institute, with Breasted, and the Museum of Fine Arts, Boston, with Reisner, were crucial to the formation of Egyptology in the United States, but America's contribution to Middle Kingdom studies is associated more closely with the scholars of a third institution, the Metropolitan Museum of Art, New York. Since 1906 the museum has carried on fieldwork at two Egyptian sites that are the source of much of what we know about the Middle Kingdom: Thebes, capital of the 11th Dynasty (excavated 1910–36), and Lisht, cemetery of the 12th Dynasty capital Itjtawy (excavated 1906–34, 1984–present). The museum appointed Albert M. Lythgoe, who had worked on the Hearst expedition with Reisner, as its first curator of Egyptian art in 1906, and he immediately retained the services of two men whose names have become linked with Middle Kingdom studies.

Arthur C. Mace (1874–1928; see fig. 29) was an Englishman who had also worked on Reisner's team. He was a cousin of W. M. Flinders Petrie, the father of all Egyptian archaeology, and had started his career sorting finds for him.[23] Primarily a field archaeologist, Mace is known above all for his brilliant reconstruction of the burial equipment of Senebtisi from Lisht and the shattered cosmetic boxes from the Middle Kingdom treasure of el-Lahun,[24] as well as for his work on objects from Tutankhamun's tomb, which he undertook as part of the Metropolitan Museum team lent by Lythgoe to Howard Carter. (Mace and Carter jointly authored the first volume of Carter's three-volume *Tomb of Tut-ankh-amen*, until recently the only publication of this famous find.)[25]

Unlike Petrie, Mace and his colleagues believed that finds could be properly understood and published only after their entire context had been excavated. His death in 1928, at the age of fifty-four, left the results of his scholarship at Lisht unpublished except for excavation reports, and his name has survived mostly in joint publications, such as his work with Reisner on the tombs at Naga el-Deir[26] and the books he wrote with Carter. Only in the Metropolitan Museum's publication of Senebtisi's tomb, which he wrote with Herbert E. Winlock, does he get top billing. The true extent of Mace's contribution is now becoming better known through the museum's new publications of the Lisht excavations, based on his field notes and recent fieldwork under the direction of Dieter Arnold.[27] Mace's skill as an epigrapher is demonstrated by the hand copies and facsimiles he made of the coffins found at Lisht.[28] Many of these coffins were too fragile to survive excavation, but thanks to Mace's patient dedication, in an area that was not his forte, their texts have been preserved. In some cases, where the wood had completely disappeared, he was even able to recover the texts from paint traces on the surrounding soil.

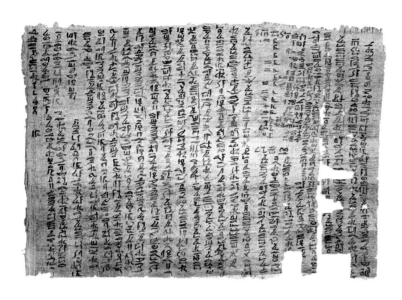

Lythgoe's second appointment in the department was equally perspicacious. Soon after retaining Mace, he hired a young student of his from Harvard, Herbert E. Winlock. Like Mace, Winlock was essentially a field archaeologist and served as director of the museum's work at Thebes. In the area of philology he is associated with one of the most important sources of Middle Kingdom texts, the archives he found in the 11th Dynasty cemetery near Deir el-Bahri. Of these, the most valuable and best known is a set of four letters and three accounts discarded in the rubble of a Middle Kingdom tomb during the reign of Senwosret I (see fig. 30).[29] These were written by (or for) a funerary priest named Heqanakht, while he was serving at Thebes, to his family at a site somewhere near the new capital at Lisht in the north, but they were never delivered.[30] Unlike monumental inscriptions and literary texts, these prosaic documents give us a picture of the everyday life and language of Egyptians at the beginning of the Middle Kingdom. They were studied for the Metropolitan Museum by the British Egyptologist Battiscombe Gunn (1883–1950) and eventually published, together with the other archives Winlock found, by the British Museum's T. G. H. James. Winlock's own philological work on Middle Kingdom texts is limited mostly to his study of the 11th Dynasty court graffiti at Shatt el-Rigal, between Edfu and Gebel el-Silsila, and those of the Middle Kingdom priests in the hills above Deir el-Bahri.[31]

Mace and Winlock were content to leave much of the real epigraphic work to the junior member of the department, whose specialty was philology. William C. Hayes (1903–63; see fig. 31) originally intended to study medieval archaeology but gained his first field experience with the University of Michigan's expedition to Carthage.[32] When he joined the Metropolitan Museum as a member of Winlock's expedition in 1927, he began to study Egyptian on his own and then, over several summers, under the tutelage of Gardiner in England. His skill at language was such that he was soon entrusted with the hieratic as well as the hieroglyphic texts from both Thebes and Lisht.

Hayes's first major contribution to Middle Kingdom philology was the complete facsimile publication and analysis of the funerary texts in the 12th Dynasty tomb of Senwosret-ankh at Lisht.[33] This important tomb contains a complete copy of the Pyramid Texts of the 5th Dynasty king Unas (r. 2356–2323 B.C.), whose pyramid was the first to be so inscribed. Hayes was able to demonstrate that Senwosret-ankh's version was derived not from Unas's pyramid itself, but from an original common to both. Although Hayes's other epigraphic work at Lisht remained unpublished during his lifetime, it now serves as invaluable source material for the Metropolitan Museum's ongoing Lisht publications.[34]

Much of Hayes's philological work had to do with New Kingdom sources, such as his studies of the 18th Dynasty royal sarcophagi and the ostraca found by the museum's Theban expedition.[35] Yet he also wrote a significant series of articles on some of the museum's major Middle Kingdom and Second Intermediate Period texts.[36] Toward the end of his life Hayes produced what is certainly his best philological work, on a fragmentary papyrus of the Second Intermediate Period bequeathed to the Brooklyn Museum by Wilbour.[37] Though it consisted of some six hundred torn pieces, he was able to recover most of its contents and to elicit from them a picture of Egyptian society, labor, administration, and foreign trade which has become a fundamental source for this hazy period in Egypt's history. Though Hayes is often remembered for *The Scepter of Egypt*, his unparalleled study of Egyptian culture based on objects from the Metropolitan Museum's collections,[38] this philological study alone has guaranteed his fame in the annals of American Egyptology.

The decade of the 1950s was bracketed by Winlock's death in 1950 and Hayes's in 1963. Between these years a fourth generation of American Egyptologists came of age, and two of these younger scholars, in particular, have enriched our understanding of the Middle Kingdom.

Henry G. Fischer joined the Metropolitan Museum in 1957 and succeeded Hayes as curator in 1963. Besides a multitude of articles on texts of the First Intermediate Period, Middle Kingdom, and Second Intermediate Period, he has produced two books on the inscriptional material of these periods from Coptos and Dendera which have set new standards for thorough philological research and publication.[39] Fischer has paid particular attention to the form of hieroglyphic signs and the architectural context of hieroglyphic inscriptions,[40] thereby giving his and subsequent generations a richer appreciation of the relationship between objects or reliefs and the texts on them.

Perhaps more than any other Egyptologist, William Kelly Simpson (b. 1928; see fig. 32) has personified America's commitment and contribution to Middle Kingdom studies. From the beginning of his career, Simpson specialized in the texts, art, and history of the Middle Kingdom. He wrote his dissertation on the pyramid site of Amenemhat I at Lisht, published and analyzed the four Middle Kingdom papyri Reisner found at Naga el-Deir,[41] and produced a masterful translation of the most important works of Middle Egyptian literature in the first American collection of Egyptian literary texts.[42]

Simpson made one of the most important American advances in Middle Kingdom epigraphy in his study of the Middle Kingdom offering chapels at Abydos.[43] Since the early 1800s Abydos has produced hundreds of private stelae, offering tables, and statues of the 12th and 13th Dynasties, now scattered in museums throughout the world. Because nearly all were excavated before the beginning of scientific archaeology, their original context has been lost. By painstakingly researching these objects in museums, publications, archives, and even obscure auction catalogues of the nineteenth century, Simpson was able to reconstruct seventy-eight groups of nonroyal monuments, involving 224 objects, which once dotted the landscape of Abydos as memorials to officials of the Middle Kingdom and their families. In doing so, he not only recovered, at least on paper, a significant group of Middle Kingdom monuments but also placed the inscriptions from these monuments in their original context.

THIS SURVEY OF AMERICA'S PART in the discovery of Middle Kingdom language and literature has, of necessity, been brief and less than all-inclusive. The work continues even today. Breasted's legacy endures at the Oriental Institute, which, in addition to fostering the ongoing work of the Epigraphic Survey, has become the premier center for education and research in Egyptian grammar in this part of the world and has spawned, in its turn, new centers of grammatical studies in other American universities. The Museum of Fine Arts, Boston, has recently resumed Reisner's excavations at Deir el-Ballas and, together with the universities of Pennsylvania and Leiden, his epigraphic work at el-Bersha. The Metropolitan Museum of Art is honoring the legacy of Winlock, Mace, and Hayes through its commitment to the publication of their fieldwork and through its new excavations in the Middle Kingdom cemeteries of Lisht and Dahshur, under the able direction of Dieter Arnold and Dorothea Arnold.

America's continuing dedication to the recovery of Middle Kingdom texts is perhaps best summed up in the words of its first Egyptologist, James Henry Breasted: "It can never be laid at my door that I taught and studied the ancient languages as an end in themselves, forgetting that they are merely a means of recovering the content and significance of ancient human life for us of today. It is the *life* of ancient men which I am trying to recover and to picture to the men of today, because I believe it will enrich *our* lives."[44]

Notes

1 Charles E. Moldenke, "The Language of the Ancient Egyptians and Its Monumental Records," *Transactions of the New York Academy of Sciences* 4 (1887): 60–74.

2 Charles E. Moldenke, *The New York Obelisk, Cleopatra's Needle* (New York: Anson D. F. Randolph, 1891; 2d ed., Lancaster, Penn: Lancaster Press, 1935).

3 T. G. H. James, in ...*The Grand Piano Came by Camel*, by Christopher C. Lee (Glasgow: Renfrew District Council, Department of Arts and Libraries, [1990]), 5.

4 James H. Breasted, *The Edwin Smith Surgical Papyrus*, OIP 3–4 (Chicago: University of Chicago Press, 1930), vol. 1: xviii.

5 Ibid.

6 Ibid., 21.

7 Wilbour's story is told in detail by John A. Wilson, *Signs and Wonders upon Pharaoh* (Chicago: University of Chicago Press, 1964), 99–109. His letters were edited for publication by Jean Capart under the title *Travels in Egypt (December 1880 to May 1891)* (Brooklyn: Brooklyn Museum, 1936).

8 Wilbour, *Travels in Egypt*, 230.

9 Wilson, *Signs and Wonders*, 106, citing Wilbour, *Travels in Egypt*, 230.

10 Edward J. Brovarski, "Naga(Nag')-ed-Dêr," *LÄ*, vol. 4, 308.

11 James H. Breasted, cited in Charles Breasted, *Pioneer to the Past: The Story of James Henry Breasted, Archaeologist* (New York: Scribner's, 1943), 65.

12 Ibid., 72.

13 Ibid., 78.

14 Ibid., 77–78.

15 James H. Breasted, *The Oriental Institute*, University of Chicago Survey 12 (Chicago: University of Chicago Press, 1933), 68, 164.

16 Pierre Lacau, *Sarcophages antérieurs au Nouvel Empire*, 2 vols., CG 11, 14, 27, 33 (Cairo: IFAO, 1904–6).

17 Adriaan de Buck, *The Egyptian Coffin Texts*, vol. 1, OIP 34 (Chicago: University of Chicago Press, 1935), xi.

18 James H. Breasted, in Breasted, *Pioneer to the Past*, 349; Alan H. Gardiner, *My Working Years* (London: Coronet Press, [1962]), 37.

19 Gardiner, *My Working Years*, 36.

20 O. Neugebauer and Richard A. Parker, *Egyptian Astronomical Texts*, 3 vols., Brown Egyptological Studies 3, 5, 6 (Providence: Brown University Press; London: Lund Humphries, 1960–64); Leonard H. Lesko, *The Ancient Egyptian Book of Two Ways* (Berkeley: University of California Press, 1972).

21 T. G. Allen, *Occurrences of Pyramid Texts with Cross Indexes of These and Other Egyptian Mortuary Texts*, Studies in Ancient Oriental Civilization 27 (Chicago: University of Chicago Press, 1950); Leonard H. Lesko, *Index of the Spells on Egyptian Middle Kingdom Coffins and Related Documents* (Berkeley, Calif.: B. C. Scribe Publications, 1979); James P. Allen, *Middle Kingdom Copies of the Pyramid Texts* (forthcoming).

22 Breasted, *Edwin Smith Surgical Papyrus*.

23 Joseph L. Smith, *Tombs, Temples, and Ancient Art*, ed. C. L. Smith (Norman: University of Oklahoma Press, 1956), 90; Lee, *Grand Piano*, 17.

24 Herbert E. Winlock, *The Treasure of El Lahun*, MMA Egyptian Expedition 4 (New York: MMA, 1934); Arthur C. Mace and Herbert E. Winlock, *The Tomb of Senebtisi*, MMA Egyptian Expedition 1 (New York: MMA, 1916).

25 James, in Lee, *Grand Piano*, 5; Howard Carter and Arthur C. Mace, *The Tomb of Tut-ankh-amen* (London: Cassell, 1923).

26 George A. Reisner and Arthur C. Mace, *The Early Dynastic Cemeteries of Naga-ed-Dêr*, 2 vols., University of California Publications, Egyptian Archaeology 2–3 (Leipzig: J. C. Hinrichs, 1908–9). Reisner appears as author of part 1; Mace, of part 2.

27 Dieter Arnold, *South Cemeteries of Lisht*, vol. 1, *The Pyramid of Senwosret I*, MMA Egyptian Expedition 22 (New York: MMA, 1988); *South Cemeteries of Lisht*, vol. 3, *The Pyramid Complex of Senwosret I*, MMA Egyptian Expedition 25 (New York: MMA, 1992). Other volumes are in preparation by Dorothea Arnold, Janine Bourriau, Felix Arnold, and Christian Hölzl.

28 James P. Allen, *Funerary Texts from Lisht*, MMA Egyptian Expedition 26 (New York: MMA, forthcoming).

29 For the dating, see Dorothea Arnold, "Amenemhat I and the Early Twelfth Dynasty at Thebes," *MMA Journal* 26 (1991): 36–37; James P. Allen, "Some Theban Officials of the Early Middle Kingdom," in *Studies in Honor of William Kelly Simpson* (Boston: MFA, forthcoming); idem, *The Heqa-nakht Papers: A New Study* (New York: MMA, forthcoming).

30 Allen, *The Heqa-nakht Papers*.

31 Herbert E. Winlock, *The Rise and Fall of the Middle Kingdom in Thebes* (New York: Macmillan, 1947), 58–90.

32 Keith C. Seele, introduction to Hayes's posthumous *Most Ancient Egypt*, ed. Keith C. Seele (Chicago: University of Chicago Press, 1964), vii.

33 William C. Hayes, *The Texts in the Mastabeh of Se'n-Wosret-'ankh at Lisht*, MMA Egyptian Expedition 12 (New York: MMA, 1937).

34 Felix Arnold, *South Cemeteries of Lisht*, vol. 2, *The Control Notes and Team Marks*, MMA Egyptian Expedition 23 (New York: MMA, 1990); Allen, *Funerary Texts from Lisht*.

35 William C. Hayes, *The Royal Sarcophagi of the XVIII Dynasty* (Princeton: Princeton University Press, 1935); idem, *Ostraca and Name Stones from the Tomb of Sen-Mut (No. 71) at Thebes*, MMA Egyptian Expedition 15 (New York: MMA, 1942); idem, "Inscriptions from the Palace of Amenhotep III," *JNES* 10 (1951): 35–36, 82–111, 156–83, 631–32; idem, "A Selection of Tuthmoside Ostraca from Dêr el-Bahri," *JEA* 46 (1960): 29–52.

36 William C. Hayes, "Royal Decrees from the Temple of Min at Coptos," *JEA* 32 (1946): 3–23; idem, "Horemkha'uef of Nekhen and His Trip to It-towe," *JEA* 33 (1947): 3–11; idem, "A Much-Copied Letter of the Early Middle Kingdom," *JNES* 7 (1948): 1–10; idem, "King Wadjkare' of Dynasty VIII," *JEA* 34 (1948): 115–16; idem, "Career of the Great Steward Henenu under Nebhepetre' Mentuhotpe," *JEA* 35 (1949): 43–49.

37 William C. Hayes, *A Papyrus of the Late Middle Kingdom in the Brooklyn Museum*, Wilbour Monographs 5 (Brooklyn: Brooklyn Museum, 1955).

38 William C. Hayes, *The Scepter of Egypt: A Background for the Study of the Egyptian Antiquities in the Metropolitan Museum of Art*, 2 vols. (New York: MMA, 1953–59; revised with additions, New York: MMA, 1990).

39 Henry G. Fischer, *Inscriptions from the Coptite Nome, Dynasties VI–XI*, Analecta Orientalia 40 (Rome: Pontificum Institutum Biblicum, 1964); idem, *Dendera in the Third Millennium B.C. down to the Theban Domination of Upper Egypt* (Locust Valley, N.Y.: J. J. Augustin, 1968).

40 See in particular Henry G. Fischer, *The Orientation of Hieroglyphs*, Egyptian Studies 2 (New York: MMA, 1977); idem, *L'écriture et l'art de l'Egypte ancienne* (Paris: Presses universitaires de France, 1986).

41 William K. Simpson, *Papyrus Reisner I* (Boston: MFA, 1963); idem, *Papyrus Reisner II* (Boston: MFA, 1965); idem, *Papyrus Reisner III* (Boston: MFA, 1969); idem, *Papyrus Reisner IV* (Boston: MFA, 1986).

42 William K. Simpson, ed., *The Literature of Ancient Egypt* (New Haven: Yale University Press, 1972).

43 William K. Simpson, *The Terrace of the Great God at Abydos: The Offering Chapels of Dynasties 12 and 13*, Publications of the Pennsylvania–Yale Expedition to Egypt 5 (New Haven: Peabody Museum of Natural History of Yale University; Philadelphia: University Museum of the University of Pennsylvania, 1974).

44 James H. Breasted, in Breasted, *Pioneer to the Past*, 354.

The Metropolitan Museum of Art's Work at the Middle Kingdom Sites of Thebes and Lisht

Dorothea Arnold

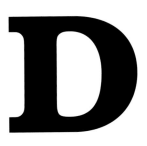

During the last decade of the nineteenth century excavations at Tanis and Bubastis, Dahshur, South Saqqara, and in the area of el-Lahun/Kahun first brought to light the art and archaeology of the Egyptian Middle Kingdom.[1] The excavators were Swiss (Edouard Naville), French (Jacques de Morgan), and British (W. M. Flinders Petrie and Guy Brunton). Until this time the artistic and architectural achievements of the Middle Kingdom had been overshadowed by the pyramids of the Old Kingdom, the monumental temples of the New Kingdom, and the finely decorated tombs preserved from both these periods. These early excavations, however, showed the Middle Kingdom to be a high point for the production of royal sculpture and portraiture, finely modeled and detailed relief sculpture, and exquisite jewelry.[2] Furthermore, even today the site of Kahun remains the most complete example we have of an ancient Egyptian town plan.

American excavators entered the field at the beginning of this century with excavations at Deir el-Ballas,[3] Dendera,[4] and el-Bersha,[5] all of which added significantly to our understanding of the Middle Kingdom. Excavations in Nubia revealed data about the previously unknown Kerma culture,[6] which flourished at this time, and about the major military and commercial presence of Egypt beyond its southern border during the Middle Kingdom.[7]

It was at Lisht and Thebes, however, that American archaeologists finally established the historical foundation of the Middle Kingdom and provided a clearer and more integrated picture of its artistic traditions. Work at both sites was carried out by excavation teams from the Metropolitan Museum of Art, New York, an institution whose collection of Middle Kingdom art is rivaled only by that of the Egyptian Museum in Cairo.

Herbert Winlock and the Early Middle Kingdom at Thebes

Herbert Winlock's achievement in establishing the history of the early Middle Kingdom (c. 2040–1970 B.C.) can be summed up by comparing the statements of

FIGURE 33
Interior of tomb of
Meketre with model
chamber as found.

57

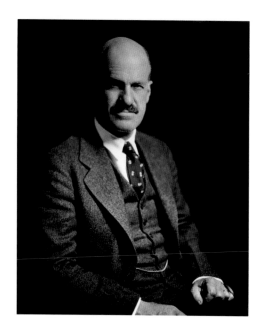

FIGURE 34
Portrait of Herbert E.
Winlock.

FIGURE 35
Map of the Theban
necropolis in the Middle
Kingdom; from Herbert E.
Winlock, "The Theban
Necropolis in the Middle
Kingdom," *The American
Journal of Semitic
Languages and Literatures*
32 (October 1915): fig. 1.

two noted historians of ancient Egypt. In 1913 Eduard Meyer wrote: "The succession of rulers and the exact history of the Eleventh Dynasty... is still fraught with numerous problems that can only be solved by new finds."[8] Thirty-seven years later Alexander Scharff would write: "The series of monarchs and early Eleventh Dynasty kings was until recently a problem that seemed almost insoluble. The problem is now largely solved thanks to the extraordinarily thorough excavations of the Metropolitan Museum of Art under the direction of H. E. Winlock."[9]

Herbert Eustis Winlock (see fig. 34) was born on February 1, 1884, in Washington, D.C., the son of an astronomer at the United States Naval Observatory. Though he showed an early interest in ancient Egypt, when he enrolled at Harvard University in 1902, he was not a model student and was placed on probation at the end of his sophomore year.[10] During his junior year, however, he excelled in courses in anthropology, Egyptology, and the fine arts, and he graduated in 1906 with an A.B. magna cum laude.[11] Among the teachers who inspired this lively twenty-two-year-old was Albert M. Lythgoe (1868–1934), curator of the Egyptian department at the Museum of Fine Arts, Boston, and head of the Harvard-Boston expedition to Giza.

In 1906 Lythgoe was appointed the first curator of the Metropolitan Museum of Art's newly formed Department of Egyptian Art and director of its excavations in Egypt. Impressed by the young Winlock from the first, Lythgoe had already asked him to join the Boston excavations in 1905. Winlock later wrote, "I accepted with a shout loud enough for the echoes of it still to fill my soul."[12]

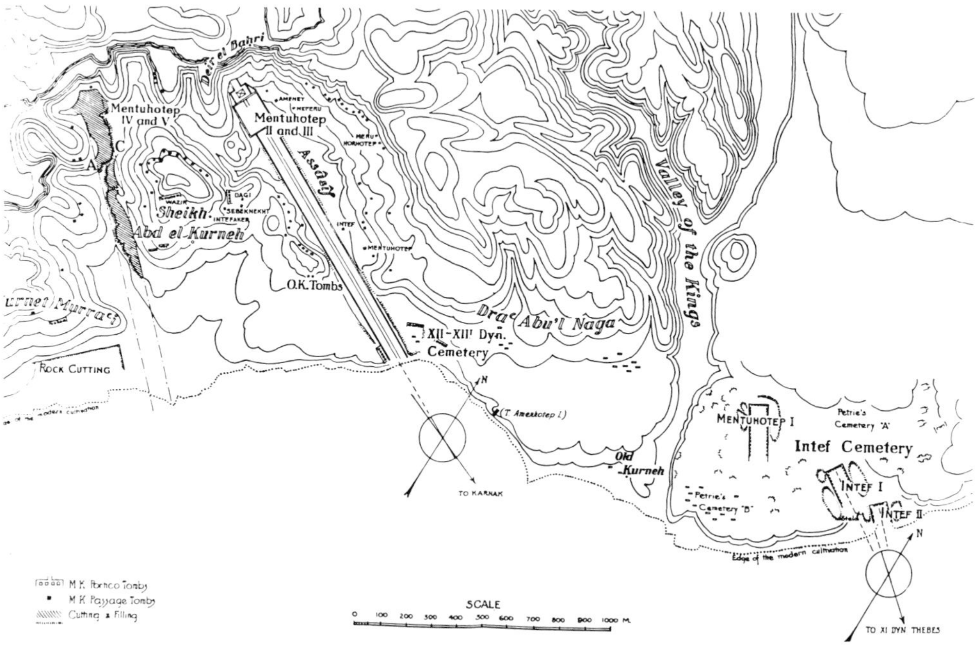

After graduation Winlock joined the Metropolitan's new Egyptian expedition at Lisht, the cemetery of the Middle Kingdom capital, Itjtawy.[13] Besides Lythgoe and Winlock, the third member of the team was Arthur C. Mace, an experienced British archaeologist, born in Hobart, Tasmania, who had worked with W. M. Flinders Petrie and with George A. Reisner at Naga el-Deir.[14] During the early years at Lisht, Mace, a painstaking and serious scholar, was Winlock's senior and mentor as they documented the rich, undisturbed burial of Senebtisi.[15]

FIGURE 36

View from above of the
unfinished royal monu-
ment of the early
Middle Kingdom in the
valley south of Deir el-
Bahri.

From 1907 until the outbreak of World War I Winlock
gained wide experience excavating at Lisht, at the temple of
Hibis in el-Kharga Oasis[16] and at Christian era monuments
at Thebes.[17] At Thebes he first encountered evidence of the
era that would become his life's work: the early Middle
Kingdom. When Norman de Garis Davies, the Metropolitan
Museum's brilliant copyist of wall reliefs and paintings, was
clearing the late 11th Dynasty tomb of the vizier Dagi (TT 103)
on the south side of the Asasif Valley, he found "some beautifully colored reliefs" by "some of the best relief artists"
(of Mentuhotep II).[18] These blocks made a strong impression
on both Winlock and the museum's president, J. Pierpont
Morgan, who continued to support excavations at Thebes.

From 1910 until he became head of the Metropolitan's
Egyptian department in 1928, Winlock spent most of each
year in Thebes. His close observation of the Theban landscape resulted in "The Theban Necropolis in the Middle
Kingdom," a 1915 article that constituted a major break-
through in reconstructing the history of the early Middle Kingdom.[19] Winlock
combined written historical sources, such as contemporary inscriptions and later
king lists, with observations of archaeological remains on the ground and careful
examination of earlier finds. His intimate knowledge of Theban topography
enabled him to identify three vast courtyards with remains of pillared porticoes,
located in the northern part of the necropolis at el-Tarif (see fig. 35), as the burial
places of the earliest rulers of the 11th Dynasty: Intef I, Intef II, and Mentuhotep
I.[20] These tombs at el-Tarif marked the northern end of the Theban necropolis in
the 11th Dynasty.

Winlock's discovery of an unfinished but undoubtedly royal monument in
a remote valley behind the hill of Sheikh Abd el-Qurna established the southern
boundary of the necropolis. One evening in 1914, while he was out exercising his
horse, "the light was exactly right," and his observant eye discerned the outlines
of a platform and a causeway leading up to it (see fig. 36).[21]

El-Tarif and this newly discovered monument flanked the Asasif Valley, at
whose apex (Deir el-Bahri) Naville had excavated the mortuary temple of King
Mentuhotep II in 1903.[22] This king had reunited Egypt about 2040 B.C. and was
considered the founder of the Middle Kingdom even by the ancient Egyptians.
Since the new site behind Sheikh Abd el-Qurna was very similar in plan to Naville's
Mentuhotep II temple, Winlock assigned the southern monument to his successor,
Mentuhotep III. He thus established a north-to-south progression for the burial

sites of the early Middle Kingdom rulers, and for the first time the Theban necropolis of the Middle Kingdom could be mapped.

Many details were added to the 1915 map (fig. 35)[23] by Winlock's subsequent excavations. Other scholars would later revise the identifications for the three royal tombs at el-Tarif[24] and ascribe the unfinished monument south of Deir el-Bahri to the first king of the 12th Dynasty, Amenemhat I (r. 1991–1962 B.C.).[25] None of these revisions diminishes the fundamental importance of Winlock's 1915 achievement. His article and map established once and for all the basic order of burial sites and rulers of the early Middle Kingdom.

The outbreak of World War I and Winlock's participation in it prevented further work at Thebes until January 1920. Since it was already late in the season, Winlock did not start at the temple site he had discovered in 1914, but turned to the seemingly less time-consuming clearance of a large tomb just north of it (TT 280) (see fig. 37). Partial clearance of the tomb already had shown that it was heavily destroyed by ancient stone robbing.[26] Some fragments of beautiful wall relief had, however, provided the name of its owner, the chancellor Meketre. In a small underground chamber of the tomb, twenty-four superb wood funerary models were found—a discovery that established once and for all Winlock's fame as an archaeologist (see figs. 33, 38).[27] "Scientific virtue rarely gets such striking or such unexpected rewards as it did on this occasion," Winlock later wrote.[28]

Winlock inevitably was drawn to investigate the central part of his 1915 map of Thebes, the Asasif Valley and Deir el-Bahri itself. In the winter of 1920–21, while clearing the temple discovered in 1914, he began to reconsider the earlier excavation of Naville at the temple of Mentuhotep II. With his sharp intellect, he spotted an inconsistency in the thinking of Naville and his colleagues, who had found the remains of six shrines dedicated to Hathor priestesses and minor queens.[29] Winlock not only recognized that these shrines predated the final phase of the temple, he also saw that errors had been made in assigning tomb shafts to the shrines—two shrines, in fact, were still without shafts.[30] Winlock immediately

FIGURE 38
Offering bearer from
the tomb of Meketre.
The Metropolitan
Museum of Art, Rogers
Fund and Edward S.
Harkness Gift, 1920,
20.3.7.

FIGURE 39
Coffin and mummy
of Mayet from the
temple of Nebhepetre
Mentuhotep at Deir
el-Bahri.

had his workmen sweep the pavement behind the shrines of Ashayet and Mayet. The "tell-tale sinking of the pavement slabs outlining a pit" behind Ashayet's shrine quickly appeared, while "another, only a little less obvious, could be seen behind Mayet's shrine."[31] In these tombs Winlock found the beautiful sarcophagus, coffin, and superb statuette of Ashayet now in the Cairo Museum (JE 47310), as well as the coffins and jewelry of five-year-old Mayet (see fig. 39).[32]

Winlock's excavations during the following decade virtually re-created the Theban early Middle Kingdom, filling out the chronological framework with a cast of human characters. There is the "garrulous old farmer-priest," Heqanakht, whose letters Winlock found in the 1920–21 season (see fig. 30).[33] Immediate and strongly personal, these letters inspired no less than Agatha Christie to turn them into a detective novel, *Death Comes as the End*,[34] even before the scholarly publication of the letters had appeared.[35]

The chancellor Khety owned one of the most beautiful tombs overlooking Deir el-Bahri (TT 311).[36] Winlock described the paintings on the limestone casing inside the hidden burial crypt: "On this were painted the equipment and provender which Khety wanted—and there was nothing mean about his desires. Jewels, perfume pots, bows, arrows, and battle axes were requisitioned by the hundreds and by the thousands.... Tables groaned with vegetables and fruits, loaves, and joints, and above was the astounding menu of the meal of the dead, running to one hundred dishes."[37]

Another of Winlock's historical sketches brings to life the priests who performed the ceremony of laying foundation deposits under the corners of the temple of King Mentuhotep II: "They may have been a very devout party but they were not very orderly, for at the northeast corner, as they moved on to the next, one of them took a short cut and carelessly stepped and slipped on one of the soft wet bricks which had just been laid so ceremoniously. It was his footprint that told us the tale."[38] Nearby Winlock found "over forty voluminous rope baskets filled with stone chips... lined up in rows as the workmen had left them" four thousand years before (see fig. 40).[39]

Winlock's reports not only testify to his talents as a writer, but they also show how for him each excavated object was a witness of human existence. His narra-

FIGURE 40
Baskets of stone chips left behind by workmen of the early Middle Kingdom, Deir el-Bahri.

FIGURE 41
Reconstruction of the façade of the temple of Nebhepetre Mentuhotep at Deir el-Bahri by W. Hauser and G. M. Peek.

tive style links ancient lives with the present-day experiences of his readers and thus bridges the gap between them. This manner of storytelling in archaeology and the aims and methods of archaeologists of the first half of the century have fallen into disrepute with modern scholars. Unlike contemporary archaeological publications, Winlock's books do not contain lists of excavated objects in the same (often abbreviated) nomenclature, and he seldom relates objects to specific archaeological strata. Indeed, the observance of stratigraphy was not central to his archaeological research because stratigraphy did not suit his primary aim, which was a reconstruction of history through the synthesis of the information provided by the finds themselves. Excavation under Winlock was focused on freeing monuments from debris. How that debris came to the place where it was found and what the relationship was between an object and the debris in which it was discovered, he seldom asked. The monuments and the objects themselves told the story, not their contexts and what had happened to them after they were lost or buried. In short, for Winlock and his team, monuments and objects were entities in themselves, not pieces in a complex network of chronological, socioeconomic, or otherwise functional relationships.

Winlock's predominantly historical and humanistic approach to the past was not without a conceptual structure. Significantly, his view of early Middle Kingdom society is most clearly expressed in visual images created under his direction, such as the site photographs of Harry Burton and the architectural reconstructions of G. M. Peek.[40] Burton, known for his many superb photographs of the Metropolitan Museum of Art's work in Thebes as well as for his photography of the tomb and treasures of Tutankhamun, produced a series of overview photographs of Deir el-Bahri and the Asasif (see fig. 42). Using a large-format camera and glass negatives to best advantage, he took clear and detailed wide-angle views of the valley and its monuments. The viewpoints of these photographs are strictly axial:

FIGURE 42
View looking over the temple of Nebhepetre Mentuhotep at Deir el-Bahri along the Asasif Valley, from the west. Photograph by Harry Burton.

from the cliffs above the temple of Mentuhotep II along the ancient causeway to the edge of the cultivation where the valley temple must have been, or from the cultivation straight up the causeway. Other views were directed from the temple toward the cliff tombs on the valley's north and south flanks or at right angles to the main east-west axis of the valley. Similarly, Winlock and Peek's reconstruction of the Mentuhotep temple showed the building in a strictly frontal view (see fig. 41),[41] while other reconstructions, both the earlier one by Naville[42] and later ones by Dieter Arnold and others, showed the temple at an oblique angle, seen from the northeast or southeast.[43]

Winlock's description of the temple and tombs emphasized the importance of the axial and frontal view to his understanding of the monuments in the valley. It was clearly his belief that the valley's monuments reflected the structure of Egyptian society in the early Middle Kingdom. As the temple of Mentuhotep II was located at the apex of the valley, with its causeway serving as the axis for orienting the tombs of his dependents, the pharaoh stood at the head and center of society. One of the basic concepts of nineteenth-century European historical thinking was that of history as a history of rulers. Egyptologists followed this tradition until the 1950s.[44] Only then did they begin to approach the history of Egypt as predominantly a social and cultural phenomenon.[45] A product of his time, Winlock followed the "history of rulers" tradition,[46] which in connection with ancient Egypt is justified to a certain extent by the important role the king played in religion and society.

According to this hierarchical view, the king's all-powerful position was supported to a large degree by his courtiers. Winlock saw their role clearly reflected in the position of their tombs. "On the hills looking down on the avenue which led to the Nebhepetre temple the courtiers were buried, ranged in death in two long

FIGURE 43
Tombs of the nobles of
the Middle Kingdom on
north flank of the Asasif
Valley at Deir el-Bahri.

ranks on either side of their earthly lord. In the higher and more prominent hills on the north side the most influential courtiers obtained sites for their tombs, and there, shoulder to shoulder, stood most of the great dignitaries of the day" (see fig. 43).[47]

Winlock also dedicated considerable research to the graffiti left by these courtiers, apparently while on a desert caravan to Nubia,[48] in the Shatt el-Rigal, a remote mountain gorge between Thebes and Aswan. In most of his writings, however, he ridicules what he saw as the pretensions of these courtiers. This tone is unmistakable in the description of Khety's tomb cited above as well as in his description of Khety's graffiti at Shatt el-Rigal, where "he wears the long skirt of a high official, and he has the rolls of fat on his belly which were the mark of a respectable and leisurely life."[49] He went on to observe, "It would be difficult to picture the distinguished persons whom [the graffiti] name, themselves spending the time and labor which obviously were required to carve these inscriptions."[50]

Winlock failed to see that here was a group of ancient Thebans whose stature and initiative—as manifest in the inventive architecture and decoration of their imposing tombs—made them important players in the politics of their time. Scholars after Winlock have used the written evidence that his excavations produced to reconstruct some of the lives and deeds of these personalities.[51] Men like Khety, Henenu,[52] Meru, and the vizier Ameny—who eventually usurped the throne, founding the 12th Dynasty and ruling as Amenemhat I—have thus regained, in part, their places in history.

Closer scrutiny of the large tombs of nobles along the Asasif and Deir el-Bahri cliffs has revealed that they do not all date to the reign of Mentuhotep II.[53] Indeed, of the whole row of tombs on the north side of the valley, only a very few, such as those of Khety (TT 311)[54] and Henenu (TT 313),[55] are contemporary with the king who reunited Egypt. The tombs of Meru (TT 240)[56] and the vizier Ipy (TT 315) and his dependent Meseh (findspot of the Heqanakht letters) have been redated to early in the reign of Amenemhat I.[57] The "bowman" Neferhotep's tomb (TT 318) dates to the 13th Dynasty.[58]

With the redating of these tombs, Winlock's reconstruction of the monuments of Deir el-Bahri and the Asasif as a reflection of 11th Dynasty society falls apart. In its place we see the gradual growth of the necropolis over three hundred or more years. The royal monument at the apex of the valley remains the focal point of activities in the valley, but its function must now be sought in the sphere of religion and ritual. The predominantly religious rather than political significance of the temple of Mentuhotep II originated during the later years of his reign, when the cult of the god Amun was installed in a sanctuary added to his mortuary temple.[59] Not long after, yearly processions were instituted, during which the god's image was transported from the temple of Karnak, on the east bank of the Nile, to Deir el-Bahri in the west.[60] This religious feast was described by one of the priests who climbed up onto the cliffs to watch the procession: "[Amun's] first festivals of Shomu, when he rises on the day of voyaging to the Valley of Nebhepetre."[61] Such sacred proceedings made the valley a very desirable resting place for the dead, since it enabled them to be present when the god journeyed over the river to Deir el-Bahri.

Does this reevaluation invalidate Winlock's image of early Middle Kingdom society? His approach to understanding ancient structures is certainly still current in archaeological thinking. Barry J. Kemp wrote in 1989: "The creation of buildings and complete settlements is a supreme act of imposing order on the natural environment....To see the shapes of towns, ancient and modern, as microcosms of society gives us the most consistent basis there is for comparing societies across space and time."[62] The only difference between this approach to archaeological remains and Winlock's is that today's archaeologists include settlements and daily life in their studies, while Winlock studied cemeteries and funerary remains. Both, however, deal with the spatial relationship of ancient buildings and see in this relationship the impact of the human mind, deducing from what Kemp calls "the visual language of ground plans"[63] the principles according to which ancient people shaped their lives.

The concept of a hierarchically structured and securely ordered Middle Kingdom society, which Winlock saw manifested in the Theban necropolis, also survives. Kemp has summed up recent evaluations of Middle Kingdom Egypt. Following current practice, his historical sources are mostly economic texts and what he calls "model communities"—the pyramid towns, frontier outposts, and Nubian fortresses with orthogonal grid layouts and standardized house types.[64] The picture he reconstructs from these sources is that of a Middle Kingdom "motivated by a vision... of a bureaucratic utopia, an unformulated ideology which acted as a pattern in the making of decisions. We find it in the inclination to formulate arithmetic devices for calculating a range of aspects of economic life, we see it in documents attempting a centralized control and direction of work and property, it lives at Kahun in a prescription for how a complete city should be arranged."[65] In essence this is not dissimilar to Winlock's understanding of the historical and social principles that underlay the axial structure of the Middle Kingdom Theban necropolis, even if a different language is employed by scholars divided by half a century.

For both Winlock and Kemp, Middle Kingdom society was rigidly structured and hierarchically ordered, providing for its citizens a secure world in which to thrive, but one that generally prohibited spontaneity and free choice. Significantly, Kemp, like Winlock—being from an age when conformity is viewed negatively—is on the lookout for traits in ancient Egypt that might mitigate its supposed lack of spontaneity and freedom. Kemp states that ultimately "this bureaucratic tendency [of the Middle Kingdom]... made no further headway." He sees better things in the New Kingdom, which he understands to have been a "less rigid system holding temporarily in check a great many individualistic ambitions."[66]

Winlock, by contrast, emphasized the human aspects of the strictly ordered Middle Kingdom society. His Thebans, simple people and nobles alike, were negligent where they should have followed strict order; they were troublesome in old age; they carried, and abandoned, baskets and sacks in the service of the architects and nobles; and they did not take the pomp and ceremony too seriously—they were, in short, normal human beings. And this, indeed, is how the people of the early Middle Kingdom have come down to us through Winlock's superb writings and lively reconstructions.

Excavations at Middle Kingdom Lisht

Lisht—or more properly el-Lisht—is a village thirty-five miles south of Cairo and just slightly south of Egypt's Middle Kingdom capital, Itjtawy, now buried beneath five to ten meters of agricultural soil. For Egyptologists the name *Lisht* designates the vast cemetery and settlement remains located on the desert margins extending from the site of Itjtawy to a village south of el-Lisht called el-Saudiya.[67] The main features of desert Lisht are two ruined pyramids on the north and south sides of a valley, or *wadi* (see fig. 44). The northern pyramid was built for Amenemhat I, first king of the 12th Dynasty, and the southern one belonged to his son and successor, Senwosret I (r. 1971–1926 B.C.).

Archaeological exploration at Lisht started in 1882, when the French Egyptologist Gaston Maspero attempted to reach the burial chambers of the two pyramids. Even then, both chambers were deeply flooded, and Maspero had to give up.[68] From 1894 to 1895 two more French archaeologists, Gustave Jéquier and Joseph Gautier, excavated at Lisht.[69] Their work confirmed the names of the owners of the two pyramids, established the general plan of the southern pyramid's temple, and recovered a number of very fine statues now in the Cairo Museum.[70]

The Metropolitan Museum of Art was granted permission to excavate at Lisht in 1906—the first excavation of the newly established Department of Egyptian Art. Between 1906 and 1934 the museum conducted fourteen seasons at the site.

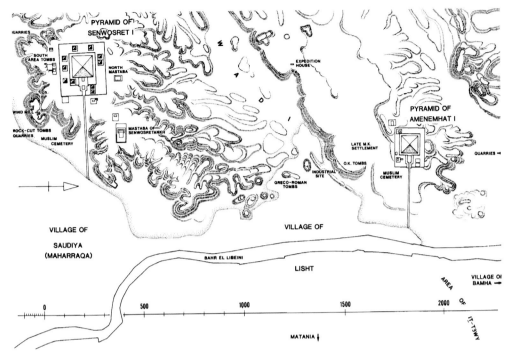

Labels on map: PYRAMID OF SENWOSRET I, QUARRIES, SOUTH AREA TOMBS, NORTH MASTABA, EXPEDITION HOUSE, WIND MILL, MASTABA OF SENWOSRETANKH, ROCK-CUT TOMBS, QUARRIES, MUSLIM CEMETERY, PYRAMID OF AMENEMHAT I, LATE M.K. SETTLEMENT, QUARRIES, INDUSTRIAL SITE, O.K. TOMBS, MUSLIM CEMETERY, GRECO-ROMAN TOMBS, VILLAGE OF SAUDIYA (MAHARRAQA), VILLAGE OF, BAHR EL LIBEINI, LISHT, VILLAGE OF BAMHA, AREA OF IT-TAWI, MATANIA, 0, 500, 1000, 1500, 2000

FIGURE 44

Plan of Lisht made by the Egyptian Expedition of the Metropolitan Museum of Art.

From 1906 to 1909 and 1912 to 1914 Lythgoe, ably assisted by Mace, was field director. As the excavations progressed, Mace eventually assumed responsibility for the northern pyramid, while Lythgoe worked in the south. During World War I the excavations at Lisht South were continued by Ambrose Lansing (1891–1959). Mace resumed work at Lisht North from 1920 to 1922. When Mace was transferred to Thebes in 1923 to assist Howard Carter in the clearance of the tomb of Tutankhamun, work at Lisht North ceased, and Lansing excavated only at Lisht South (1923–25 and 1931–34), assisted by the young William C. Hayes from 1931 onward.

When the museum ceased work at Lisht in 1934, Winlock, who was now director of the museum, described Lisht as "a site which has been signally productive, both for the science of Egyptology and for the collection of the Metropolitan Museum."[71] Realizing that the potential of Lisht for the "science of Egyptology" could not be fully realized without full publication of the 1906–34 field records, the museum began a reexamination of certain features at the site in 1984. This research is still under way.[72] By 1994 three volumes had appeared on Lisht South, and others are in preparation.[73]

Lythgoe was of vital importance the growth of the museum's Egyptian collection. Educated in Bonn, where he studied with the historian Alfred Wiedemann, Lythgoe got his archaeological training with George A. Reisner at Naga el-Deir from 1899 to 1904.[74] Lythgoe's collaborator, Mace, had begun his excavation career under Petrie at Hu.[75] Mace had met Lythgoe at Naga el-Deir, and when Lythgoe was appointed to the Metropolitan, he immediately asked Mace to join his excavation team. Although Mace is most famous for his work in the tomb of Tutankhamun,[76] his work at Lisht was at least as important for Egyptology. Between 1907 and 1922 he was in charge of the excavation at and around the pyramid of Amenemhat I at Lisht North. Only one of his important finds, however, the tomb of Senebtisi, was published in full, in an exemplary, and now rare and valuable, book.[77] To publish the results of all Mace's work at Lisht North is a primary concern at present of the Metropolitan's Department of Egyptian Art.[78]

FIGURE 45
Detail of stone repairs to the pyramid of Senwosret I at Lisht South.

The excavations in the south cemetery of Lisht were taken over by Lansing in 1916 and continued until 1934. Lansing had been trained at Leipzig under Georg Steindorff and became assistant curator in the Department of Egyptian Art at the Metropolitan in 1922. During the 1932–33 and 1933–34 seasons Hayes joined the team. Hayes later became curator of the department, a post he held until his death in 1963, and was the author of the masterful *Scepter of Egypt* (2 vols., 1953–59). He had received his Ph.D. from Princeton in 1935 with a ground-breaking thesis on royal sarcophagi of the 18th Dynasty.[79] At Lisht Hayes's scholarly influence is clearly documented in the hundreds of tomb cards that he prepared on the finds that filled the storerooms after more than ten seasons of work.[80] In 1937 he published the beautifully decorated and inscribed burial chamber of the tomb of Senwosret-ankh at Lisht South.[81]

Until the Lisht excavations are published in full, it is difficult to sum up the wealth of evidence for the art, architecture, and history of the Middle Kingdom discovered there. At the present time, however, this evidence would seem to indicate that the picture of the Middle Kingdom as a "bureaucratic utopia," characterized by "centralized control and direction of work and property"—based on the model community of Kahun or the Nubian military fortresses—was not universally true.[82] In the cemeteries of Lisht we see an unprecedented level of individual choice drawing on a broad range of funerary traditions. The 13th Dynasty settlement at Lisht North, unlike other pyramid towns,[83] was not constrained by standardized house plans, a grid layout, or an enclosure wall.

Large-scale building activities at Lisht[84] started during the last decade of the reign of Amenemhat I.[85] In both Amenemhat I and Senwosret I's pyramids ample evidence testifies that Egyptian architects and masons of the early 12th Dynasty had to relearn pyramid building. One can still see the innumerable repairs made to the casing stones of both pyramids due to the stonemasons' lack of experience. No pyramids on this scale had been erected for more than 150 years (see fig. 45).[86]

Much thought has been given to the fact that a great number of limestone and granite blocks of the Old Kingdom were built into Amenemhat's pyramid.[87] Whatever the purpose or reason might have been for this substantial reuse of Old Kingdom stone from relief-decorated structures,[88] these blocks are certainly a sign that the king's architects and sculptors had ample opportunity to study Old Kingdom temple architecture and decoration.

The learning process, however, did not lead to slavish copying of Old Kingdom monuments. In the pyramid complex of Amenemhat I elements characteristic of the funerary temple of Mentuhotep II at Deir el-Bahri might have been incorporated: a vertical rock face, for instance, was cut on the east and south sides of the pyramid to create the impression that it stood on a raised platform.[89] A number

of objects are further proof of the capi-
tal's continued contacts with Thebes,
or at least Upper Egypt. An altar found
in the canal north of el-Lisht—at the
site of Itjtawy—is dedicated to the
Theban gods Amun and Montu,[90] and
a fragment of a stone bowl with the
name of the last king of the 11th
Dynasty, Mentuhotep IV, and dedicated
to Hathor of Dendera, was found in the
Lisht North cemetery. Amenemhat I
had his name added to this bowl, presumably when he rededicated it at a
Hathor sanctuary at Lisht.[91]

To build the pyramid temple for Amenemhat I, the king's architects used
blocks from an earlier building of that king. The reliefs on these reused blocks
show scenes commemorating Amenemhat I's *sed* festival (thirty-year jubilee) and
mention his son, Senwosret, as being "the king himself," which strongly indicates
that Senwosret I was already ruling together with his father as coregent when this
earlier building was decorated.[92] These blocks were found in the foundations of
the pyramid temple, which was—as far as can still be ascertained—a rather small
and insignificant structure (see figs. 46, 47).[93]

On the whole, Senwosret's pyramid and temple at Lisht South were, despite
evidence of inexperienced stone handling, a much more accomplished architectural
achievement; the building of his father's monument had clearly provided useful

experience. A new structural system with radiating walls to strengthen the pyramid core increased stability. The pyramid temple plan is almost a pure revival of 6th Dynasty prototypes.[94] The same is true for the relief decoration, which shows, however, the individual styles of various sculptors' schools.[95] The causeway had first been planned as an open avenue like that of Amenemhat I, both going back to the Theban causeway of Mentuhotep II at Deir el-Bahri. In a later stage the causeway of the Lisht South pyramid was enclosed like those of the Old Kingdom, but royal statuary was still lined up along the causeway walls.[96]

When Hayes described the Lisht South cemetery in *The Scepter of Egypt*, he followed almost word for word the manner in which Winlock had described the tombs in the Asasif Valley and Deir el-Bahri at Thebes (see above): "Round about the royal enclosure were the tombs of Se'n-wosret's many courtiers, officials and priests."[97] Closer research into the dates of the large mastaba tombs that surround both Lisht pyramids reveals, however, that only very few tombs are contemporary with the kings whose pyramids towered over them. In the north only the large structure at the southwest corner of the pyramid complex is contemporary with either Amenemhat I or the early years of Senwosret I's reign.[98] This tomb has been ascribed to a man named Rehuerdjersen by Hayes and others.[99] The king's mother, Nofret, might have been buried nearby, as shown by an offering plate dedicated to her, but her tomb has not been identified.[100]

According to the pottery and the known career of one of their owners, the vizier Intefiqer,[101] the mastabas on the east side of Amenemhat's pyramid date to the reign of Senwosret I. On the basis of his name the tomb of a man called Senwosret which lies farther away from the pyramid to the southwest is already at least of that date, if not later.[102] About a third of the tombs that surround the pyramid have shafts with square plans, a type that died out around the middle of the 12th Dynasty;[103] the rest, with rectangular shafts, belong after the reign of Senwosret I. Not many objects found in these tombs can be dated to the early 12th Dynasty, and almost none before the later years of Senwosret I's reign.[104] A great number of burials at Lisht North can be dated to the late 12th and 13th Dynasties, thus attesting to the continued use of the area throughout the Middle Kingdom.[105]

At Lisht South a similar range of dates for the tombs can be observed. There is one shaft tomb northwest of the pyramid that was used in the early years of Senwosret I's reign for the burial of the lady Ankhet.[106] The mastaba of Mentuhotep, vizier of Senwosret I,[107] located at the southeast corner of the king's pyramid, can be dated late in the king's reign, and the same may be true of the tomb of Khety[108] and some of the mastabas south of the pyramid.[109] The tombs of Imhotep[110] and Senwosret-ankh[111] are demonstrably of the reign of Amenemhat II, the successor of Senwosret I, and the mastaba west of Senwosret-ankh, which contained the burial of the lady Hapy, is perhaps slightly earlier than the two others.[112] Tomb shafts containing 13th Dynasty burials were located south of the royal causeway between the causeway and the tomb complex of the vizier Mentuhotep.[113]

From this brief overview of both Lisht cemeteries, it is clear that during the reign of each king only a few particularly favored people were allowed to build tomb structures in the pyramid cemeteries. Most tombs, of both commoners and nobles, were built around the royal monuments after the king's demise, perhaps for religious reasons rather than as a mark of their position in the state hierarchy.

A number of motives must have led individuals to choose Lisht as a burial site even when the later kings of the 12th and 13th Dynasties elected to be buried elsewhere (Lahun, Hawara, Dahshur). One reason, perhaps, was that Itjtawy continued to function as the capital and a royal residence. Considerable personal choice is also evident in the diversity of tomb structures in these cemeteries. At both Lisht North and South the variety of tomb structures subsumed by archaeologists under the term *mastaba* is striking indeed. Only a few, like that of Imhotep in the south,[114] were actual rectangular mastabas with solid-rubble cores. Many others were partly solid but had niches or chapels built into them, decorated with reliefs, like that of Rehuerdjersen at Lisht North. Other tomb superstructures were chapel-like buildings that only looked from the outside like solid-core mastabas; such a structure was built for the vizier Mentuhotep at Lisht South. Decoration again varied from none, as in Imhotep's case, to relief in the chapel, to inscriptions on the outside (Mentuhotep), to niched decoration (Senwosret-ankh). In fact, none of the roughly two dozen large tomb structures at Lisht is much like another.

Mastaba and mastaba-like tomb structures had a long history by the beginning of the 12th Dynasty, and most tomb types at Lisht had precursors in the Old Kingdom. The Lisht tomb owners, or their architects, apparently did not invent any of the forms used; they found them in Old Kingdom prototypes. The choice was which prototype to follow and how to combine the elements.[115]

There was also a certain degree of selection in funerary equipment.[116] The tomb of Imhotep is a notable example.[117] The ritual equipment chosen for his burial included two fairly large wood boats, two model-sized boats, a shrine with an Anubis fetish, and two statues of divinities wearing royal crowns. These were deposited at various locations around the superstructure of his tomb (see fig. 48).[118] Most of these objects can be linked to two-dimensional representations of Egyptian

FIGURE 48
Ritual statuary and shrine in situ in the enclosure wall of the mastaba of Imhotep at Lisht South.

funeral rites that occur in many 12th Dynasty tombs. Imhotep alone chose to be accompanied in death by the real thing. Since he had Pyramid Texts from the Old Kingdom inscribed on the inside of his sarcophagus pit, his tomb also demonstrates an interest in what were already ancient rituals.[119] Senwosret-ankh, at Lisht South, also chose Pyramid Texts for his tomb.[120]

If natural growth and individual choice played a significant role in the development of the cemeteries at Lisht North and South, this is even truer in the Lisht North settlement. The village was founded, for reasons unknown to us, during the late 12th Dynasty, with a few self-contained houses built in the cemetery south of the pyramid of Amenemhat I. The number of houses grew until, during the 13th Dynasty, the settlement covered most of the cemetery area to the south, east, and west of the pyramid. Some houses were even built against the slope of the pyramid (see fig. 49), and many covered the entrances of previously used tomb shafts. Other shafts were probably still in use for internments, and new shafts were dug between the houses and, in some cases, inside them.[121]

This community was not strictly planned. In the end there seems to have been a somewhat crooked street in the southern portion of the village, with some open space around a still-standing tomb chapel; houses randomly filled the rest of the area. Alterations went on continuously. Large rooms were subdivided by walls, doors opened in other walls, rooms were added as required. The houses were not poor, but fair-sized structures with living rooms plastered and painted in a uniform fashion with a multicolored dado. Wood columns carried the roofs of larger rooms, and many houses had an upper story or at least a stairway to the rooftop. In one house a workshop was established for the production of faience objects. The kiln debris from this industry spread over a considerable area, and the kiln had many layers, indicating use over a long period.

Intensive study of the material from earlier seasons as well as selective reexcavation will be necessary to understand this settlement fully. At present one feature of the village as it flourished throughout the 13th Dynasty, and perhaps even into the Hyksos period, stands out. A great deal of foreign pottery was in use there. A trial excavation of dump material from the settlement has shown that on average 3.4 percent of all the sherds found originally came from large storage jars that were manufactured in Canaan.[122] If these dumps are a representative sample of the pottery in the village, we can deduce that each household possessed at least one large Canaanite jar. We do not know what was imported from Canaan in these containers, and it is possible that the original contents were intended for use by the royal residence or a noble household at Itjtawy. The residents of the Lisht North village might have obtained the empty jars and reused them as storage vessels. The presence of these jars, nevertheless, is a strong indication of the intensive trading that went on during the 13th Dynasty between Egypt, Canaan, and the Mediterranean. The appearance of some luxury goods at Lisht thus becomes more understandable.[123]

One of these fine imports that has attracted considerable attention from scholars since its discovery is the so-called Dolphin Jar (fig. 50).[124] Neutron activation analysis has shown that this jar was manufactured of Canaanite clay, probably somewhere in the region of Gaza.[125] It is decorated with a design of dolphins and large water birds in dark purplish brown manganese paint on a light reddish yellow ground; the shape is characteristic of Canaanite jugs. The organization of the design lacks the structured, geometrical quality of Tell el-Yahudiya pottery.[126] Found in the plundered shaft of tomb 879 among funeral goods, the vase could have been part of the burial equipment, or it could have come to rest in the tomb with debris moved down from the house that was built over it. In either case the presence of this exquisite item of imported pottery should be seen against a background of large-scale trading between Egypt and Canaan in the eighteenth century B.C.—trade that possibly was conducted through the city of Avaris (Tell el-Dab'a) in the eastern Delta, where Canaanite people had settled by this time.[127] A Canaanite-looking clay figurine of a deity[128] and the name of a man's mother, "the Asiatic,"[129] indicate that Canaanites might even have been part of the population of Itjtawy and probably also Lisht village.[130] Other, less numerous imports of Aegean pottery in the village debris indicate trade relations with the Minoan culture.[131] All in all, the settlement at Lisht North appears to have been a lively place, industrious and well aware of the world outside Egypt.

Notes

The author would like to acknowledge the assistance of Susan Allen in the writing of this essay

1 W. M. Flinders Petrie, *Tanis*, pt. 1, *1883–4*, Egypt Exploration Fund, 2d Memoir (London: Trubner, 1885); idem, *Tanis*, pt. 2, *Nesbesheh (Am) and Defenneh (Tapahnes)*, Egypt Exploration Fund, 4th Memoir (London: Trubner, 1888); Edouard Naville, *Bubastis (1887–1889)*, Egypt Exploration Fund, 8th Memoir (London: Kegan Paul, Trench, and Trubner, 1891); Jacques de Morgan, *Fouilles à Dachour, mars–juin 1894* (Vienna: Adolphe Holzhausen, 1903); W. M. Flinders Petrie, *Kahun, Gurob, and Hawara* (London: Kegan Paul, Trench, and Trubner, 1890); idem, *Illahun, Kahun, and Gurob, 1889–90* (London: David Nutt, 1891); Guy Brunton, *Lahun I: The Treasure*, British School of Archaeology in Egypt and the Egyptian Research Account, 20th Year, 1914 (London: British School of Archaeology in Egypt, 1920); W. M. Flinders Petrie, Guy Brunton, and M. A. Murray, *Lahun II*, British School of Archaeology in Egypt and the Egyptian Research Account, 26th Year, 1920 (London: British School of Archaeology in Egypt, 1925).

2 Hans G. Evers collected, studied, and illustrated the masterworks of Egyptian sculpture in the Middle Kingdom; see *Staat aus dem Stein: Denkmäler, Geschichte und Bedeutung der ägyptischen Plastik während des Mittleren Reichs* (Munich: F. Bruckmann, 1929). Cyril Aldred devotes almost a third of the plates in *Jewels of the Pharaohs* (New York: Thames and Hudson, 1971) to the jewelry of Middle Kingdom queens and princesses.

3 This site was excavated in 1900 by George A. Reisner, Albert M. Lythgoe, and F. W. Green, but the results remain unpublished; see Peter Lacovara, "The Hearst Excavations at Deir el-Ballas: The Eighteenth Dynasty Town," in *Studies in Ancient Egypt, the Aegean, and the Sudan: Essays in Honor of Dows Dunham*, ed. William K. Simpson and W. M. Davis (Boston: MFA, 1981), 120–24. The Museum of Fine Arts, Boston, resumed work at the site in 1980; for excavation results, see Peter Lacovara, *Deir el-Ballas: Preliminary Report on the Deir el-Ballas Expedition, 1980–86* (Winona Lake, Ind.: American Research Center in Egypt, 1990). See also Henry G. Fischer, *Inscriptions from the Coptite Nome, Dynasties VI–XI*, Analecta Orientalia 40 (Rome: Pontificum Institutum Biblicum, 1964), 103–23.

4 Clarence S. Fisher, as director of the Eckley B. Coxe Jr. Expedition for the University Museum, University of Pennsylvania, conducted excavations at Dendera from 1915 to 1918. The excavation finds from the Middle Kingdom remain largely unpublished, although some Dendera material appeared in Ray Anita Slater, "The Archaeology of Dendereh in the First Intermediate Period" (Ph.D. diss., University of Pennsylvania, 1974).

5 The results of Reisner's excavations at el-Bersha in 1915 on behalf of Harvard University and the Museum of Fine Arts, Boston, remain unpublished. Boston resumed excavations at the site in 1989 in collaboration with the University of Pennsylvania Museum of Archaeology and Anthropology and Leiden University. For a preliminary report, see Edward Brovarski et al., *Bersheh Reports I* (Boston: MFA, 1992).

6 George A. Reisner, *Excavations at Kerma, Parts I–III*, Harvard African Studies 5 (Cambridge: Peabody Museum, Harvard University, 1923); idem, *Excavations at Kerma, Parts IV–V*, Harvard African Studies 6 (Cambridge: Peabody Museum, Harvard University, 1923); Dows Dunham, *Excavations at Kerma, Part VI* (Boston: MFA, 1982).

7 Dows Dunham, *Second Cataract Forts*, 2 vols. (Boston: MFA, 1960–67). These excavations also produced major works of Middle Kingdom sculpture, most notably the statue of the lady Sennuwy, now in the Museum of Fine Arts, Boston (see fig. 97); see William S. Smith, *The Art and Architecture of Ancient Egypt*, 2d rev. ed. (Baltimore and Harmondsworth: Penguin Books, 1981), 180–81, figs. 171–72.

8 Eduard Meyer, *Geschichte des Altertums*, vol. 1, pt. 2, *Die ältesten geschichtlichen Völker und Kulturen bis zum sechzehnten Jahrhundert* (1913; reprint, Stuttgart: J. G. Cotta, 1954), 254 (author's translation).

9 Alexander Scharff, "Geschichte Ägyptens von der Vorzeit bis zur Grundung Alexandreias," in *Ägypten und Vorderasien im Altertum*, by Alexander Scharff and Anton Moortgat (Munich: F. Bruckmann, 1950), 87 (author's translation).

10 Herbert E. Winlock, *Excavations at Deir el Bahri, 1911–1931* (New York: Macmillan, 1942), vii.

11 I am indebted to Patrice Donoghue of the Harvard University Archives for this information.

12 Winlock, *Excavations at Deir el Bahri*, vii.

13 Albert M. Lythgoe, "The Egyptian Expedition," *BMMA* 2 (April 1907): 61–63.

14 See Christopher C. Lee, ...*The Grand Piano Came by Camel: Arthur C. Mace, the Neglected Egyptologist* (Edinburgh and London: Mainstream Publishing, 1992). Mace would eventually be "lent" by the Metropolitan Museum to Howard Carter in 1922 to work in the tomb of Tutankhamun. The author is grateful to Mace's daughter, Mrs. Margaret Orr, for her recollections about Winlock and her father.

15 Arthur C. Mace and Herbert E. Winlock, *The Tomb of Senebtisi at Lisht*, MMA Egyptian Expedition 1 (New York: MMA, 1916). It is not easy today to identify which parts of this masterful publication belong to its respective authors.

16 Herbert E. Winlock, *The Temple of Hibis in El Khargeh Oasis*, vol. 1, *The Excavations*, MMA Egyptian Expedition 13 (New York: MMA, 1941).

17 Herbert E. Winlock, *The Monastery of Epiphanius at Thebes*, vol. 1, *The Archaeological Material*, MMA Egyptian Expedition 3 (New York: MMA, 1926).

18 Winlock, *Excavations*, 1–2.

19 Herbert E. Winlock, "The Theban Necropolis in the Middle Kingdom," *American Journal of Semitic Languages and Literatures* 32 (October 1915): 1–37.

20 Ibid., 13–24, fig. 1.

21 Herbert E. Winlock, *The Rise and Fall of the Middle Kingdom in Thebes* (New York: Macmillan, 1947), v.

22 Edouard Naville, H. R. Hall, and E. R. Ayrton, *The XIth Dynasty Temple at Deir el-Bahari*, 3 vols., Memoirs of the Egypt Exploration Fund 28, 30, 32 (London: Egypt Exploration Fund, 1907, 1910, 1913). The first excavations at the site had been undertaken by Lord Dufferin in 1859; see I. E. S. Edwards, "Lord Dufferin's Excavations at Deir el-Bahri and the Clandeboye Collection," *JEA* 51 (1965): 16–28.

23 Winlock, "Theban Necropolis," fig. 1.

24 Dieter Arnold, *Gräber des Alten und Mittleren Reiches in el-Tarif*, Deutsches archäologisches Institut, Abteilung Kairo, Archäologische Veröffentlichungen 17 (Mainz: Philipp von Zabern, 1976), 22. Arnold assigns the three tombs (in south-to-north order) to Intef I, Intef II, and Intef III.

25 Dorothea Arnold, "Amenemhat I and the Early Twelfth Dynasty at Thebes," *MMA Journal* 26 (1991): 10–12.

26 Georges Daressy, "Trois points inexplorés de la nécropole thébaine," *ASAE* 2 (1901): 134; M. Robert Mond, "Report of Work in the Necropolis of Thebes during the Winter of 1903–1904," *ASAE* 6 (1905): 77–78.

27 Winlock, *Excavations*, 17–19.

28 Herbert E. Winlock, "Digger's Luck: Remarkable Models Discovered in an Egyptian Tomb 4,000 Years Old," *Scribner's Magazine* 69 (February 1921): 207–21; idem, *Excavations*, 17–29; idem, *Models of Daily Life in Ancient Egypt: From the Tomb of Meket-Re at Thebes*, MMA Egyptian Expedition 18 (Cambridge: Harvard University Press, 1955).

29 Naville, Hall, and Ayrton, *The XIth Dynasty Temple*, vol. 1, 47–51, pls. I–II.

30 Winlock, *Excavations*, 35–37.

31 Ibid., 38.

32 Ibid., 38–46, pls. 6–11.

33 Herbert E. Winlock, "Hekanakht Writes to His Household," *Scribner's Magazine* 73 (March 1923): 288–96; idem, *Excavations*, 58–67, pl. 33.

34 Agatha Christie, *Death Comes as the End* (New York: Harper Paperbacks, 1992), ix–x.

35 T. G. H. James, *The Hekanakhte Papers and Other Early Middle Kingdom Documents*, MMA Egyptian Expedition 19 (New York: MMA, 1962).

36 Winlock, *Excavations*, 68–71, pls. 15–16.

37 Ibid., 71.

38 Winlock, *Excavations*, 52; Winlock, *Rise and Fall*, 39.

39 Winlock, *Excavations*, 52.

40 See, e.g., a reconstruction drawing by G. M. Peek, published in Dieter Arnold, *The Temple of Mentuhotep at Deir el-Bahari from the Notes of Herbert Winlock*, MMA Egyptian Expedition 21 (New York: MMA, 1979), pl. 41.

41 For the Mentuhotep II temple, see Winlock, *Rise and Fall*, 38–42; Dieter Arnold, *Temple of Mentuhotep*, 37–45; idem, *Der Tempel des Königs Mentuhotep von Deir el-Bahari*, vol. 1, *Architektur und Deutung*, Deutsches archäologisches Institut, Abteilung Kairo, Archäologische Veröffentlichungen 8 (Mainz: Philipp von Zabern, 1974), 62. Arnold has discussed in detail his reasons for not reconstructing a pyramid on top of the temple as Winlock did (ibid., 28–31; *Temple of Mentuhotep*, 34–35).

42 Naville, Hall, and Ayrton, *The XIth Dynasty Temple*, vol. 2, pl. 1.

43 Dieter Arnold, *Mentuhotep*, vol. 1, fig. opp. p. 7.

44 James H. Breasted, *A History of Egypt: From Earliest Times to the Persian Conquest* (New York: Scribner's, 1912); William C. Hayes, "The Middle Kingdom in Egypt: Internal History from the Rise of the Heracleopolitans to the Death of Ammenemes III," in *Early History of the Middle East*, vol. 1.2 of *The Cambridge Ancient History*, 3d ed. (Cambridge: Cambridge University Press, 1971), 464–531; Alan H. Gardiner, *Egypt of the Pharaohs: An Introduction* (Oxford: Clarendon Press, 1961).

45 John A. Wilson, *The Burden of Egypt: An Interpretation of Ancient Egyptian Culture* (Chicago: University of Chicago Press, 1951); Hermann Kees, *Das alte Ägypten: Eine kleine Landeskunde* (Berlin: Akademie-Verlag, 1955); and, most recently, Erik Hornung, *Geist der Pharaonenzeit* (Zurich: Artemis, 1989).

46 E.g., in his final book on the Middle Kingdom, *The Rise and Fall of the Middle Kingdom at Thebes*, Winlock's table of contents (p. xi) lists chapter headings (e.g., "The Rulers of Upper Egypt in the Eleventh Dynasty") with subheadings for each king.

47 Ibid., 68.

48 Ibid., 58–76.

49 Ibid., 62.

50 Ibid., 66.

51 Wolfgang Schenkel, *Memphis, Herakleopolis, Theban: Die epigraphische Zeugnisse der 7.–11. Dynastie Ägyptens*, Ägyptologische Abhandlungen 12 (Wiesbaden: Harrassowitz, 1965).

52 William C. Hayes, "Career of the Great Steward Heneu under Nebhepetre Mentuhotpe," *JEA* 35 (1949): 43–49.

53 James P. Allen, "Some Theban Officials of the Early Middle Kingdom," in *Studies in Honor of William K. Simpson* (Boston: MFA, forthcoming).

54 Ibid.

55 Ibid.

56 Ibid.

57 Dorothea Arnold, "Amenemhat I," 36–37; ibid.

58 Dorothea Arnold, "Amenemhat I," n. 196.

59 Dieter Arnold, *Temple of Mentuhotep*, 42.

60 Herbert E. Winlock, "Graffiti of the Priesthood of the Eleventh Dynasty Temples at Thebes," *American Journal of Semitic Languages and Literatures* 58 (April 1941): 146–62; idem, *Rise and Fall*, 79–86, pls. 40–45.

61 Winlock, *Rise and Fall*, pl. 40, no. 1.

62 Barry J. Kemp, *Ancient Egypt: Anatomy of a Civilization* (London: Routledge, 1989), 137.

63 Ibid.

64 Ibid., 149–80.

65 Ibid., 180.

66 Ibid.

67 This village was known as el-Maharraqa in the nineteenth and early twentieth centuries.

68 Charles Edwin Wilbour, *Travels in Egypt (December 1880 to May 1891): Letters of Charles Edwin Wilbour*, ed. Jean Capart (Brooklyn: Brooklyn Museum, 1936), 249–51, 344–45.

69 Joseph-Etienne Gautier and Gustave Jéquier, *Mémoire sur les fouilles de Licht*, Mémoires publiés par les membres de l'Institut français d'archéologie orientale du Caire 6 (Cairo: IFAO, 1902).

70 Ibid., 12, pls. 9–13.

71 Herbert E. Winlock, "The Egyptian Expedition, 1933–1934," *BMMA* 29, pt. 2 (November 1934): 3.

72 Since 1984 the following scholars have worked at the site: Dieter and Dorothea Arnold, Günther Heindl, Christian and Regina Hoelzl, James and Susan Allen, Cheryl Haldane, Adela Oppenheim, and Ray A. Slater. Architects were Raymond Theler, Marcel Gruber, and Joseph Dorner. Draftsmen have included Lara Bernini, Barry Girsh, Peter Janosi, Lisa Majerus, Peter Nikitsch, William P. Schenck, Angela Schwab, and Richard Velleu. Student assistants were Felix Arnold and Sarah Orel.

73 Dieter Arnold, *The South Cemeteries of Lisht*, vol. 1, *The Pyramid of Senwosret*, MMA Egyptian Expedition 22 (New York: MMA, 1988); Felix Arnold, *The South Cemeteries of Lisht*, vol. 2, *The Control Notes and Team Marks*, MMA Egyptian Expedition 23 (New York: MMA, 1990); Dieter Arnold, *The South Cemeteries of Lisht*, vol. 3, *The Pyramid Complex of Senwosret I*, MMA Egyptian Expedition 25 (New York: MMA, 1992). In preparation are James P. Allen, *Funerary Texts from Lisht*; Dieter Arnold, *The Pyramid of Amenemhat I at Lisht*; idem, *Mastabas of the Middle Kingdom at Lisht and Dahshur*; Dorothea Arnold, *The Mastaba of Imhotep*; Felix Arnold et al., *The Settlements*; Janine Bourriau, *Selected Tomb Groups from Lisht North*; and Janine Bourriau and Geoffrey T. Martin, *Scarabs and Seal Impressions from Lisht*.

74 George. A. Reisner, *The Early Dynastic Cemeteries of Naga-ed-Dêr,* vol. 1, University of California Publications, Egyptian Archaeology 2 (Leipzig: J. C. Hinrichs, 1908); Arthur C. Mace, *The Early Dynastic Cemeteries of Naga-ed-Dêr,* vol. 2, University of California Publications, Egyptian Archaeology 3 (Leipzig: J. C. Hinrichs, 1909).

75 See n. 7 above, and W. M. Flinders Petrie, *Diospolis Parva: The Cemeteries of Abadiyeh and Hu, 1898–99,* with chapters by Arthur C. Mace, Memoir of the Egypt Exploration Fund 20 (London: Egypt Exploration Fund, 1901).

76 Howard Carter and Arthur C. Mace, *The Tomb of Tut-ankh-amen* (New York: George H. Doran Co., 1923).

77 Mace and Winlock, *Senebtisi.*

78 See note 73 above.

79 William C. Hayes, *Royal Sarcophagi of the XVIIIth Dynasty,* Princeton Monographs in Art and Archaeology, Quarto Series 19 (Princeton: Princeton University Press, 1935).

80 These tomb cards provide the primary documentation of tomb group and excavation locus, giving sketch plans, inventory, and small sketches to scale of finds, translations of inscriptions, and the excavators' observations.

81 William C. Hayes, *The Texts in the Mastebeh of Se'n-Wosret-'ankh at Lisht,* MMA Egyptian Expedition 12 (New York: MMA, 1937).

82 Another point against too strict a view of Middle Kingdom centralization and suppression of individualism is the richness of regional styles in evidence throughout the 11th and most of the 12th Dynasties; see Janine Bourriau, "Patterns of Change in Burial Customs during the Middle Kingdom," in *Middle Kingdom Studies,* ed. Stephen Quirke (New Malden, U.K.: SIA Publishing, 1991), 3–20. It is quite possible that the "bureaucratic utopia" was true only for the last two reigns of the 12th Dynasty and then only for part of society.

83 Petrie, *Illahun,* 5–8, pl. 14.

84 Recent work by Ahmed Abd el Hamid, the inspector of antiquities for Lisht, has uncovered remains of First Intermediate Period tombs south of the southern pyramid, overlooking the cultivation west of el-Saudiya. These tombs will be published by the MMA Egyptian Expedition series.

85 Discussion of the coregency of Amenemhat I and his son Senwosret I has recently been renewed by Claude Obsomer, "La date de Nésou-Montou (Louvre C1)," *RdE* 44 (1993):

103–33. See Dorothea Arnold, "Amenemhat I," n. 47, for a summary of current literature on coregencies in the 12th Dynasty. A coregency is likely, based on the evidence from Lisht to date, but the question will have to be readdressed when the reliefs from the northern pyramid are published.

86 The pyramid that the Herakleopolitan king Merikara may have erected at Saqqara was certainly small, since no trace of it is visible today. For the possible existence of this pyramid, see Cecil M. Firth and Battiscombe Gunn, *Excavations at Saqqara: Teti Pyramid Cemeteries,* vol. 1 (Cairo: IFAO, 1926), 8.

87 Hans Goedicke, *Re-used Blocks from the Pyramid of Amenemhet I at Lisht,* MMA Egyptian Expedition 20 (New York: MMA, 1971).

88 Dieter Arnold, "Hypostyle Halls of the Old and Middle Kingdom," in *Studies in Honor of William K. Simpson.*

89 I. E. S. Edwards, *The Pyramids of Egypt,* rev. ed. (London: Penguin Books, 1991), 206; Arthur C. Mace, "Excavations at Lisht," *BMMA* 17 (December 1922): pt. 2, 5, fig. 1.

90 Aly El-Khouly, "An Offering-Table of Sesostris I from El-Lisht," *JEA* 64 (1978): 44, pl. 9.

91 MMA 09.180.543: Herbert E. Winlock, "Neb-Hepet-Re Mentu-hotpe of the Eleventh Dynasty," *JEA* 26 (1940): 116–19, pl. 21; Dorothea Arnold, "Amenemhat I," 14–15, figs. 15–17.

92 MMA 08.200.5, 6, 9, 10, 113: Albert. M. Lythgoe, "The Egyptian Expedition II," *BMMA* 2 (July 1907): 115–16, fig. 6 on p. 117 (MMA 08.200.5); Arthur C. Mace, "The Egyptian Expedition III," *BMMA* 3 (October 1908): 184, fig. 1 (MMA 08.200.6); William Kelly Simpson, "Studies in the Twelfth Egyptian Dynasty I–II: II, The Sed Festival in Regnal Year 30 of Amenemhet III and the Periodicity of the Festival in Dynasty XII," *JARCE* 2 (1963): 60–63; Hayes, *Scepter,* vol. 1, 172–73, figs. 103–4 (MMA 08.200.5, 9, 10, 113). See also n. 85 above.

93 William K. Simpson, in his unpublished dissertation on the North Pyramid of Lisht, considered the possibility that the building in which the *sed*-festival blocks were found was not Amenemhat's pyramid temple but a later building that replaced it.

94 Dieter Arnold, *The Pyramid of Senwosret I,* 56–57, and plans.

95 Note the difference between the relief in Hayes, *Scepter,* vol. 1, 186, fig. 114, and the relief in this exhibition (cat. no. 59).

96 Dieter Arnold, *Pyramid of Senwosret I,* 18–20, figs. 1–2, pls. 3–7, 76–77, 105.

97 Hayes, *Scepter,* vol. 1, 183.

98 Arthur C. Mace, "The Egyptian Expedition: Excavations at the North Pyramid of Lisht," *BMMA* 9 (October 1914): 14–15, figs. 7–8 on pp. 8–9. The pottery found in a foundation deposit discovered under this monument has not yet been published but is similar to that found in Senwosret I's pyramid foundation deposits; see Dorothea Arnold, "The Pottery," in Dieter Arnold, *Pyramid of Senwosret I,* 106–9, figs. 52–54, pls. 61d, 63d.

99 Hayes, *Scepter,* vol. 1, 177. Rehuerdjersen cannot, however, be the owner of the stela illustrated on p. 333, fig. 221 (MMA 12.182.1), which is of a later date. See Rita Freed, "Stelae Workshops of Early Dynasty 12," in *Studies in Honor of William K. Simpson.*

100 MMA 22.1.21: Hayes, *Scepter,* vol. 1, 177; Mace, "Excavations at Lisht," 12, fig. 11; Dieter Arnold, *Pyramid Complex,* 22–23, n. 26.

101 William K. Simpson, *Papyrus Reisner II* (Boston: MFA, 1965), 21.

102 Mace, "The Egyptian Expedition III," 188.

103 This is amply attested at Lisht South. Large tomb structures, however, often possessed rectangular shafts at an earlier time.

104 The occurrence of globular jars with narrow necks is a fairly reliable indicator of a date late in the reign of Senwosret I; see Dorothea Arnold, "The Pottery," 142–43, fig. 72: nos. 27, 131, 141. Pottery predating the change in ceramic style that occurred during the middle years of Senwosret I's reign was found predominantly in the foundation deposits of the Lisht North pyramid temple.

105 The burial of the lady Senebtisi (see note 15 above) is one of these later burials; see Dorothea Arnold, "The Area of the Northwest Corner of the Causeway," in Dieter Arnold, *Pyramid of Senwosret I,* 37, n. 114; Bourriau, "Patterns of Change," 17–18.

106 Dorothea Arnold, "Pottery," 55–58, pls. 66–69.

107 William K. Simpson, "Mentuhotep, Vizier of Sesostris I, Patron of Art and Architecture," *MDAIK* 47 (1991): 331–40; Dieter Arnold, *Mastabas of the Middle Kingdom.*

108 Ambrose Lansing, "I. Excavations on the Pyramid of Sesostris I at Lisht: Seasons of 1916–17 and 1917–18," *BMMA* 15 (July 1920): 3–6, figs. 2–3; Khety's coffin (MMA 32.1.22) will be published in Allen, *Funerary Texts.*

109 Ambrose Lansing, "The Egyptian Expedition, 1931–1932: The Museum's Excavations at Lisht," *BMMA* 28 (April 1933): 20–21, figs. 16–17. The wood models could be a generation later than Senwosret I; earlier pottery was found in some of the shafts.

110 Albert M. Lythgoe, "The Egyptian Expedition II: Excavations at the South Pyramid of Lisht in 1914," *BMMA* 10 (February 1915): 6–22.

111 Ambrose Lansing, "The Egyptian Expedition: The Excavations at Lisht," *BMMA* 28 (November 1933): 9–38.

112 Ambrose Lansing, "The Egyptian Expedition: The Excavations at Lisht," *BMMA* 29 (November 1934): pt. 2, 27–41.

113 Mentuhotep's tomb as well as remains of a brick structure north of it, with numerous plundered shafts, will be published in Dieter Arnold, *Mastabas of the Middle Kingdom*.

114 Lythgoe, "Egyptian Expedition II," 6–22.

115 Stephan Seidlmayer's argument that the types available at the beginning of the Middle Kingdom consolidate again in the 12th Dynasty does not seems to be borne out

by the Lisht evidence; see *Gräberfelder aus dem Übergang vom Alten zum Mittleren Reich*, Studien zur Archäologie und Geschichte Altägyptens 1 (Heidelberg: Heidelberger Orientverlag, 1990), 399–412.

116 Bourriau, "Patterns of Change," 7–9.

117 Lythgoe, "Egyptian Expedition II," 6–22.

118 One of the large boats is MMA 14.3.23; the two model boats (MMA 14.3.21–22) were represented only by remains of stern and prow and ritual objects that had been attached to them. The Anubis shrine and fetish are MMA 14.3.18–20. The divinity wearing the red crown is MMA 14.3.17; that with the white crown is in the Egyptian Museum, Cairo (JE 44951).

119 These texts will be published in Allen, *Funerary Texts*.

120 Hayes, *Texts in the Mastebeh*, passim.

121 For the village, see all the excavation reports of the MMA expedition at Lisht between 1906 and 1922, especially Arthur C. Mace, "Excavations at Lisht," *BMMA* 16 (November 1921): 10–14. The excavators at the beginning of the century did not recognize the importance of this settlement and were unable to date it properly. Excavation of one house area was resumed in 1991; the results

of this excavation and earlier seasons are forthcoming in Felix Arnold et al., *Settlements*.

122 Dorothea Arnold, Felix Arnold, and Susan Allen, "Canaanite Imports at Lisht, the Middle Kingdom Capital of Egypt," *Ägypten und Levante* 5 (1995, in press).

123 Barry J. Kemp and Robert S. Merrillees, *Minoan Pottery in Second Millennium Egypt* (Mainz: Philipp von Zabern, 1980); Robert S. Merrillees, "Syrian Pottery from Middle Kingdom Egypt," *Australian Journal of Biblical Archaeology* 2 (1973): 51–59.

124 MMA 22.1.95: Helene J. Kantor, "The Relative Chronology of Egypt and Its Foreign Correlations before the Late Bronze Age," in *Chronologies in Old World Archaeology*, ed. Robert W. Ehrich (Chicago: University of Chicago Press, 1965), 23–24, fig. 5; Hayes, *Scepter*, vol. 1, 12–13, fig. 4; Kemp and Merrillees, *Minoan Pottery*, 220–25; Janine Bourriau, "The Dolphin Vase from Lisht," in *Studies in Honor of William K. Simpson*.

125 Patrick E. McGovern et al., "The Archaeological Origin and Significance of the Dolphin Vase Determined by Neutron Activation Analysis," *Bulletin of the American School of Oriental Research*, no. 296 (1994): 31–41.

126 Kantor saw Minoan influence in this decoration ("Relative Chronology," 23).

127 Manfred Bietak, "Avaris and Piramesse: Archaeological Explorations in the Eastern Nile Delta," Mortimer Wheeler Archaeological Lecture 1979, *Proceedings of the British Academy, London* 65 (1979): 272–73. See also *Pharaonen und fremde Dynastien im Dunkel*, exh. cat. (Vienna: Museen der Stadt Wien, 1994), 290–92.

128 MMA 22.1.1625: Mace, "Excavations at Lisht," 9, fig. 7.

129 Allen, *Funerary Texts*, from the base of a statue found at Lisht North.

130 The presence of Asiatics is already attested at Kahun: Petrie, *Illahun*, 9–10, pl. 1; Ulrich Luft, "Asiatics in Illahun: A Preliminary Report," *Atti, Sesto Congresso internazionala di egittologia*, vol. 2 (Turin: Organizing Committee of the Sixth International Congress of Egyptology), 292; Rosalie David, "Religious Practices in a Pyramid Workmen's Town of the Twelfth Dynasty," *Bulletin of the Australian Centre for Egyptology* 2 (1991): 35–36.

131 Kemp and Merrillees, *Minoan Pottery*, 1–6.

The American Archaeological Focus on Ancient Palaces and Temples of the New Kingdom

David O'Connor

The New Kingdom (c. 1550–1070 B.C.) is one of the best-known periods in Egyptian history in terms of specific events, relatively well-documented processes (such as the development of an empire), and general culture. Its constituent dynasties— the 18th, 19th, and 20th—have been much studied by Egyptologists, and some of its rulers—Akhenaten, Tutankhamun, and Ramesses II—are those most familiar to the interested public. Neither circumstance is surprising, since the documentation and archaeology of the New Kingdom are the best preserved of the entire Egyptian Bronze Age (c. 3100–1070 B.C.) and are associated with such spectacular discoveries as the relatively unplundered tomb of Tutankhamun and the apparent monotheism of Akhenaten.

The New Kingdom was a particularly expansive period. Because of the relative efficiency of their internal governance, its pharaohs were able to build an extensive empire, stretching to Canaan and northern and central Nubia, and a complex network of diplomatic and trading contacts extending far beyond, to the Aegean, Anatolia and the Near East, southern Nubia and Punt, and Libya. Politically and socially dominant, the Egyptian kingship thus controlled vast wealth, by antiquity's standards, and lavished it in part on sometimes enormous temples as well as on sprawling palace complexes. Society as a whole, although characterized by a sharp division between a wealthy elite and the rest of the populace, was relatively prosperous and divided into several socioeconomic classes.[1]

Archaeological remains of the period are found throughout Egypt. The temples of Thebes and of southern sites such as Abydos and Abu Simbel are sometimes startlingly well preserved, although their equivalents in middle and northern Egypt have not fared as well, since their fine stonemasonry was repeatedly pillaged in later centuries as a source of building materials. But beyond the major monuments, innumerable cemeteries, of both elite and commoner, and many town and village ruins still exist, most buried below the modern flood plain.

It was, therefore, well-nigh inevitable that any substantial American archaeological project in Egypt over the last one hundred years would encounter New Kingdom remains, none of which can be counted as insignificant. Temples and colorfully decorated tombs of royalty and elite are eye-catching, but lower-order cemeteries and the cities and towns documenting ancient Egypt's social complexity are, from other perspectives, equally important. An abundance of New Kingdom material is recorded in the publications and archival records of American Egyptologists, but the highlights—all that we can cover in any detail here—are, in fact, temples and palaces.

No American excavated New Kingdom cemeteries comparable in the richness of their social complexity to those uncovered by George A. Reisner at Giza and Naga el-Deir for the Old Kingdom and First Intermediate Period, or by Clarence S. Fisher at Dendera for the First Intermediate Period and the Middle Kingdom. For the most part the major achievements in terms of New Kingdom settlement archaeology were those of the Germans and British at Amarna and of the Institut français d'archéologie orientale, Cairo, at Deir el-Medina on the west bank at Thebes.[2] But Reisner's excavations (now resumed by the Museum of Fine Arts, Boston) at the unusual and short-lived early New Kingdom "royal city" at Deir el-Ballas, and of several Nubian fortresses with substantial New Kingdom components, should be noted.

With regard to temples and palaces, American endeavors focused on Thebes and, to a more limited but important degree, Memphis, the longest lived of Egypt's royal cities, centers of governance and long-term (if not continuous) residence by pharaohs. The significant Ramesside temples of Abydos engaged little American attention, although Herbert E. Winlock did recover from there a significant, if small, chapel of Ramesses I,[3] and more recently excavations by Stephen Harvey, under the aegis of the Pennsylvania-Yale expedition to Abydos (see fig. 52), have made important discoveries about a long-neglected, largely destroyed complex of the pharaoh Ahmose, including perhaps the first actual depictions to be recovered of his war against the Hyksos.[4] Similarly, the well-preserved New Kingdom temples of Nubia received little archaeological attention from Americans, except for Reisner's excavations at the vast but not well-preserved temple of Amun-Re at Gebel

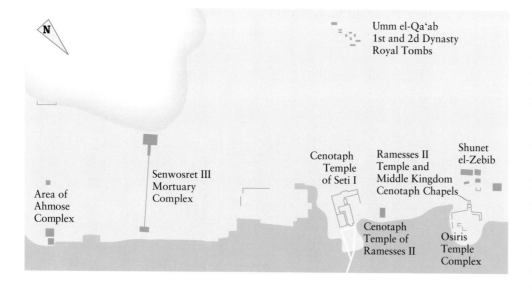

FIGURE 52
Abydos.

Barkal, in Upper Nubia.[5] The superb record of the Beit el-Wali temple of Ramesses II, made during the Nubian Salvage Campaign in the 1960s, was an epigraphic rather than an archaeological venture.[6]

In their work with Theban temples, however, American institutions have made exceptionally important contributions to New Kingdom archaeology, and this is even more true of palaces at Thebes (Malqata), Memphis, and Deir el-Ballas. Substantial and important structures in ancient Egypt, palaces were largely built of mud brick rather than stone, which, by the New Kingdom, was commonly used for major temples. The mud-brick palaces are rarely located and excavated because they did not survive as well as stone temples and are embedded within, or covered over by, ancient urban matrices. It is noteworthy that, apart from the palaces of Amarna, every major New Kingdom palace excavation has been conducted by American Egyptologists.

In concentrating on temples and palaces, however, I do not wish to overlook some other significant contributions to our knowledge of the New Kingdom, though they belong more to the realm of art history and epigraphy than archaeology. These include the long-term work of the Oriental Institute of the University of Chicago on Theban temples and tombs and some important Metropolitan Museum of Art (New York) publications of the latter. More specifically archaeological projects involve the Theban Valley of the Kings. In the first decade of the twentieth century Theodore M. Davis (1837–1915), a copper magnate from Rhode Island, funded the excavation of several significant if badly ruined and disturbed tombs within the valley,[7] and more recently Kent R. Weeks has carried out a detailed topographical and architectural survey (see figs. 53, 54) of inestimable value (now being followed up by excavation in the unique tomb KV5, which he has identified as the possible burial place of the many sons of Ramesses II),[8] which is a notable complement to another major American achievement, Elizabeth Thomas's encyclopedic study of the royal tombs.[9] On the east bank the Brooklyn Museum has excavated at the Mut temple complex,[10] focusing primarily on post–New Kingdom remains, and the universities of Pennsylvania and Toronto have jointly studied the Akhenaten temple blocks from east Karnak, subsequently followed by excavations at the site by Toronto.[11]

The excavations I will consider in this essay are particularly illuminating for our understanding of Egyptian kingship, a much-debated institution[12] in the New Kingdom. In chronological order, by reign or kingship, these excavations include: Hatshepsut's temple at Deir el-Bahri, by the Metropolitan Museum of Art (1912–36); Malqata, the "palace city" of Amenhotep III, near Medinet Habu, by the Metropolitan Museum of Art (1910–18), with subsequent work by the University of Pennsylvania Museum of Archaeology and Anthropology (1971–77); a ceremonial

palace of Merneptah at Memphis, by the University of Pennsylvania Museum of Archaeology and Anthropology (1915–20); and the mortuary temple of Ramesses III at Medinet Habu, by the Oriental Institute of the University of Chicago (1924–29).

This series of important excavations focused on the archaeology of New Kingdom kingship might suggest a careful plan of research coordinated among institutions and scholars. In reality, as is so often the case, they were more the result of accidental, unexpected developments or individual scholarly initiatives. At Medinet Habu the Oriental Institute was interested first in epigraphy, not archaeology, although the need for the latter soon became evident and was, in some ways, superbly met. Herbert E. Winlock and his team at Deir el-Bahri were for a long time much more interested in early (11th Dynasty) remains than those of Hatshepsut's temple, which had already been somewhat ruthlessly investigated by Edouard Naville on behalf of the Egypt Exploration Society. And, while Fisher was keen to excavate within urban contexts (unlike most Egyptologists, he had earlier worked on excavations in Mesopotamia, where a primary focus has always been monumental complexes within urban contexts), it was only the more-or-less chance discovery of part of Merneptah's throne room by others that drew him to Memphis. Nevertheless, these seemingly accidental circumstances led to the outstanding results that in their totality represent a specifically American contribution to New Kingdom archaeology.

Deir el-Bahri

Deir el-Bahri was the single most important of the Metropolitan Museum's several concessions at Thebes.[13] The leading figure in the work was Herbert E. Winlock, of whom John A. Wilson wrote: "Few other men could bring ancient Egypt back to such vivid life in their published reports."[14] A witty, even-tempered man and a good administrator, Winlock was an exceptionally able archaeologist, displaying just the qualities needed for exploring the 18th Dynasty at Deir el-Bahri—careful, painstaking work in often discouraging and "unprofitable" conditions, and sustained brilliance in reconstructing complicated situations from the most fragmentary evidence. Inevitably some of these reconstructions were subsequently modified, but the overall reliability of Winlock's work has held true.

FIGURE 56
Mortuary temple of
Hatshepsut at Deir
el-Bahri, 1995.

Deir el-Bahri consists of a deep bay in the high, rugged sides of the Nile gorge (see fig. 55). It first became important in the late 11th Dynasty, when Nebhepetre Mentuhotep (r. 2061–2010 B.C.)—a pharaoh who reunited Egypt after a period of internal fragmentation and civil war—built an unusual and innovative funerary monument there. Many of his officials and their dependents were buried in rock-cut tombs along the northern arc of the cliffs defining Deir el-Bahri. Nebhepetre's monument, and an associated cult place of Hathor, goddess of the west or the funerary realm at Thebes, were venerated throughout the Middle and into the New Kingdom. In the fifteenth century B.C. Hatshepsut (r. c. 1473–1458 B.C.), one of only two female pharaohs of the New Kingdom, built her own larger mortuary temple next to Nebhepetre's (see fig. 56).[15] It followed a similar pattern of a large court followed by a "terraced" temple, built upon a series of platforms of increasingly higher elevations. Subsequently Hatshepsut's monument was defaced and "closed down" by her erstwhile coruler and eventual sole successor, Tuthmosis III (r. 1479–1425 B.C.), who built a replacement temple of his own there.[16]

In its totality Hatshepsut's temple covered a very large area (about two hectares), much of which came to be excavated by Winlock and his colleagues. First they explored the far end of its approach causeway, looking for Hatshepsut's valley temple. Later Winlock excavated most of the temple's enormous first court (approximately one hectare), which earlier excavators had largely neglected. In addition he studied many aspects of the still-standing architecture and detected important changes made in the plan and extent of the temple as Hatshepsut and her advisers developed new ideas—a rare opportunity to study the evolutionary development of a major New Kingdom monument during a single reign.

Finally Winlock excavated two enormous pits or depressions, a daunting and often wearisome task, but one yielding extremely valuable results. One pit had actually been cut into the causeway of the Nebhepetre temple; the other was a huge quarry, cut to recover shale, lying north of Hatshepsut's temple. From both, hundreds of statue fragments were recovered, enabling Winlock to reconstruct—in concept and line drawings, and sometimes in actuality—the entire rich statuary program of this great temple, a rare achievement and one that is due, ironically, to the savage treatment the temple and its statuary had received soon after Hatshepsut's death. Temple statuary was not usually destroyed but was gradually removed from its original context, so the reconstruction of such programs is usually difficult or impossible. Winlock's unique work in the study of the complex roles of statuary within Egyptian temples provided a basis for Roland Tefnin's more recent (1979) and brilliant analysis of the Deir el-Bahri statuary,[17] as well as a model for ongoing research into the complex statuary forms found in the mortuary temple of Amenhotep III.[18]

At the beginning of his work Winlock added to the list of known Theban royal mortuary temples (some have never been identified), for he found and, in an archaeological sense, brilliantly deciphered the scanty remains of a very ambitious building. Lying at the foot of Nebhepetre's causeway was a mortuary temple begun by Ramesses IV (r. 1163–1156 B.C.), continued by Ramesses V (r. 1156–1151 B.C.) and Ramesses VI (r. 1151–1143 B.C.), and planned to be twice the size of the Ramesseum (Ramesses II's mortuary temple), one of the largest ever built. This new temple, however, was never completed.

Working within Hatshepsut's temple, Winlock recovered a number of foundation deposits, such as groups of model tools, representative materials, and other items ritually deposited in pits distributed over the temple site (see cat. no. 76). He persuasively demonstrated that their apparently random pattern of distribution actually reflected the changing plan and increasing size of the temple. Originally Hatshepsut's temple approximated Nebhepetre's in plan and scale, but over time her architects became increasingly ambitious and innovative. Winlock applied painstaking excavation techniques capable of recovering the most fragile details, such as a series of shallow artificial pools in the first court, still crusted with crackled mud.

Malqata: A Unique Palace City

A little south of the well-preserved mortuary temple of Ramesses III (r. 1194–1163 B.C.) in western Thebes is the much less impressive site, even after excavation, of Malqata. Spread out over the low desert are a vast expanse of denuded brick walls (occasionally with painted dadoes surviving), fragments of collapsed ceilings and their painted decoration, and heaps of ancient rubbish scattered around the site's perimeter. But archaeologically this is one of the most unusual of New Kingdom, indeed of Egyptian, sites: a complex of palaces, villages, ceremonial structures, a temple, service buildings, servants' quarters and manufactories, a veritable palace city covering more than thirty-three hectares.[19] Individual structures within it were correspondingly large; the king's palace, for example, occupying three-quarters of a hectare, was almost as big as the great mortuary temple of Ramesses II.

Because Malqata was a one-period site in the open desert, built and occupied by Amenhotep III (r. 1391–1353 B.C.) and abandoned soon after, its remains attracted early interest, but little was known about it until Winlock began excavations there in 1910 on behalf of the Metropolitan Museum.[20] Earlier Georges Daressy

FIGURE 57
The University of
Pennsylvania Museum's
excavations to
delineate palace walls
at the palace-city
of Amenhotep III
at Malqata.

had uncovered the remains of a painted palace floor at Malqata, and also for the Metropolitan Museum, Percy E. Newberry and Robb de Peyster Tytus had delineated some structures and recovered large fragments of brilliantly painted frescoes that had once covered their mud-plastered walls and ceilings.[21] Malqata was also famous as a place where literally hundreds of attractive minor objects (whole or fragmentary) could be picked up from the surface: brightly colored faience rings, amulets, and beads and scraps of pottery painted with unusual designs in blue and other colors, a rarity among Egyptian ceramics, which were usually monochrome, undecorated, and drab.

The Metropolitan Museum's scholars were interested in a fuller understanding of the palatial complex and hoped to recover a rich array of minor objects of the New Kingdom, which, with Egyptian approval, would be an important addition to the museum's collections. Once work had begun, an unexpected factor encouraged large-scale clearance at the site. The Metropolitan's excavation funds shrank as a result of World War I, and many of the museum's erstwhile excavators in Egypt entered the army; Winlock, for example, was posted to Fort Monroe, Virginia. But the museum wanted to keep its large Egyptian work force employed and available for expanded excavations when the war ended. Malqata, with its open spaces and relatively uncomplicated archaeology, seemed ideal for this purpose, and work continued under Ambrose Lansing's direction.[22]

Much of the area was excavated, and archaeologically the results were of great interest. Many of Malqata's buildings, however, remain in moist, alluvial soil covered over by modern farmland; originally the site was even larger. Winlock and others identified many significant components.[23] To the north, a temple dedicated to Amun was linked to the celebration of Amenhotep's *sed* festivals (royal ceremonies ritually providing regeneration and new vitality to the pharaoh) in his thirtieth, thirty-fourth, and thirty-seventh regnal years. South of the temple were ceremonial structures, which are poorly understood, and farther south again a fascinating set of palaces, including Amenhotep's and another for his queen, Tiye.

The king's palace is unlike any other excavated palace in Egypt and is probably the most akin to an actual residential palace. Multicolumned ceremonial halls, with adjacent throne rooms, their columns and throne daises still traceable, are followed by an extensive suite of private apartments (see fig. 57). Many painted fragments recovered throughout the palaces provide invaluable evidence about the decoration of such structures.

The purpose of the Malqata complex is still debated. Winlock thought it was built specifically for the *sed* festivals, as do others. Barry Kemp, for example, describes it as "a kind of festival showground created for the great pageants of kingship."[24] It is possible, however, that Malqata was a genuine residential complex, lived in by both pharaoh and court whenever he visited Thebes. It was at least most likely modeled on true residential palaces, complexes of which stood at Amarna and probably occupied about the same area.

The Metropolitan Museum's excavations left one major feature unexplored. Next to the palace, and extending out over the flood plain, enormous, regularly laid-out spoil heaps of sand, gravel, and some alluvium outlined a huge rectangle. Some suggested the mounds were natural; others believed they were the wall remains of an arena of some kind. Yet others thought they defined the location of a larger harbor basin, cut into the flood plain and subsequently filled in by silts deposited by the annual Nile inundation. Winlock, like other scholars, believed the harbor was really a pleasure lake cut for Queen Tiye and recorded on several commemorative scarabs, but these were later shown to refer to an irrigation basin located far from Thebes.

This feature was a key interest of a University of Pennsylvania Museum expedition that returned to Malqata from 1971 to 1977, directed by this author and Barry Kemp of Cambridge University (see figs. 58, 59).[25] Excavations in and around the great mounds demonstrated that they were indeed the material removed from a vast artificial basin cut into the flood plain adjacent to the palace city and contemporaneous with it. The basin or harbor underwent two phases, being expanded in the second to an awesome size of about two hundred hectares.

Although other Nile harbors existed in Egypt, the excavated examples are all relatively small and attached to temples (or, once in Nubia, to a fortress), so the functions and scale of the Malqata harbor are somewhat mysterious. It undoubtedly could have been used to bring construction materials to the site (and the alluvial soil excavated from it may well have been used for the hundreds of thousands, even millions, of bricks used for the palace city), and presumably continued to serve practical purposes thereafter, but it is much larger than necessary for either purpose.

FIGURE 58
Some members of the University of Pennsylvania Museum's Malqata excavation team and visitors. *Left to right*: Karen Foster, unidentified, Harry James of the British Museum, Labib Habachi, Mrs. James, David O'Connor, and Zahi Hawass.

FIGURE 59
Excavation of 18th Dynasty houses along the edge of the harbor mounds at Malqata by the University of Pennsylvania expedition.

Fundamentally the harbor should be seen as conceptually linked to the palace city but in ways we can only guess at. The spoil heaps were carefully landscaped to resemble rows of hills, so the whole was perhaps intended to evoke the geography of primeval times, when the world emerged from the waters of Nun, an event of great significance to the Egyptians. The harbor might have been used for water-borne royal ceremonies in which the pharaoh reenacted the course of the sun god over the sky, itself envisaged as a navigable interface between the orderly cosmos and the endless liquidity of Nun, which surrounded that cosmos. Thus, as in many other ways, pharaoh's ceremonial and governmental life could be represented as an earthbound version of the sun god's rulership of the cosmos as a whole.

The vast palatial complex of Amenhotep III at Malqata seems to have been intended for short-term use, as was another, even more unusual palace city, excavated by George A. Reisner at Deir el-Ballas (1900–1902) and subsequently reinvestigated (1980 to present) by Peter Lacovara for the Museum of Fine Arts, Boston (see fig. 60).[26] Extending along the low desert adjacent to the flood plain for a considerable distance (almost two kilometers), this palace city was developed, perhaps, in the late Second Intermediate Period by Theban pharaohs already engaged in a struggle for Egyptian independence from the Canaanite Hyksos, who dominated northern and middle Egypt. Much of the construction seems to date to Ahmose (1550–1525 B.C.), the expeller of the Hyksos and first pharaoh of the 18th Dynasty. The site was abandoned soon after, suggesting that it was intended for a specific, short-term use.

In fact, as Lacovara persuasively suggests, Deir el-Ballas was an intentionally short-lived town, developed as a base from which Ahmose could launch campaigns against the Hyksos. Its overall plan is significant, for it seems based on a preexisting model of a royal city and might represent an embryonic version of a city type finding fullest expression (in terms of excavated remains) in the famous town of Amarna.

Despite the anticipated brevity of its lifespan, the core palace at Deir el-Ballas must have been most impressive. Within a vast enclosed space more than 4.5 hectares in area, a series of very large, multicolumned halls surrounded a casement-built platform, which probably supported a throne room with columned ante-hall as well as other chambers. This unusual layout, as compared with other New Kingdom palaces, probably related to its special character. The large, columned halls, like those of Malqata, were presumably intended for large gatherings of people involved in specific royal ceremonies and perhaps banquets, and all give a distinctively military cast to Deir el-Ballas—indeed, the entrance corridor to the main hall was embellished with paintings of soldiers.

A second so-called palace was located at Deir el-Ballas, but this was more likely a grandiosely scaled observation post, although the inclusion of many columns again suggests a relationship to royal appearances and ceremonial function.

The Palace of Merneptah

From Malqata and Deir el-Ballas, it is appropriate both chronologically and conceptually to move to the palace of Merneptah and another major contribution to the archaeology of the New Kingdom by an American institution.[27] Clarence S. Fisher (see fig. 61), Egyptian curator at the University Museum of the University of Pennsylvania (now the University of Pennsylvania Museum of Archaeology and Anthropology), began excavations in 1915 at Dendera in southern Egypt and at Memphis, the latter work continuing until 1920.

FIGURE 61
Clarence S. Fisher
in Philadelphia in the
1920s or 1930s.

Although Fisher's archaeological strategies and techniques at times betray the limitations of his day, he was a professional architect and a trainee of Reisner, so in other ways his work was exceptionally good. His eye for detail was often acute: a field photograph from Dendera actually shows him kneeling in a grave shaft and laboriously rethreading ancient beads on new string so as to preserve their original order.

Yet, if Winlock saw and appreciated the comedic aspects of life, Fisher tended to be part of them; he sometimes became obsessed by the personal tensions that inevitably develop on excavations. Once, for example, Fisher was so incensed by the supposed insubordination of a young assistant that he denounced the latter's "pronounced Bolsheviki ideas," which made "him assert an independence of all authority" to the University Museum's then-director. The director queried the eminent Egyptologist Francis Llewellyn Griffith (1862–1934), who had recommended the young man to Fisher, and Griffith, angered, responded he couldn't conceive the young man would "express Bolsheviki ideas or anything bordering on insubordination unless someone or something [a veiled reference to Fisher!] has driven him to a state of lunacy!"[28]

Whatever his personal foibles, Fisher triumphed in his excavation of Merneptah's palace, the best-preserved royal palace ever discovered in Egypt (see fig. 51). Merneptah (r. 1224–1214 B.C.), a son and successor of Ramesses II, had built a very large ceremonial palace at Memphis, occupying about 3,276 square meters, almost the same impressive scale as the comparable segments of the famous mortuary temple of Ramesses III at Medinet Habu. The basic structure was mud brick with a vast roof of timber; the gigantic columns and massive doorways were limestone. Relatively early in its history (but well after Merneptah's death), the great palace caught fire. Its massive roof and the upper parts of its brick walls collapsed, and many of its stone columns and doorways fell over. The Egyptians left the palace ruins to be covered over by the subsequent development of ancient Memphis, and hence the palace plan and, more unusually, its stone elements (usually removed from other palaces to be reused elsewhere) were relatively well preserved.

Thanks to this, and to Fisher's careful recording and study of the remains, the three-dimensional aspects of this palace can be reconstructed with a greater degree of accuracy than usual. Laid out in rectangular fashion along a north-to-south axis (typical of New Kingdom palaces, whereas temples usually had an east-west axis), Merneptah's palace probably had an elevated façade incorporating a columned entry hall opening onto a large court with side colonnades, its walls perhaps eleven meters high. Beyond the court the roofed segment of the palace included a columned hall, with a columned throne room behind; its stone dais—decorated with carved and brightly painted figures of prostrate foreigners—is perhaps the best-preserved example ever discovered. Behind, a suite of rooms was intended for the pharaoh's private use over short spans of time (that is, not as a long-term residence) and included a shower-bath emplacement, its walls lined with stone slabs covered with apotropaic figures that would magically protect the pharaoh when he was stripped of his regalia, themselves a means of warding off supernatural danger. Akin to a standard temple in shape as well as plan, Merneptah's palace, like a temple, was probably rich in cosmological meanings.

Fascinating as this individual palace is, it was probably only part of a larger whole, an enclosed complex of more than six hectares which was never comprehensively excavated. One entrance to this enclosure, however, was located by Fisher, and its enormous gateway jambs (like many other elements) are now displayed in the University of Pennsylvania Museum, thanks to the generosity of the Egyptian government. Their decoration takes up cosmological themes in a series of panels telling the story of kingship's creation (with the ur-pharaoh played by Merneptah). Later the gateway and its double-columned portico became a place of popular cult, and the many votive stelae recovered by Fisher, dedicated to Ptah and the other deities of Memphis, provide a rare glimpse into popular religion.

Medinet Habu: The Mortuary Temple of Ramesses III

In Thebes, in southern Egypt, the mortuary temple of Ramesses III at Medinet Habu is the best preserved of the many temples that once stretched along the low desert at the foot of the western cliffs, behind which lies the Valley of the Kings (see fig. 62). Farther north, the more ruined but still massive remains of the mortuary temple of Ramesses II were more romantic, with their fallen colossus that inspired Percy Bysshe Shelley's poem "Ozymandias" (see fig. 76), but Medinet Habu still provides the best overall impression of what such temples actually looked like in their more standardized, Ramesside phase (19th–20th Dynasties, 1307–1070 B.C.).

Today visitors to the cleared courts and halls of Medinet Habu can refer to guidebooks illustrated by detailed plans of both the temple and its surrounding complex (covering almost six hectares), and sometimes by superb three-dimensional renditions of the temple's original appearance, before its thousands of square feet of wall scenes and texts had been largely stripped of their brilliant color (see fig. 63) by exposure to the elements. Earlier in this century the situation was very different: the temple interior, although partially cleared and studied by Auguste Mariette in 1859–63, was still only partly defined, and the surrounding complex was a chaos of obscure archaeological remains overlaid by sand and excavation spoil.

This situation began to change dramatically in 1924, thanks to a major American initiative undertaken by the Oriental Institute of the University of Chicago and its inspired leader, James Henry Breasted. Breasted had long been concerned that the extant scenes and texts already exposed in countless Egyptian monuments were deteriorating physically, and usually before they had been properly recorded. The Oriental Institute would do just that through its field operations in Egypt, with Medinet Habu as a leading target.

Soon after the epigraphic recording had begun, however, Breasted realized that a proper architectural survey of the temple had to be undertaken so that the recorded scenes and texts could be accurately correlated with the architecture. As in epigraphy, here also Breasted strove for perfection, seeking to make Medinet Habu a model for detailed architectural recording that could be applied to the other major monumental buildings of ancient Egypt. He chose for the task the brilliant architectural historian Uvo Hölscher (1878–1963), who had already written monographs on the high gateway of Medinet Habu and on pharaoh Khafre's monuments at Giza; he had also participated in the careful German excavations at Amarna.

Hölscher's years of excavation and research resulted in the definitive study of the typical royal mortuary temple of the late New Kingdom,[29] a type of structure that was also used by pharaohs such as Seti I (r. 1306–1290 B.C.), Ramesses II, Merneptah, and Ramesses IV. Moreover, Hölscher—no doubt sensitized by his work at the great urban center of Amarna—soon saw that Medinet Habu provided a wonderful opportunity to study the whole complex of related buildings and enclosure walls that typically surrounded a mortuary temple (see fig. 64).

In fact, the excavation of the entire complex was carried out in an amazingly short time, thanks to a lavish application of funds and well-supervised labor. Hundreds of local workers were employed, and ten dump cars traveling on five hundred meters of railway track carried away the enormous amounts of debris

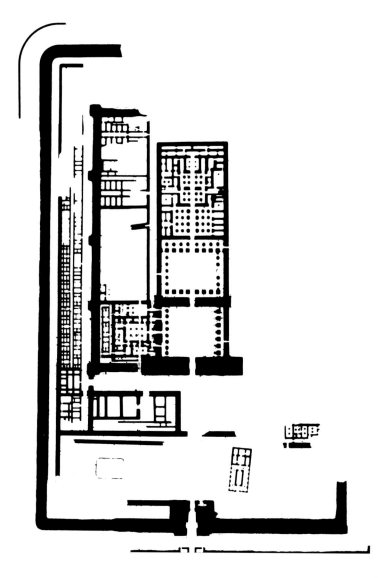

generated by the excavation. Hölscher not only successfully defined the plan of the original complex but also traced its continuing history into Coptic times, carefully identifying the building levels of the different periods. Unfortunately, as was often the case in his day, he seems to have paid little attention to stratigraphy outside of building levels, and hence substantial information may have been lost, although the recent discovery of his long-lost field notebooks may modify that impression.

Hölscher did succeed in identifying the many components of the site. As well as the temple proper, with its colonnaded court and roofed halls and sanctuaries, there was a royal palace, attached to an outer court, and an extraordinary eastern gateway, massive and fortified yet containing scenes on the walls of its interior chambers of the king interacting with his wives and daughters. Beyond palace and temple were a garden and other structures and, to the north, administrative offices and the great storehouses for the grains, wines, and other products of the temple estates. One massive mud-brick wall faced with towers enclosed the whole, and beyond it lay yet another wall, the intervening space filled with the residences of priests and dependents. Hölscher combined his architectural notations with the work of the epigraphers recording the scenes and texts of the temple to produce—besides detailed plans and elevations—some superb reconstructed views (see fig. 65).

In addition, Hölscher excavated north of Medinet Habu and located the remains of the last of the 18th Dynasty mortuary temples, built for the pharaoh Ay (r. 1323–1319 B.C.), Tutankhamun's successor, and used subsequently for the pharaoh Horemheb (r. 1319–1307 B.C.).[30] Hölscher also made a special study of the Ramesseum, which evidently had served as a model for much of Ramesses III's temple.

In both Medinet Habu and the Ramesseum Hölscher paid special attention to palaces. Here, and in other Ramesside temples, the palace was always attached to the south side of an outer court of the temple and consisted essentially of a "window of appearance" opening onto the court, a columned hall and throne room, and a short-term residential suite. The façades of such palaces, covered with emblematic scenes of pharaoh dominating Egypt's foreign enemies under the aegis of Amun-Re, and sometimes, as a lesser theme, Egyptians dominating foreigners in wrestling matches (reflective of actual events), probably indicate what actual

FIGURE 65
Reconstructed view
of the audience hall
from the first palace
of Ramesses III
at Medinet Habu.

palaces looked like; Hölscher provided an extremely fine rendering of the Medinet Habu palace façade.[31]

Many believe that these palaces were actually used when the pharaoh visited the temple while it was being built, or later, before his death, for ritual purposes. It is quite likely, however, that the palace is entirely a simulacrum, a full-scale model intended for the "use" of the deceased pharaoh. The inspiration probably came from an actual palace, an "administrative" one located north of the approach to Karnak temple, which in its turn provided the basic model for the mortuary temple itself.

LOOKING BACK OVER THE AMERICAN ACHIEVEMENT in New Kingdom archaeology, one is struck by the massiveness of the contribution and by its exceptionally high quality. Scholars and archaeologists such as Winlock, Fisher, and Hölscher were on the cutting edge of their day (just as American epigraphers were in their sphere of activity). The product, unfortunately, was more variable. Hölscher's superb and massive volumes on Medinet Habu are a monument in themselves, but Winlock and his colleagues never published full accounts of their work on

Hatshepsut's temple or at Malqata, and Fisher was even less forthcoming on the palace of Merneptah at Memphis. Full publication of these invaluable archives is just as important as the excavations themselves and subsequent studies.

As for the future, many aspects of New Kingdom archaeology still challenge the archaeologist and may come to engage the attention of American scholars. Some reinvolvement in New Kingdom archaeology on the part of American institutions has already been noted, but the major American field projects today are focused on other periods (e.g., Mark Lehner's work at Giza) or include important New Kingdom components as part of larger, multiperiod projects (e.g., the Pennsylvania–Yale–Institute of Fine Arts, New York University, expedition to Abydos). Of the many exciting opportunities that might be taken up by American institutions, one stands above all others: the full archaeological survey of ancient eastern Thebes, primarily a New Kingdom and post–New Kingdom city, but one that has been explored only in segments, not as an urban whole. Here, in collaboration with Egyptian colleagues, a splendid opportunity exists for some farsighted American institution.

Notes

1 On New Kingdom Egypt, see Alan H. Gardiner, *Egypt of the Pharaohs: An Introduction* (Oxford: Clarendon Press, 1961), chaps. 8–11; David O'Connor, "New Kingdom and Third Intermediate Period, 1552–664 B.C.," in *Ancient Egypt: A Social History,* by Bruce G. Trigger et al. (Cambridge: Cambridge University Press, 1983), 203–32; and T. G. H. James, *Pharaoh's People: Scenes from Life in Imperial Egypt* (Chicago: University of Chicago Press, 1984).

2 For New Kingdom urbanism, see David O'Connor, "Urbanism in Bronze Age Egypt and Northeast Africa," in *The Archaeology of Africa: Foods, Metals, and Towns,* ed. Thurstan Shaw (New York: Routledge, 1993), 570–86; Fekri Hassan, "Town and Village in Ancient Egypt: Ecology, Society, and Urbanization," in ibid., 551–69; Barry J. Kemp, *Ancient Egypt: Anatomy of a Civilization* (New York: Routledge, 1989), pt. 3, 183–317; and Peter Lacovara, "State and Settlement: Deir-el-Ballas and the Development, Structure, and Function of the New Kingdom Royal City" (Ph.D. diss., University of Chicago, 1993).

3 Herbert E. Winlock, *Bas-Reliefs from the Temple of Rameses I at Abydos,* MMA Papers 1 (New York: MMA, 1921).

4 Stephen Harvey, "Monuments of Ahmose at Abydos," *Egyptian Archaeology* 4 (1993): 3–5.

5 Dows Dunham, *The Barkal Temples* (Boston: MFA, 1970).

6 Herbert Ricke, George R. Hughes, and Edward F. Wente, *The Beit el-Wali Temple of Ramesses II,* OINE 1 (Chicago: University of Chicago Press, 1967).

7 Theodore M. Davis, *The Tomb of Iouiya and Touiyou* (London: A. Constable, 1907); idem, *The Tomb of Sipthah: The Monkey Tomb and the Gold Tomb* (London: A. Constable, 1908); idem, *The Tomb of Queen Tiyi* (London: A. Constable, 1910); and idem, *The Tombs of Harmhabi and Touatankhamanou* (London: A. Constable, 1912).

8 Kent R. Weeks et al., "The Berkeley Map of the Theban Necropolis: Report of the Sixth, Seventh, and Eighth Seasons," *NARCE,* no. 136–37 (Winter–Spring 1987): 1–14.

9 Elizabeth Thomas, *The Royal Necropolis of Thebes* (Trenton: T. W. Moorman and D&W Blue Print Co., 1966).

10 Richard Fazzini, "Mut-Tempel, Karnak (Mut Precinct)," *LÄ,* vol. 4 (1980), cols. 248–51.

11 Ray W. Smith and Donald B. Redford, *The Akhenaten Temple Project* (Warminster, U.K.: Aris and Phillips, 1976).

12 See, most recently, David O'Connor and David P. Silverman, eds., *Ancient Egyptian Kingship* (Leiden: E. J. Brill, 1994).

13 On the Metropolitan excavations, see Herbert E. Winlock, "Excavations at Thebes in 1912–13, by the Museum's Egyptian Expedition," *BMMA* 9 (January 1914): 11–23; Ambrose Lansing, "The Egyptian Expedition, 1915–16," *BMMA* (supp.) 12 (1917): 7–26; Herbert E. Winlock, "The Egyptian Expedition, MCMXXI–MCMXXII," *BMMA* 17 (December 1922): pt. 2, 3–48; idem, "The Egyptian Expedition, 1922–23," *BMMA* 18 (December 1923): pt. 2, 3–39; Ambrose Lansing, "The Egyptian Expedition, 1923–24," *BMMA* 19 (1924): pt. 2, 3–43; Herbert E. Winlock, "The Egyptian Expedition, 1924–25," *BMMA* 21 (March 1926): pt. 2, 3–32; idem, "The Egyptian Expedition, 1925–27," *BMMA* 23 (February 1928): pt. 2, 3–58; idem, "The Egyptian Expedition, 1927–28," *BMMA* 23 (December 1928): sec. 2, 3–28; idem, "The Egyptian Expedition, 1928–29," *BMMA* 24 (November 1929): sec. 2, 3–34; idem, "The Egyptian Expedition, 1929–30," *BMMA* 25 (December 1930): sec. 2, 3–28; idem, "The Egyptian Expedition, 1930–31," *BMMA* 27 (March 1932): sec. 2, 3–37; William C. Hayes, "The Egyptian Expedition, 1934–35," *BMMA* 30 (November 1935): sec. 2, 3–36; Ambrose Lansing and William C. Hayes, "The Egyptian Expedition, 1935–36," *BMMA* 32 (January 1937): sec. 2, 3–39.

14 John A. Wilson, *Signs and Wonders upon Pharaoh: A History of American Egyptology* (Chicago: University of Chicago Press, 1964), 184.

15 On Hatshepsut, see Donald B. Redford, *History and Chronology of the Eighteenth Dynasty of Egypt: Seven Studies* (Toronto: University of Toronto Press, 1967), 57–87.

16 Jadwiga Lipinska, *The Temple of Tuthmosis III: Architecture* (Warsaw: PWN-Editions scientifiques de Pologne, 1977).

17 Roland Tefnin, *La statuaire d'Hatshepsout: Portrait royal et politique sous la 18e dynastie* (Brussels: Fondation égyptologique reine Elisabeth, 1979).

18 Arielle P. Kozloff and Betsy M. Bryan, *Egypt's Dazzling Sun: Amenhotep III and His World,* exh. cat. (Cleveland: Cleveland Museum of Art, 1992), 73–260.

19 On New Kingdom palaces, see David O'Connor, "City and Palace in New Kingdom Egypt," *Cahier de recherches de l'Institut de papyrologie et d'égyptologie de Lille* 11 (1989): 73–87; Fran Weatherhead, "Painted Pavements in the Great Palace at Amarna," *JEA* 78 (1992): 179–94.

20 H. G. Evelyn-White, "The Work of the Egyptian Expedition, *BMMA* 7 (October 1912): 184–90; idem, "The Egyptian Expedition, 1914–15," *BMMA* 10 (December 1915): 253–56; Ambrose Lansing, "The Egyptian Expedition, 1916–17," *BMMA* (supp.) 13 (March 1918): 3–14; Robb de P. Tytus, *A Preliminary Report on the Re-excavation of the Palace of Amenhetep III* (New York: Winthrop Press, 1903).

21 Tytus, *Preliminary Report,* 9.

22 Lansing, "Egyptian Expedition, 1915–16"; idem, "Egyptian Expedition, 1916–17"; idem, "Egyptian Expedition, 1923–24"; Lansing and Hayes, "Egyptian Expedition, 1935–36."

23 Winlock, "Egyptian Expedition, 1922–23"; idem, "Egyptian Expedition, 1924–25."

24 Kemp, *Ancient Egypt,* 213.

25 David O'Connor and Barry J. Kemp, "An Ancient Nile Harbor: University Museum Excavations at the Birket Habu," *International Journal of Nautical Archaeology and Underwater Exploration* 3, no. 1 (1974): 101–36.

26 Lacovara, "State and Settlement."

27 David O'Connor, "Mirror of the Cosmos: The Palace of Merenptah," in *Fragments of a Shattered Visage: The Proceedings of the International Symposium on Ramesses the Great,* ed. Edward Bleiberg and Rita Freed, Monographs of the Institute of Egyptian Art and Archaeology 1 (Memphis: Memphis State University, 1991), 167–98.

28 O'Connor and Silverman, *Ancient Egyptian Kingship,* 23–24.

29 On Hölscher's work at Medinet Habu, see Uvo Hölscher, *Medinet Habu,* vol. 1, pt. 2, *The Architectural Survey, 1924–28* (Chicago: University of Chicago Press, 1929); idem, *Medinet Habu,* vol. 2, pt. 1, *The Architectural Survey, 1928–29* (Chicago: University of Chicago Press, 1930); idem, *Medinet Habu,* vol. 3, pt. 2, *The Architectural Survey, 1929–30* (Chicago: University of Chicago Press, 1931); idem, *Excavations at Ancient Thebes 1930/31* (Chicago: University of Chicago Press, 1932).

30 Hölscher, *Excavations at Ancient Thebes,* 47–53.

31 Hölscher, *Medinet Habu,* vol. 1, pt. 2, 47.

New Kingdom Epigraphy

Lanny Bell

pigraphy, unlike archaeology, is rarely perceived or depicted as glamorous or romantic.[1] Like archaeology, however, epigraphy is not an end in itself. It is essential to the gathering of reliable and complete primary data for research into many aspects of ancient Egyptian culture,[2] including studies in philology, art, history, religion, and society. Original monuments are in constant danger of being damaged or destroyed; if this occurs before they have been copied adequately, their full potential is lost forever. Herein lies the primary importance of epigraphy. But making a complete epigraphic record of a monument is by no means a simple matter. It involves much more than standing in front of a wall and drawing whatever one sees, mechanically and mindlessly. Epigraphy is an art, creative and synthetic, as well as a technical and objective science. The skilled epigrapher employs intuition and insight gained from experience. As Jaromír Málek has recently written:

> To produce an accurate copy, the epigraphist must understand the texts and scenes so that he is not deceived by accidental features. . . .
>
> Subjective knowledge and experience are used to obtain a record which is made as objective as possible by eliminating the irrelevant and accidental, and thus stressing the essential. Every line on the surface of the monument is examined and a decision made as to whether it is part of the original design to be recorded or is accidental, e.g., the result of damage to the monument or a flaw in the material. Damaged areas are carefully studied: the epigraphist must rescue the minutest traces still discernible without succumbing to the temptation to add non-existent features based on wishful thinking. It is here that experience is of great importance: a completed copy shows how an epigraphist (or, better, an epigraphic team) saw and interpreted a text or a scene in its entirety, and this places it in a category quite distinct from that of photography.[3]

FIGURE 66
From left: Charles F. Nims, Douglas A. Champion, and George R. Hughes of the Epigraphic Survey checking and correcting copies of text and reliefs at Medinet Habu, 1951–52

I have already dealt extensively with the subject of Egyptian epigraphy against the background of my own nearly two decades of field experience with the New Kingdom monuments of Luxor.[4] My emphasis here will be on the history of some remarkable individuals and the institutions they represented as I summarize their outstanding contributions to the development of American Egyptology. I must restrict my discussion to published volumes and to major projects documenting the decoration of monuments in the field. Practically, this limits me to two institutions that have mounted epigraphic expeditions to record the standing monuments of Egypt: the Oriental Institute of the University of Chicago and the Metropolitan Museum of Art, New York. In fact, Chicago's Epigraphic and Architectural Survey and the Metropolitan's Graphic Section, chiefly Norman and Nina de Garis Davies, are often paired in discussions of epigraphic theory and practice.[5] Just as the Epigraphic Survey technique provides a standard against which other publications of temple decoration can be compared, so the Davieses' volumes provide the standard for exactness and completeness in tomb copying.[6] Both the Epigraphic Survey and the Davieses strove to give equal treatment to text and scene: each text was reproduced within its scene, and every scene was reproduced with its accompanying text (see fig. 67).

FIGURE 67
Nefertari Kneeling in Adoration, facsimile of wall painting from Nefertari's tomb in the Valley of the Queens by Nina de Garis Davies, 1922. Metropolitan Museum of Art 30.4.144.

The year 1865 coincidentally saw the birth of the two men who would formulate American epigraphic practices at New Kingdom monuments, James Henry Breasted and Norman de Garis Davies. Their paths converged on several occasions: Davies accompanied Breasted's expedition to Nubia in 1906–7; both came to concentrate their epigraphic efforts in ancient Thebes; and Breasted inspired John D. Rockefeller Jr. to fund the publication of Nina Davies's colored drawings in the sumptuous two-volume *Ancient Egyptian Paintings* (1936).[7] (Breasted had already convinced Rockefeller to fund the first four folios of *The Temple of King Sethos I at Abydos* [1933–58], a joint publication of the Archaeological Survey of the Egypt Exploration Society and the Oriental Institute.)[8]

Breasted, the brilliant academician, organizer, publicist, and fund-raiser, established the Epigraphic Survey in 1924. Right from the start he envisaged it as a team effort that would utilize the latest technical aids and employ specialists with diverse skills to document mostly Ramesside temples for his newly founded

Oriental Institute. An archetypal university product of his time, operating within the context of a dynamic intellectual environment, Breasted set up his project self-consciously and with a great deal of introspection, writing extensively about what he was doing and why.

In contrast, Davies, the consummately skilled British draftsman and artist, worked essentially on his own.[9] He joined the Egyptian Expedition of the Metropolitan Museum of Art in 1907 after nearly a decade with the Egypt Exploration Society, for which he produced twelve volumes in the Archaeological Survey series. Albert M. Lythgoe had established the Metropolitan's Egyptian Expedition with a graphics division[10] to provide "a record through copies, drawings and photographs of the principal painted tombs of Thebes,"[11] and it was greatly to his credit that he quickly secured the services of the preeminently qualified Davies. Accompanied and assisted by his professional wife, tracing the decoration primarily of 18th Dynasty private tombs,[12] Davies seems to have set about his task conscientiously, sensitively, and energetically, with a minimum of fuss and bother.

To be sure, the needs of the copyist, working conditions, and available space are quite different in tombs and temples. Apart from the possibility that they might conceal buried treasures, the relatively small tombs in the Theban necropolis had long attracted both scientific and popular notice,[13] due in no small part to the astonishingly well preserved colors in the exquisite paintings some of their offering chapels still contained, with their vivid depictions of "daily life." The decoration of the majestic Theban temples, however, had lost most of its original paint and seemed much less interesting to the casual observer confronted by repetitive, often bewildering, and endless-seeming offering scenes. Nonetheless, the projects of the Oriental Institute and the Metropolitan, both concentrating on monuments demonstrably suffering from misuse and neglect, complemented each other nicely.

In 1892, when the young Breasted undertook graduate studies in Egyptology in Berlin, he stepped into a revitalized scholarly milieu: "The era of intuitive and individualistic Egyptologists was drawing to a close and… discipline was being introduced into the young science. Two corollaries of this were that co-operative activity was necessary to establish the new régime and that the existing documents must be re-examined in the light of a better understanding. None of the new school was willing to take an old copy or an old translation at its face value. They wanted to make their own firsthand copies and translations. The notation 'verified by my own collation' was essential to the final study of any document."[14]

Actually the course of Breasted's scholarly interests was greatly influenced by the work of the preceding generation of Egyptologists. The year 1859 had seen the publication of the final fascicle of Karl Richard Lepsius's twelve-volume

Denkmäler aus Ägypten und Äthiopien, presenting the first fruits of the epigraphic accomplishments of the great Prussian expedition to Egypt and Nubia in 1842–45. Two years before, in 1857, Auguste Mariette, with the backing of Ferdinand de Lesseps (1805–94), had convinced the Khedive Said Pasha (r. 1854–63) to create the Service des antiquités de l'Egypte (now the Supreme Council of Antiquities) and the Bulaq (now Cairo) Museum and to establish an Egyptian national antiquities policy. The Egypt Exploration Society was established in 1882, with its Archaeological Survey created in 1889,[15] under the watchful guidance of the extraordinary British philologist Francis Llewellyn Griffith. Distraught over the loss of ancient monuments still ongoing when he first saw Upper Egypt, Griffith wrote:

If a small portion of the sums of money that, in the name of scientific research, have been spent in Egypt on treasure-hunting for antiquities, on uncovering monuments and exposing them to destruction, on unwatched excavations from which the limestone sculptures have gone straight to the kiln or the village stonemason—if a small portion of this had been utilised in securing systematically throughout the country accurate and exhaustive copies of the inscriptions above ground and in danger, the most important part of all her evidence of her past that Egypt has handed down to our day would have been gathered intact, instead of mutilated beyond recovery.[16]

In 1894 Breasted took a honeymoon trip up the Nile as far as Aswan and saw firsthand the problems of monumental decay and damage that had already inspired Mariette and Griffith to action. When he arrived at the University of Chicago in 1895, he was keenly aware of the danger to the ancient monuments and was determined to do something about it. It was a dramatic event four years later, at one of the most famous sites in all of Egypt, that suddenly focused not only Breasted's but the world's attention on the problem. The peaceful dawn of October 3, 1899, was unexpectedly shattered when a shift in an unstable foundation at Karnak suddenly brought eleven gigantic columns crashing down with a deafening roar, two careening precariously against the Second Pylon, the others coming to rest in a jumble in the broken debris of column drums and architraves on the hypostyle hall floor.[17] Breasted's first practical response was to undertake his 1905–7 Nubian expeditions. In his preliminary report of 1906 he stated the case for epigraphy in terms that would characterize all his subsequent appeals:

Probably there are few Egyptologists who do not realize that the monuments of Egypt still in situ *are rapidly falling to ruin. Such catastrophes as that in the great hall of Karnak have been uncomfortable reminders of the slow but ceaseless decay*

which is undermining them.... It would seem, however, that while the structural decay and barbarous demolition of the monuments are sufficiently well known, the invisible but steady disintegration of surfaces of intact walls, especially those of the temples, involving the gradual disappearance of inscriptions and reliefs, is not generally understood. Add to this the wanton vandalism of modern visitors and native dealers, who hack out cartouches and heads, or especially well-made hieroglyphs, and the rate at which temple records are disappearing is appalling. One need only examine a series of photographs of the great geographical list of Palestinian towns recorded by Sheshonk at Karnak, and if the negatives have been made at intervals during the last twenty years, the surface of the wall from photograph to photograph may be seen slowly dissolving and the record upon it fading into blank masonry before one's eyes.[18]

FIGURE 68
Chicago House entrance, grounds, and residence building, 1995.

FIGURE 69
The courtyard of the residence building at Chicago House, 1973.

FIGURE 70
Chicago House staff, 1977. *Front row, left to right*: Ann Roth, Martha Bell, William Murnane, Raymond Johnson, Mark Ciccarello, Richard Jaeschke, Eric Krause, Reg Coleman, Marie Coleman. Director Lanny Bell is standing at far right with permanent members of Chicago House staff.

Breasted was the leading American exponent for a concerted campaign of salvage epigraphy.[19] He possessed the qualities—rarely associated with a scholar-administrator managing an academic institution—of clear vision combined with a genius for communicating his ideas in such a way as to catch the imagination of his audience, successfully persuading them to accept his point of view, adopt his cause, and underwrite the costs of his endeavors. Taking full advantage of all the publicity and international excitement generated by the discovery of the tomb of Tutankhamun in 1922, he was able to set up the Epigraphic Survey in 1924; the present Chicago House was opened in Luxor in 1931 (see fig. 68). Built as the well-appointed base for housing and feeding a large staff during the annual six-month seasons, Chicago House was equipped with offices, studios, library, and darkroom facilities, as well as storerooms and workshops (see figs. 69, 70). Meanwhile, Davies, living simply in a small but comfortable house,[20] had already been working quietly in the Theban necropolis on Metropolitan Museum Egyptian Expedition projects for seventeen years.

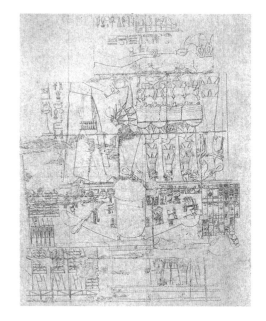

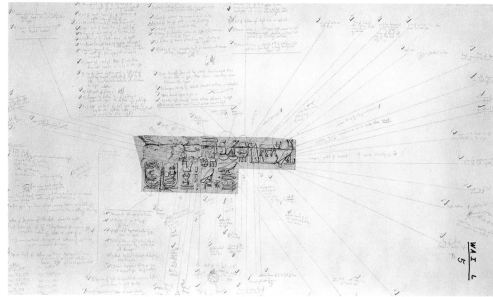

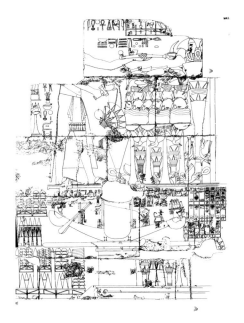

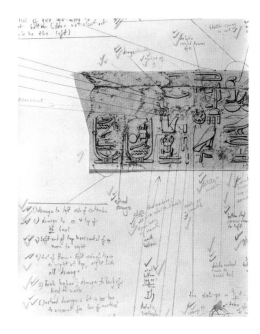

FIGURES 71–74
Sample Epigraphic
Survey materials, docu-
mentation of Scene
WA I (Tutankhamun
offering before bark of
Amun), Luxor temple,
clockwise from top left:
blueprint, collation
sheet, detail of collation
sheet, publication plate.

Breasted selected Luxor as the
headquarters for his new expedition
because of the concentration and
variety of New Kingdom monuments
located there. From among the endangered monuments desperately in need
of thorough and meticulous recording,
Breasted concentrated on the reign of
Ramesses III (1194–1163 B.C.), the last
great builder of the New Kingdom.
He had first ascertained that this king's
impressive structure at Medinet Habu
was the best preserved of all the royal
("funerary") temples and that its reliefs
contained important historical information (see fig. 66). For comparison,
he proposed to record the other, likewise largely unpublished, monuments of
Ramesses III at Thebes. This approach, valid as a sort of sampling technique,
recognizes that knowing a single monument as completely as possible, and knowing one pharaoh's monuments in the greatest possible detail, is tantamount to
knowing something about every other monument of the same type and about the
monuments of all the rulers who built or decorated in the same area.

Breasted proposed to make not mere hand copies or approximate drawings but
strict facsimiles[21] to the extent possible in the reduction of three-dimensional reliefs
to two-dimensional drawings (see figs. 71–74).[22] With an eye to future research needs,
he argued for completeness in each project. He insisted that whatever was still visible
in the decoration—not just the attractive sections or those easiest to document—must

FIGURE 75
Epigraphic Survey
staff member Mark
Ciccarello checking
a drawing from a
scene on a column in
the colonnade of
Tutankhamun, Luxor
temple, 1977–78.

be recorded, even on the most damaged wall surface. As a cultural historian he was concerned with the whole wall, in its broadest context, and stressed its architectural setting and the interplay of art and inscription, scene and text, in it.[23] Furthermore, all work was to be done at or close to the wall to facilitate constant reference and checking (see fig. 75).

Breasted recruited a former student, Harold Hayden Nelson (1878–1954), as the survey's first (and longest-serving) field director (1924–47). An unsung hero of American Egyptology,[24] Nelson proved to be a leader in the interpretation of data.[25] This important and long-neglected aspect of epigraphy is all too often confined to brief prefatory remarks in volumes of epigraphic plates. Nelson first produced a "road map" to the decoration of the temples, resulting in the publication of his *Key Plans Showing Locations of Theban Temple Decorations* (1941).[26] He thus developed the means by which to refer to the location of any scene in any Theban temple. Nelson then began photo documentation of as many decorated walls as he could.

An early advocate of photography, Breasted took the German photographers Friedrich Koch and Horst Schliephack with him on his Nubian campaigns of 1905–7, when he went as far south as the sites of Meroe, Musawwarat el-Sufra, and Naqa' in the Sudan.[27] Breasted expressed his optimism about the use of photography in archaeology in his popular *Egypt through the Stereoscope: A Journey through the Land of the Pharaohs* (1905): "In the preparation of the following pages, I have constantly had my eyes within the hood of the stereoscope, and I cannot forbear to express here the growing surprise and delight with which I observed, as the work proceeded, that it became more and more easy to speak of the prospect revealed in the instrument as one actually spread out before me.... The mind looks... with essentially all the sensations of having seen the reality; an actual visit to the place can do little more."[28]

Today stereo-pair photography is employed in contour mapping,[29] in the making of photogrammetric drawings of monumental decoration,[30] and for other archaeological purposes.[31] In epigraphy, photography is vital as a complement or control to line drawings for its unique capacity to convey an accurate impression of the style of carved surfaces as well as their three-dimensionality in the play of light and shadow across them.[32]

Even before Breasted's time, photography had been touted by its enthusiastic pioneers as a miracle time-saver that could expedite and simplify the documenting of ancient monuments. When François Arago introduced photography to the French Academy of Sciences in 1839, he catalogued the medium's many advantages: "To copy the millions and millions of hieroglyphs covering only the exterior of the great monuments of Thebes, Memphis, Karnak, twenty years and scores of draftsmen are required. With the daguerreotype, a single man could execute this immense task... [and] the new images will surpass in fidelity and local color the work of the most capable among our painters."[33]

In epigraphic terms the most important photographers of New Kingdom monuments for American institutions have been the British national Harry Burton (1879–1940) and the American Charles Francis Nims (1906–1988). Nims first went to work for the Epigraphic Survey as an epigrapher in 1935, became its photographer[34] in 1946, and served as its fourth field director from 1964 until his retirement in 1972. Burton, like Davies, was hired by Lythgoe; he worked for the Metropolitan Museum from 1914 until his death.[35] Burton's photographs have graced many volumes of the Metropolitan's tomb publications, just as Nims's have for the Oriental Institute (in addition to serving as the concealed base for a great many Epigraphic Survey drawings).[36] The Chicago House photo archive now contains well over sixteen thousand negatives of monuments, mostly in the Theban area and primarily temples;[37] the Metropolitan Museum's collection of Burton photographs of Theban monuments, mostly private tombs, numbers thirty-two hundred negatives.[38]

Because a single photograph necessarily gives an incomplete impression of a wall, the success of any attempt to publish a monument solely in photographs is limited. This is especially the case with carved relief, which, even when photographed under favorable circumstances, is particularly affected by lighting conditions.[39] An exemplary recent publication based on photographs, substantially those of Burton, is Erik Hornung's *The Tomb of Pharaoh Seti I*.[40] Mention must also be made of the fine publications by Alexandre Piankoff, assisted by Natacha Rambova,[41] in the Bollingen Foundation series Egyptian Religious Texts and Representations: *The Tomb of Ramesses VI* (1954) and *The Shrines of Tut-Ankh-Amon* (1955).[42] A compromise is represented by a publication of the University of Pennsylvania–University of Toronto Akhenaten Temple Project,[43] which reproduces photographs of individual *talatat* blocks, most reassembled into "temporary scenes," with missing elements frequently reconstructed in line drawings.

During his Nubian expeditions Breasted began experimenting with drawing directly on photographic prints to record significant epigraphic features that did not show up clearly.[44] From this would develop the "Chicago method" of

epigraphy, as refined and fully worked out by Nelson—with the collaboration of epigraphers Caroline Ransom Williams, William F. Edgerton, and John A. Wilson—during the first two field seasons of the Epigraphic Survey.[45]

Breasted and his colleagues were not the first to use such a drawing technique. They were preceded by John Beasley Greene (1832/33–1856),[46] the second American known to have photographed in Egypt (see fig. 76).[47] Granted permission to excavate in Thebes, Greene cleared approximately the lower third of the right wing of the Second Pylon at Medinet Habu; he then photographed all thirty-eight lines of the great historical inscription of Ramesses III's year 8 in a single negative. He proceeded to draw directly upon the print, which, after removal of the photographic image, became the basis for the publication of his copy of the text.[48]

Ricardo Caminos has observed that Félix Guilmant made a "virtually complete record in facsimile of Ramesses IX's tomb,"[49] published in 1907, using the method later elaborated by the Epigraphic Survey. The Oriental Institute's Sakkarah Expedition (1930–36) employed this recording method,[50] as did Keith Seele[51] and Nelson[52] (both Epigraphic Survey staff members) on their own epigraphic projects.[53] Amice C. Calverley used a modified form of it in her work at Abydos,[54] and Serge Sauneron applied the technique at Esna;[55] in addition, it has been adopted by the Egyptian Centre d'études et de documentation sur l'ancienne Egypte.[56] The latest Theban tomb publication from the Metropolitan Museum of Art contains newly collated drawings made by Charles Wilkinson in 1930–31 "directly onto enlarged prints of Harry Burton's photographic negatives."[57] Nevertheless, the most important aspect of the Epigraphic Survey's rigorous method was, and remains, its reliance on a coordinated team effort to attain a high degree of

precision and reliability. Strictly speaking, an individual working alone is not actually employing the Chicago method—
even if the technical aspect of preparing the drawings is the
same—since the epigraphy is done without the benefit of
the extensive checks and balances of the team system.

Breasted long ago observed that "the future will certainly
hold us responsible for some adequate and permanent record
of the documents accessible to us."[58] Today the Oriental
Institute's Epigraphic Survey continues its recording in Luxor,
with annual six-month field seasons at Chicago House
(see fig. 77), and the publishing of the excavation records
of the Metropolitan Museum—including some tombs
excavated by Herbert E. Winlock—proceeds steadily in
an ambitious program.

I can do no better in conclusion than to cite reviews
of the output of each endeavor. Concerning the Epigraphic
Survey publication of the battle reliefs of Seti I at Karnak,
Kenneth A. Kitchen wrote: "One cannot do other than reiterate the capital importance and splendid quality of this latest Chicago epigraphic production. If only
all the war-reliefs (and for that matter, all the temples!) were so fortunate in their
choice of epigraphers!" One need not look far for similar superlatives applied to
the work of Norman and Nina Davies for the Metropolitan Museum. Margaret
A. Murray began her review of *The Tomb of Nefer-hotep at Thebes*: "When
a publication is issued in the joint names of Mr. and Mrs. de Garis Davies it is a
guarantee of accuracy in the reproduction of the sculptures and sympathy in the
explanation of the scenes." In his review of Davies's posthumous *The Tomb of
Rekh-mi-Rē' at Thebes*, T. George Allen remarked that "Davies' keen observation
of archaeological details is evident not only in his plates but in his text. To have
recorded conscientiously in dependable form for future study as many ancient monuments as Davies has gives him a valid claim to scientific immortality."[59]

Notes

I dedicate this essay to the life and memory of Ricardo A. Caminos (1915–92), the news of whose death in London reached me as I was finishing the first version of my manuscript. Caminos was a renowned epigrapher and sometime staff member of the Epigraphic Survey, and his treatment of "The Recording of Inscriptions and Scenes in Tombs and Temples" in Caminos and Henry G. Fischer, Ancient Egyptian Epigraphy and Palaeography (New York: MMA, 1976), 3–25, has proven invaluable in writing the present article, as well as in my class entitled Introduction to Egyptian Epigraphy.

1 In his review of *The Tomb of Rekh-mi-Rē at Thebes* (*JEA* 31 [1945]: 115), R. O. Faulkner speaks of "that Cinderella of Egyptological science, the recording of standing monuments."

2 See Charles F. Nims, "The Publication of Ramesside Temples in Thebes by the Oriental Institute," in *Textes et langages de l'Egypte pharaonique*, vol. 2, Bibliothèque d'étude 64 (Cairo: IFAO, 1973), 90.

3 Jaromír Málek, "Egyptian Epigraphy as Practised at Memphis," *EES Newsletter*, no. 3 (October 1988): 4–5. See also the comments of Françoise Le Saout, as quoted by Claude Traunecker, in "Les techniques d'épigraphie de terrain: Principes et pratique," in *Problems and Priorities in Egyptian Archaeology*, ed. Jan Assmann, Günter Burkard, and Vivian Davies (London and New York: KPI, 1987), 270–71.

4 Lanny Bell, "The Epigraphic Survey and the Rescue of the Monuments of Ancient Egypt," in *The Ancient Eastern Mediterranean, Centennial Symposium, 1889–1989*, ed. Eleanor Guralnick (Chicago: Chicago Society of the Archaeological Institute of America, 1990), 7–15 (for an abridged version of the above, see idem, "The Oriental Institute's Epigraphic Survey and the Rescue of the Monuments of Ancient Egypt," *KMT* 1, no. 3 [1990]: 38–41); idem, "The Epigraphic Survey: The Philosophy of Egyptian Epigraphy after Sixty Years' Practical Experience," in *Problems and Priorities*, 43–55, pls. 1–6; idem, with William Murnane and Bernard Fishman, "The Epigraphic Survey (Chicago House)," pts. 1–2, *NARCE*, no. 118 (1982): 3–23; 119 (1982): 5–13.

5 Hermann Kees, review of *Medinet Habu*, vol. 1 (OIP 8, 1930), in *Göttingische gelehrte Anzeigen*, no. 5 (1931): 182; Serge Sauneron, *Esna*, vol. 2, *Le temple d'Esna* (Cairo: IFAO, 1963), vii; idem, *L'Egyptologie* (Paris: Presses universitaires de France, 1968), 84; Kenneth A. Kitchen, "Ramesside Texts," in *Textes et langages*, 88; John Baines and Jaromír Málek, *Atlas of Ancient Egypt* (New York: Facts on File, 1980), 29; Françoise Le Saout, "Les techniques de relevés épigraphiques," in *Karnak: L'Egypte grandiose*, Histoire et archéologie 61 (Dijon: Archéologia, 1982): 91; and E. S. Bogoslovsky, review of *Hieroglyphic Texts from Egyptian Stelae, Pt. 10*, *Bibliotheca Orientalis* 42 (1985): 88.

6 John A. Wilson, *Thousands of Years: An Archaeologist's Search for Ancient Egypt* (New York: Charles Scribner's Sons, 1972), 52. See also Málek, "Egyptian Epigraphy," 5; Cyril Aldred, "Anna Macpherson Davies," *JEA* 51 (1965): 196–97; W. V. Davies, "Thebes," in *Excavating in Egypt: The Egypt Exploration Society 1882–1982*, ed. T. G. H. James (Chicago: University of Chicago Press, 1982), 68; and T. G. H. James, "The Archaeological Survey," in *Excavating in Egypt*, 151.

7 Alan H. Gardiner, *Ancient Egyptian Paintings* (Chicago: University of Chicago Press, 1936). See also James H. Breasted, *The Oriental Institute* (Chicago: University of Chicago Press, 1933), 91, 224–28; Alan H. Gardiner, *My Working Years* (Privately printed, 1962), 19–20, 47, 52–53.

8 See James, "Archaeological Survey," 152–55; Barry J. Kemp, "Abydos," in *Excavating in Egypt*, 85; Breasted, *The Oriental Institute*, 91–93, 228–33; Gardiner, *My Working Years*, 53–55.

9 James, "Archaeological Survey," 149. The longest serving of the assistants assigned to the Davies team in Thebes was Charles K. Wilkinson (1897–1986), who worked for the Egyptian Expedition as draftsman from 1920 to 1934; see Charles K. Wilkinson and Marsha Hill, *Egyptian Wall Paintings: The Metropolitan Museum of Art's Collection of Facsimiles* (New York: MMA, 1983), 8–10, 14; Aldred, "Anna Macpherson Davies," 197–98.

10 See Marsha Hill, "The Life and Work of Harry Burton," in Erik Hornung, *The Tomb of Pharaoh Seti I* (Zurich: Artemis, 1991), 28; Wilkinson and Hill, *Egyptian Wall Paintings*, 10.

11 Aldred, "Anna Macpherson Davies," 196.

12 A listing of Davies's books is found in Warren R. Dawson and Eric P. Uphill, *Who Was Who in Egyptology*, 2d ed. (London: Egypt Exploration Society, 1972), 78. To get an idea of the full range of the activities of the Davies couple in the Theban necropolis, see PM, 1st ed., vol. 1, 201–6; Helen Murray and Jaromír Málek, "Theban Tomb Tracings Made by Norman and Nina de Garis Davies," *Göttinger Miszellen* 37 (1980): 31–36; Wilkinson and Hill, *Egyptian Wall Paintings*, 163–64.

13 For an assessment of the importance of the nineteenth-century epigraphic record of Theban tombs now "lost," see Lise Manniche, *Lost Tombs: A Study of Certain Eighteenth Dynasty Monuments in the Theban Necropolis* (London and New York: Kegan Paul, 1988), esp. 1–2. For a brief history of modern activities in the Theban necropolis, see idem, *City of the Dead: Thebes in Egypt* (Chicago: University of Chicago Press, 1987), 93–130.

14 John A. Wilson, "Biographical Memoir of James Henry Breasted: 1865–1935," in *Biographical Memoirs of the National Academy of Sciences*, vol. 18, 5th memoir (Washington, D.C.: U.S. Government Printing Office, 1937), 98–99.

15 For the early history of the Archaeological Survey, see James, "Archaeological Survey," 141–46.

16 Ibid., 144.

17 Claude Traunecker and Jean-Claude Golvin, *Karnak: Résurrection d'un site* (Fribourg: Office du livre, 1984), 161–62.

18 James H. Breasted, "First Preliminary Report of the Egyptian Expedition," *American Journal of Semitic Languages and Literatures* 23 (1906–7): 1–3.

19 See James H. Breasted, "Luxor and Armageddon: The Expansion of the Oriental Institute of the University of Chicago," *Art and Archaeology: The Arts through the Ages* 22 (November 1926): 163.

20 For a photograph of Davies's house and the Metropolitan Museum expedition house, see Wilkinson and Hill, *Egyptian Wall Paintings*, 14–15.

21 See Bell, "Epigraphic Survey: The Philosophy," 43–44.

22 See Traunecker, "Techniques d'épigraphie de terrain," 269, 274–75.

23 Edna R. Russmann, review of *The Temple of Khonsu*, vol. 1, in *Serapis* 7 (1981–82): 104.

24 See William J. Murnane, ed., *The Great Hypostyle Hall at Karnak*, vol. 1, pt. 1, *The Wall Reliefs*, OIP 106 (Chicago: Oriental Institute, University of Chicago, 1981), ix.

25 Nelson's articles, "The Identity of Amun-Re of United-with-Eternity," *JNES* 1 (1942): 127–55, and "Certain Reliefs at Karnak and Medinet Habu and the Ritual of Amenophis I," *JNES* 8 (1949): 201–37, 310–45, were truly ground-breaking.

26 OIP 56, reprinted with additions and corrections in 1965.

27 The resulting nearly eleven hundred photographic images have been published in microfiche format. The Oriental Institute, *The 1905–1907 Breasted Expeditions to Egypt and the Sudan: A Photographic Study*, 2 vols. (Chicago: University of Chicago Press, 1975).

28 Quoted from the edited and abridged version, James H. Breasted, *Egypt: A Journey through the Land of the Pharaohs* (New York: Camera/Graphics Press, 1978), 8, which reproduces the original hundred stereo views.

29 E.g., Kent R. Weeks, "The Berkeley Map of the Theban Necropolis," *NARCE*, no. 105 (Summer 1978): [24]; idem, "The Berkeley Map of the Theban Necropolis," *NARCE*, no. 109 (Summer 1979): app., 3–6; idem, "The Berkeley Map of the Theban Necropolis, Report of the Third Season, 1980," *NARCE*, no. 113 (Winter 1980): [48].

30 See, e.g., Christiane Desroches-Noblecourt and Charles Kuentz, *Le petit temple d'Abou Simbel*, vol. 2 (Cairo: Centre de documentation et d'étude sur l'ancienne Egypte, 1968), pls. 11, 17, 34, 37, 61, 64, 65, 101, 126; anon., "Under the Sign of Maat, Goddess of Precision," *UNESCO Courier* (February 1960): 40–43. See also Mark E. Lehner, "The ARCE Sphinx Project: A Preliminary Report," *NARCE*, no. 112 (Fall 1980): 5–6, figs. 1–2; Shinji Fukai et al., *Taq-i Bustan*, vol. 3, *Photogrammetric Elevations*, Tokyo University Iraq-Iran Archaeological Expedition, Institute of Oriental Culture Report 19 (Tokyo: Yamakawa, 1983).

31 Traunecker, "Techniques d'épigraphie de terrain," 269, n. 23.

32 Breasted, "First Preliminary Report," 4–5.

33 Nissan N. Perez, *Focus East: Early Photography in the Near East (1839–1885)* (New York: Harry N. Abrams, 1988), 15. See also Kathleen Stewart Howe, *Excursions along the Nile: The Photographic Discovery of Ancient Egypt*, exh. cat. (Santa Barbara: Santa Barbara Museum of Art, 1993), 22–25.

34 See Nims's entry, "Photography and the Archaeologist, Part II: Photographic Equipment and Techniques in Archaeological Photography," in *The Encyclopedia of Photography; The Complete Photographer: The Comprehensive Guide and Reference for All Photographers*, ed. Willard D. Morgan, vol. 15 (New York: Greystone Press, 1964), 2735–45. See also the Oriental Institute's *Archaeological Newsletter*, 28 July 1953.

35 See Hill, "Life and Work of Harry Burton," 27–30.

36 Nims's excellent documentary photographs appear in The Epigraphic Survey, *The Tomb of Kheruef: Theban Tomb 192*, OIP 102 (Chicago: Oriental Institute, University of Chicago, 1980), the only tomb published to date by the survey.

37 See *The Registry of the Photographic Archives of the Epigraphic Survey*, OIC 27 (Chicago: Oriental Institute, University of Chicago, 1995).

38 See the partial list "Tombs Photographed by the Metropolitan Museum of Art up to May 1926," in PM, 1st ed., vol. 1, 207.

39 Breasted, "First Preliminary Report," 5, 10.

40 For the use of Burton's photos to complement the epigraphic publication of a tomb, see Heike Guksch, "Das Grab des Benja, gen. Paheqamen, Theben Nr. 343: Nachtrag zur Publikation des Grabes, Archäologische Veröffentlichungen 7, Mainz 1978," *MDAIK* 38 (1982): 195–99, pls. 31–51.

41 Michael Morris, *Madam Valentino: The Many Lives of Natacha Rambova* (New York: Abbeville Press, 1991), chap. 12, esp. 235–43.

42 This publication is a photographic complement to Alexandre Piankoff, *Les chapelles de Tout-Ankh-Amon*, Mémoires publiés par les membres de l'Institut français d'archéologie orientale du Caire 72 (Cairo: IFAO, 1951–52).

43 Ray W. Smith and Donald B. Redford, *The Akhenaten Temple Project*, vol. 1, *Initial Discoveries* (Warminster, U.K.: Aris and Phillips, 1976).

44 Breasted, "First Preliminary Report," 5–6.

45 Wilson, *Thousands of Years*, 52–54; Nims, "Publication of Ramesside Temples in Thebes," 91.

46 Conflated with John Baker Greene (c. 1830–c. 1886) in Dawson and Uphill, *Who Was Who in Egyptology*, 124; Bruno Jammes, "John B. Greene, An American Calotypist," *History of Photography* 5 (October 1981): 305, n. 4; Louis Vaczek and Gail Buckland, *Travelers in Ancient Lands: A Portrait of the Middle East, 1839–1919* (Boston: New York Graphic Society, 1981), 194. A short biographical entry on Greene is to be found in Perez, *Focus East*, 173, cf. 128. Joel M. Snyder, professor in the Department of Art, University of Chicago, has informed me that Greene's middle name was actually Beasley, not the "Bulkley" cited by Perez from Vaczek and Buckland, and followed by Rainer Wick, ed., *Die Pioniere der Photographie, 1840–1900: Die Sammlung Robert Lebeck* (Weingarten: Kunstverlag Weingarten, 1989), 69—nor, for that matter, the "Buckley" cited in Gary Edwards, *International Guide to*

Nineteenth-Century Photographers and Their Works (Boston: G. K. Hall, 1988), 228. For the correct name, see Michèle Auer and Michel Auer, *Encyclopédie internationale des photographes de 1839 à nos jours* (Geneva: Editions Camera Obscura, 1985) (this latter reference brought to my attention by John Larson); Howe, *Excursions along the Nile*, 28, 160.

47 Greene seems to have been preceded in this by Leawitt Hunt, who was active in 1851–52; see Perez, *Focus East*, 178.

48 This reference has been called to my attention by Joel Snyder; see his "Inventing Photography," in *On the Art of Fixing a Shadow* (Boston: Bulfinch Press, 1989), 36, n. 29. See Greene's *Fouilles exécutées à Thèbes dans l'année 1855: Textes hiéroglyphiques et documents inédits* (Paris: Firmin Didot Frères, 1855), 3, pls. I–III. See also Emmanuel de Rougé, "Notice de quelques textes hiéroglyphiques récemment publiés par M. Greene," reprinted in Gaston Maspero, ed., *Bibliothèque égyptologique* 23 (1910), 47; Jammes, "John B. Greene," 309, n. 12.

49 Caminos and Fischer, *Ancient Egyptian Epigraphy and Palaeography*, 10.

50 James H. Breasted and Thomas George Allen, foreword to *The Mastaba of Mereruka*, OIP 31 (Chicago: University of Chicago Press, 1938), vol. 1, xviii.

51 See Keith C. Seele, *The Tomb of Tjanefer at Thebes*, OIP 86 (Chicago: University of Chicago Press, 1959), v.

52 See Murnane, *Wall Reliefs*, ix–x.

53 And presumably also Schott, likewise an Epigraphic Survey staff member; see Siegfried Schott, *Wall Scenes from the Mortuary Chapel of the Mayor Paser at Medinet Habu*, Studies in Ancient Oriental Civilization 30 (Chicago: University of Chicago Press, 1957), 5; as well as Parker (another survey staff member): see Richard A. Parker, Jean Leclant, and Jean-Claude Goyon, *The Edifice of Taharqa by the Sacred Lake of Karnak*, Brown Egyptological Studies 8 (Providence: Brown University Press; London: Lund Humphries, 1979), ix.

54 John Baines, "Recording the Temple of Sethos I at Abydos in Egypt," *Bulletin of the Ancient Orient Museum* (Tokyo) 11 (1990): 70–71.

55 Serge Sauneron, *Esna*, vol. 1, *Quatre campagnes à Esna* (Cairo: IFAO, 1959), 166.

56 Gamal Mokhtar, "Registration of the Hieroglyphic Texts: The Technique Adopted by the Cairo Centre of Documentation," in *Textes et langages de l'Egypte pharaonique*, vol. 3, Bibliothèque d'étude 64 (Cairo: IFAO, 1974), 280.

57 Peter F. Dorman, *The Tombs of Senenmut: The Architecture and Decoration of Tombs 71 and 353* (New York: MMA, 1991), 94.

58 Breasted, "First Preliminary Report," 4.

59 Kenneth A. Kitchen, review of *The Battle Reliefs of King Sety I*, *Bibliotheca Orientalis* 45 (1988): 320; Margaret A. Murray, review of *The Tomb of Neferhotep at Thebes*, *Ancient Egypt* 18 (1933): 122; T. George Allen, review of *The Tomb of Rekh-mi-Rē' at Thebes*, AJA 50 (1946): 314.

Some American Contributions to the Understanding of Third Intermediate and Late Period Egypt

Richard A. Fazzini

he Third Intermediate and Late Periods span close to eight centuries of complex Egyptian history and cultural development (1070–332 B.C.).[1] American individuals and institutions excavating or recording monuments in Egypt, as well as American-assisted or supported projects, have made significant contributions to our knowledge of ancient Egypt during these eras.

Indeed, the efforts of one of America's earliest Egyptologists, Charles Edwin Wilbour, continue to shape our understanding of late Egyptian history and culture. Wilbour collected Egyptian antiquities in the nineteenth century, and the study of his collection of papyri, bequeathed to the Brooklyn Museum in 1947, has helped illuminate varied aspects of Egyptian civilization in the Late Period and early Ptolemaic era.[2] Perhaps the best known of Wilbour's papyri documents and illustrates an oracle given by Amun-Re in his chief temple at Karnak, on the east bank of the Nile at Thebes, in year 14 of King Psamtik I (r. 664–610 B.C.) of the 26th Dynasty.[3] The event commemorated reflects the fact that not until the end of the 26th Dynasty did the god Amun cease to be the theoretical sovereign of a large portion of southern Egypt. This sovereignty, centered in Thebes, appears to have begun in the time of Herihor, high priest of Amun in the late 20th to early 21st Dynasties.

Thebes, Egypt's Southern Metropolis

American Egyptologists have been significantly involved in excavating, documenting, and studying the Third Intermediate and Late Periods at Thebes. One of the better-preserved temples in the Theban area is that of the lunar deity Khonsu at Karnak. Khonsu was important in his own right and as the son of Amun and the goddess Mut. The Epigraphic Survey of the Oriental Institute, University of Chicago, whose main goal is to record and publish Theban temple decoration, has worked in the Khonsu temple many times since the 1930s. In 1979 and 1981 the institute published the decoration of the temple's first hypostyle hall — adorned for Herihor and the 20th Dynasty's last king, Ramesses XI (r. 1100–1070 B.C.), with some interesting scenes and restorations by the 30th Dynasty king Nectanebo II (r. 360–343 B.C.)—and of its court, adorned for Herihor but including images of the first of the 21st Dynasty's high priests of Amun, named Painedjem.[4]

This previously unpublished or inadequately published decoration provides important data for the study of the end of the New Kingdom and the beginning of the Third Intermediate Period. For example, the careful study of a scene published in the nineteenth century removed the evidence for the long-accepted theory that Herihor was the father of the high priest of Amun, Paiankh.[5] Equally important, the Khonsu temple's images of Herihor and Painedjem I include scenes of them not only as high priests but also—and unusually—as kings. These decorations thus offer meaningful evidence for discussions of the nature of their "kingships."[6] Indeed, the Epigraphic Survey's Khonsu publications have been one basis for recent arguments that Herihor followed Paiankh in office and that his kingship began on the death of Ramesses XI.[7] They have also resulted in discussions of the kingship of Herihor and Painedjem I in terms of an evolution of Egyptian kingship toward shared rule between actual kings and king-gods.[8] The Epigraphic Survey's work also led to the realization that the Khonsu temple's court and the hypostyle hall of Karnak's Amun temple were linked by various elements of decoration[9] and that a similar relationship existed as early as the reign of Ramesses IV (r. 1163–1156 B.C.) and possibly even at the time of an earlier Khonsu temple.[10]

American Egyptologist Helen Jacquet-Gordon recorded, in part while a fellow of the American Research Center in Egypt (ARCE) in 1986–87, graffiti on the Khonsu temple's roof, for publication under the auspices of the Oriental Institute.[11] Her earlier publication of two of these graffiti resulted in the addition of the previously unknown king Iny to the eighth-century B.C. rulers of Thebes.[12] Whether Iny belongs to a northern 23d Dynasty or to a Theban 23d Dynasty[13] remains to be determined. It is certain, however, that the recently much-discussed view that the 23d Dynasty was not a unilinear dynasty residing at Leontopolis in the Delta, but consisted of several groups of kings in different places, can be traced to an important article by American Egyptologist Klaus Baer (1930–87), a long-time member of the Oriental Institute faculty.[14]

Although identification of the Delta city of Bubastis as the capital of the 22d Dynasty is problematic,[15] the 22d Dynasty has traditionally been called Bubastite, as has the 22d Dynasty portico in the forecourt of Karnak's Amun temple. The portico's inscriptions and figural reliefs, the most important 22d Dynasty temple decoration at Thebes, were recorded by the Epigraphic Survey between 1934 and 1952 and published in 1954.[16] Survey renderings of the topographical list in Shoshenq I's (r. 945–924 B.C.) triumphal smiting scene became a main basis for the study of the king's major and successful military campaign in Palestine and of the history of the era in Egypt and the adjacent Near East.[17] Moreover, the portal's lengthy and somewhat later texts known as the Chronicles of Prince Osorkon are also major historical documents. Described by their main interpreter, Ricardo Caminos, as "among the most comprehensive and factual accounts of individual accomplishment that have been vouchsafed to us from Pharaonic Egypt,"[18] the chronicles concern civil warfare and struggles for the control of Thebes. They also shed interesting light on various aspects of Egyptian society and culture.[19]

The important 1979 publication by Brown University of another monument at Karnak—a building of unique plan beside the Amun temple's sacred lake, built or rebuilt by the 25th Dynasty king Taharqa (r. 690–664 B.C.)—was indebted to work by the Epigraphic Survey.[20] It was written by American Egyptologist Richard Parker (1905–93) and French Egyptologists Jean Leclant and Jean-Claude Goyon. The first Wilbour Professor of Egyptology at Brown, Parker had earlier been an epigrapher with, and for a time field director of, Chicago's Epigraphic Survey. For a recording project of the survey, he first studied the decoration of the unusual subterranean rooms of Taharqa's Lake Edifice as comparative material for elements in the Re chapel of the 20th Dynasty king Ramesses III's temple at Medinet Habu, on the Nile's west bank.[21] Various links connect the temple decoration in the Lake Edifice and at Medinet Habu.

Medinet Habu and its Small Temple were holy places for centuries before the 21st Dynasty, by which time, at the latest, the site and especially the Small Temple had become associated with the Mound of Djeme: a "mound of creation" and the tomb or cenotaph for primordial deities of creation identified with Amun and his first terrestrial manifestations, and for Osiris as well. With it developed rituals, theoretically conducted every ten days, linking Amun of Karnak and Amun of Luxor, on the Nile's east bank, to their divine ancestors and their renewing powers.[22] Goyon has argued that Taharqa's building was used for rituals complementing those at Djeme and related to Amun's union with various forms of the sun god and Osiris (night sun), Amun's rebirth as the sun, and (as with the Djeme rituals) the confirmation and renewal of royal power.[23]

French Egyptologist Claude Traunecker has proposed that Taharqa's Lake Edifice may have served as a substitute cult place for the rites of Djeme, thereby eliminating the need for a large procession back and forth across the Nile every tenth day. He suggests that the same function might have been filled somewhat earlier by the chapel of Osiris Heqa-Djet (ruler of eternity), whose 23d Dynasty reliefs include a depiction of the rites of the Mound of Djeme.[24]

The chapel of Osiris Heqa-Djet was at least one of the first of the small chapel-temples of Osiris built at Karnak in the Third Intermediate and Late Periods, and

its 25th Dynasty decoration accounts for a significant share of the temple reliefs known from the reign of Shebitku (698–690 B.C.). Its even rarer decoration by the 23d Dynasty kings Osorkon IV (r. 777–749 B.C.) and Takeloth III and divine worshiper Shepenwepet I includes elements, some unusual or unique, that are important to our understanding of the era's history and culture (see fig. 79). The chapel's decoration, especially of the 23d Dynasty, was a major interest of a combined mission of Toronto's Society for the Study of Egyptian Antiquities and the State University of New York at Binghamton in the early 1970s, codirected by Canadian Egyptologist Donald Redford and American Egyptologist Gerald Kadish, who was also an epigrapher for the project.[25]

The Canadian-American expedition and its excavations also dealt with the site's history and its place in the architectural history of Karnak. This is reflected, for example, in Redford's comments to date on the structures, especially an Isis chapel and Osiris chapels, located with the Heqa-Djet chapel in the northeast quadrant of the 30th Dynasty Amun precinct (which was not part of the precinct in the Third Intermediate Period), and by his discovery that this part of Karnak can be associated with the "great mound of the god of Wese (Thebes)," which he identifies as a tomb of Osiris.[26]

Despite its focus on an 18th Dynasty king, the Akhenaten Temple Project is relevant to this essay. The University Museum, University of Pennsylvania (now the University of Pennsylvania Museum of Archaeology and Anthropology), initiated the project in 1966, and in 1972 the University of Toronto became a participant, with Redford as director. In addition to shedding light on Akhenaten's temples, excavations begun in 1975 established a sequence of archaeological phases for East Karnak, a significant part of ancient Thebes during many periods of its history, including the Third Intermediate through Macedonian periods (see fig. 80).[27] This has led to important increases in our knowledge of the uses of different parts of East Karnak during those eras, of some aspects of the ancient city's layout, and of more limited subjects such as domestic architecture.[28] Among the significant nondomestic buildings investigated by the project were the temple and temenos (temple enclosure) at East Karnak labeled C.[29] The present temple proved to be Ptolemaic, but excavations revealed the remains of a 26th Dynasty–fourth-century B.C. temenos, possible evidence of a 25th Dynasty temple, and evidence suggesting that the temple might long have been dedicated to Khonsu-the-Child.[30]

Definitely associated with the child form of Khonsu is Temple A at South Karnak, parts of which have been excavated by the Brooklyn Museum Archaeological Expedition to the Temple Precinct of the Goddess Mut, an ongoing project conducted with the assistance of the Detroit Institute of Arts, with Richard Fazzini as project director and co–field director with William Peck. The Mut precinct encloses religious structures of the New Kingdom to early Roman period as well as the remains of pre–New Kingdom domestic structures and habitations of the Ptolemaic and Roman periods.[31] The expedition is concerned with the

FIGURE 80
East Karnak, with the remains of a seventh-century B.C. gate in the foreground. The gate may have been set into an eastern wall for Thebes and is oriented toward the Amun Temple, the eastern precinct gate of which is visible 187 meters to the west.

history and function of the site as a whole over its entire period of use and with the preservation and restoration, wherever possible, of its structures. Of particular importance for this essay are the site's monuments of the 25th and 26th Dynasties.

The expedition's work has added evidence supporting both Paul Barguet's statement that much of the present Temple A is a 25th Dynasty work[32] and Gerhard Haeny's observation of significant 25th Dynasty rebuilding in the Mut temple,[33] not to mention the probable addition of porches to the temple's façade. The expedition has discovered a gateway of the 25th Dynasty king Taharqa (see figs. 81, 82) set into a wall, which might represent an expansion of the Mut precinct beyond its New Kingdom limits to include Temple A, whose function seems to have changed over time. Initially it was probably a temple of Amun, but

FIGURE 81
Excavations of the
Brooklyn Museum Mut
expedition. Visible in
the foreground are the
partially excavated
south (right) half of
a gateway of King
Taharqa and some of
the late Ptolemaic and
Roman period struc-
tures in which it was
buried. The gateway is
aligned precisely with
the main (east-west)
axis of the precinct's
Temple A to the east
(rear). The front of the
Mut Temple is visible at
upper right.

FIGURE 82
The west face of the
north (left) half of the
Taharqa gateway, Mut
precinct. The king is
depicted entering the
precinct and being
received by Amun atop
symbols of the union of
Upper and Lower
Egypt. On the south
half of the gateway Mut
welcomed Taharqa atop
similar symbols.

it appears to have later become a temple to Khonsu-the-Child or to have become or also functioned as one of the earliest *mammisi*, structures for conducting the rituals celebrating the birth of a child god with whom the king could be identified.[34]

Whatever the precise nature of Temple A, it proved to contain a small chapel of the 25th and/or 26th Dynasty dedicated to a queen or divine worshiper.[35] In the vicinity of Temple A the reused remains of a small and unusual early 26th Dynasty chapel dedicated to healing magic were also uncovered.[36] Moreover, the bases of sphinxes on the approach to Temple A contain a number of reused blocks of Mentuemhet (one of Thebes's most powerful officials in the late 25th and early 26th Dynasties), including lintels from two small chapels, one of which could fit the in situ remains of a chapel discovered in the area. These add weight to the Mentuemhet inscriptions, long known from the Mut precinct, claiming responsibility for important architectural work there.[37]

In the 1920s and 1930s the Oriental Institute's Architectural Survey, directed by German archaeologist and architect Uvo Hölscher, conducted excavations over much of Medinet Habu which yielded valuable information about the site's Third Intermediate Period–Coptic religious, funerary, and domestic structures and objects. Indeed, the Oriental Institute is still recording and publishing these excavations, a task made easier by the recent rediscovery of long-lost excavation field records.[38] Of continuing concern to the Epigraphic Survey is the Small Temple, various parts and decorations of which date from the 18th Dynasty to Roman times,[39] and its connection to the Mound of Djeme.

Chicago's excavations at and just west of Medinet Habu have included tombs and funerary chapels dating from the 20th to 26th Dynasties, including those of the ninth-century B.C. king Horsiese (see fig. 78),[40] several divine worshipers

of the 23d to 25th–26th Dynasties, and a 26th Dynasty queen.[41] Relevant, in part, to beliefs concerning the Mound of Djeme, these structures, even prior to complete publication, have increased our knowledge of the funerary architecture, art, and customs of their eras.[42] The Medinet Habu excavations also yielded important data for the study of domestic architecture of the Third Intermediate and Late Periods.[43]

Farther north on the Theban west bank, Metropolitan Museum of Art excavations led by Ambrose Lansing and especially by Herbert E. Winlock added significantly to the study of the Theban necropolis, funerary customs, and funerary arts. Almost all the discoveries were in the large bay in the cliffs known as Deir el-Bahri and on the great plain before it called the Asasif.[44] Most of the funerary monuments excavated by the Metropolitan Museum were 21st to 26th Dynasty burials in undecorated tombs without above-ground chapels, but many contained decorated coffins, papyri (e.g., cat. no. 91), and other funerary furnishings that continue to figure in studies of such monuments[45] and, quite often, of the identities of their owners and the history of the late 20th to 21st Dynasties.[46] The Metropolitan expedition did, however, discover and clear the tomb of the early 26th Dynasty vizier Nespeqashuty (TT 312),[47] a monument seemingly reusing in part the remains of a Middle Kingdom tomb and decorated with reliefs harking back in style and content to much earlier eras (see fig. 83). The expedition also cleared the debris from the already-known early 26th Dynasty decorated tomb of Pabasa, chief steward of the God's Wife of Amun Nitocris I (TT 279; see cat. no. 105).[48]

The Temple at Hibis

In the el-Kharga Oasis, well west and slightly south of Thebes, is the ancient city of Hibis. Here the Metropolitan Museum of Art excavated, recorded, and helped restore the temple of Amun-Re,[49] one of the best-preserved Egyptian temples of the pre-Ptolemaic Late Period. Some of its walls bear rare reliefs of the 27th Dynasty (Egypt's first period of domination by Achaemenid Persia) and significant 30th Dynasty decoration.[50] The main work of excavation, directed by Winlock, was completed during the first season of fieldwork, in 1909–10. After a hiatus caused by World War I, photographer Harry Burton and artist Norman de Garis Davies, among others, continued recording the temple until 1939. Their efforts resulted in the publication of three monographs on the temple and its decoration.[51] The interpretation of some of its unusual decoration (especially the sanctuary's adornment with more than 650 divine figures) is still under discussion.[52] Some features, such

as the columns' composite plant capitals[53] or the solar and Osirian chapels,[54] antic-
ipate elements of Ptolemaic temples and, indeed, form links between the Ptolemaic
era and much earlier periods.

For various reasons the Metropolitan Museum's expedition was not able to
record all the in situ decoration of the temple or all its stray blocks; nor was it
able to complete the final checking of some drawings. Publication of the decoration
was thus accompanied by limited descriptions and comments. Completing this
work is a major goal of another American mission, the Hibis Temple Project,
directed by Eugene Cruz-Uribe. Since the first field season of 1984–85 Cruz-
Uribe has published several articles and a monograph that include translations of
inscriptions and commentaries on the texts and images.[55] The mission's study has
prompted proposals on the temple's dating, particularly that much of what has
been called 27th Dynasty is actually the work of the 26th Dynasty king Psamtik II
(r. 595–589 B.C.).[56]

Memphis, Egypt's Northern Metropolis

Memphis remained a religious and administrative center of Lower Egypt during
the Third Intermediate and Late Periods. In the first decade of this century W. M.
Flinders Petrie directed excavations, supported in part by American institutions,
of some of the mounds that are the remains of the ancient city.[57] Two are relevant
to this discussion. One was the site of a 21st Dynasty building of the time of King
Siamun (r. 978–959 B.C.). Its precise nature and plan are not known, but it might
have been dedicated to "Amun, lord of lapis-lazuli."[58] Built mainly of mud brick,
the building yielded a number of limestone doorjambs and lintels, including one
now in the Carnegie Museum of Natural History, Pittsburgh (cat. no. 92). Their
decoration has been a valuable source for our knowledge of royal and high priestly
art of their time, and their inscriptions by major Memphite priests have proved
important for genealogical and historical studies.[59]

The other relevant structure excavated by Petrie was a fortified palace, probably to be attributed to the 26th Dynasty king Apries (r. 589–570 B.C.), significant
for the history of Egyptian architecture and as a possible reflection of the somewhat unsettled nature of its times.[60] Built mainly of mud brick, the palace had
a large decorated limestone doorway, whose interesting archaizing reliefs showing
religious rituals have stylistic and iconographic ties to royal works of earlier periods, especially the Old Kingdom.[61]

The onset of World War I prevented the Romanian government from using a
permit to excavate at Memphis, thus allowing the University Museum, University
of Pennsylvania, to succeed Petrie, whose excavations it had supported.[62] The
museum's expedition, led by Clarence S. Fisher between 1915 and the early 1920s,

focused on a significant palace, of which relatively few have been preserved or excavated, in this case, one belonging to the 19th Dynasty king Merneptah (r. 1224–1214 B.C.). The project is mentioned here because clearing this structure entailed clearing the later stratified town remains over and around it. Fisher published little of the expedition's results,[63] but for more than three decades Alan Schulman has been systematically publishing the more than two hundred inscribed stone objects from the excavation. Works postdating the New Kingdom include stelae, reliefs, and statuary.[64]

A second University Museum expedition, led by German Egyptologist Rudolf Anthes (1896–1985) in conjunction with the Egyptian Antiquities Department, conducted two seasons of fieldwork at Memphis in 1955 and 1956.[65] Working mainly in and near the southwest corner of the Ptah temple's temenos wall, the expedition uncovered strata, pottery, and even inscribed objects from the Third Intermediate and Late Periods.[66] In fact, it contributed greatly to our understanding of the stratigraphy and post-Ramesside history of part of Memphis.[67]

A member of the Anthes-directed expedition, John Dimick, became interested in the remains of one structure at Memphis and ultimately helped develop another expedition to investigate this monument associated with the cult of the Apis bulls.[68] With Dimick as consultant and with funding from the Dimick Foundation, between 1982 and 1986 the Apis House Project conducted six seasons of survey and excavation on behalf of New York University's Institute of Fine Arts, under the auspices of ARCE. The project director was Bernard V. Bothmer (1912–93), then Lila Acheson Wallace Professor of Ancient Egyptian Art at the Institute of Fine Arts, and the field directors were British archaeologists and Egyptologists Michael Jones and Angela Milward Jones, who rapidly published preliminary reports.[69]

An Apis bull was considered an earthly intermediary to the god Ptah and, indeed, his son and a manifestation of the god. Only one Apis bull lived at a time, and when it died, it was believed to become the Osirian manifestation of the deity. Prior to the Apis House Project a structure in the southwest quadrant of the Ptah temple had sometimes been dated to the reign of the 22d Dynasty king Shoshenq I[70] and tentatively identified with the "stall," known from classical writers, where the living Apis was housed, and/or the place where the deceased Apis was embalmed.[71] The Apis House Project[72] yielded more evidence that part of the structure was a place of embalming. We also know that the building, a work of the fourth century B.C. built on two artificial terraces on different levels, replaced earlier structures, including one of probable 25th to 26th Dynasty date. The fourth-century B.C. edifice might well date to the reign of the 30th Dynasty king Nectanebo II (360–343 B.C.).

There are, of course, several famous cemeteries related to Memphis. Among them is Giza, renowned for its Old Kingdom monuments, of which a significant number were excavated by George A. Reisner. During the 1924–26 season he investigated one structure relevant to this discussion: the temple of Isis, Mistress of the Pyramids (see fig. 84).[73] The temple's sanctuary includes the mortuary chapel of a subsidiary pyramid of Khufu's Great Pyramid. Other parts of the temple are of the 21st Dynasty and later; they include a columned hall, a kiosk, and flanking chapels, some with burial shafts.

In 1980–81 Michael Jones and Angela Milward Jones undertook a detailed architectural survey of the temple, and French Egyptologist Christiane Zivie-Coche studied its texts as part of ARCE's Sphinx–Isis Temple Project, of which James Allen was project director and Mark Lehner, field director.[74] Since then, Zivie-Coche, using the records of the Reisner excavations, has produced for the Museum of Fine Arts, Boston, a study of the temple and its architectural, historical, and cultural contexts at Giza.[75] This publication and the remains of the temple contribute particularly to our knowledge of archaizing in art and religion; the growth of the cult of Isis, whose large temples, as their inscriptions and physical remains attest, do not predate the Late Period;[76] the use of temple grounds (relating to somewhat earlier usages at Tanis and Medinet Habu)—and, here, an actual functioning temple building (beginning in the late 22d–23d Dynasty)—for burials, which relates to later usages at Sais;[77] and the association of a priestly family with the temple and of its and Isis's connections with the cult of long-dead kings.

The Delta

Several of Egypt's ruling dynasties of the Late Period arose in the Delta, from cities such as Sais, Mendes, and Sebennytos. An expedition to Mendes (Tell el-Rub'a), in the northeast Delta, was undertaken by New York University's Institute of Fine Arts, with the assistance of the Brooklyn Museum, the Detroit Institute of Arts, and Chicago's Oriental Institute, from 1964 to 1966 and, following a long hiatus caused by the 1967 Arab-Israeli war, from 1976 through 1981. Bothmer, then of the Brooklyn Museum and the Institute of Fine Arts, was project director, and Donald P. Hansen of the Institute of Fine Arts was field director until 1979, when he was succeeded by Karen L. Wilson.

One of the objects of the expedition's investigations was a large temple at the site. All that had been known of this temple was a single standing colossal granite naos (7.85 meters tall) inscribed for King Amasis (r. 570–526 B.C.) of the 26th Dynasty (see figs. 85, 86). Excavations in the early seasons of the Mendes expedition revealed major foundations for significant parts of the temple, not all of which proved to be as late as the 26th Dynasty. The excavators uncovered colossal limestone foundations (yielding foundation deposits for Amasis) supporting the standing naos and three more like it, of which parts were preserved. These shrines were dedicated to Re, Shu, Geb, and Osiris as manifestations of Mendes's main deity, Banebdjed.[78] The expedition also discovered the upper half of a 26th Dynasty sculpture of a god, which Bothmer published as an image of Shu and possibly a cult image from one of the naoi.[79]

FIGURE 85
View of Mendes, looking south toward the sanctuary of the temple, before excavation. Visible is the standing granite naos of King Amasis.

FIGURE 86
View of Mendes, looking south toward the sanctuary of the temple, following excavation in the 1960s by the Institute of Fine Arts, New York University. In addition to the standing naos of King Amasis, the photograph shows pieces of three other colossal naoi inscribed for Amasis, the remains of the massive limestone platform and paving on which the naoi sat, and the large mud-brick walls containing the sand that served as the foundation for the stonework.

Until the 1979 season fieldwork at Mendes was concentrated in the precinct of the temple of Banebdjed, containing tombs and burials of the Old Kingdom and earlier. With the passing of the field directorship to Wilson, the expedition focused on obtaining an unbroken ceramic sequence for Mendes and on excavating outside the precinct to recover materials of a type not previously found at Mendes. The first goal was not realized because desired Middle and New Kingdom strata were not located; instead, interesting Third Intermediate to Late Period strata were uncovered.[80]

Mendes was the home of the kings of the 29th Dynasty, and a huge sarcophagus in the temple precinct has long been tentatively ascribed to King Nepherites I (r. 399–393 B.C.) because of a large shabti found in it. In 1977 the expedition undertook a limited excavation that did not result in the identification of the sarcophagus's owner but did yield fragments of limestone reliefs, including one of Nectanebo I, as well as some private statuary of the 26th and 27th Dynasties.[81]

Since 1990 a consortium of the Universities of Illinois, Washington, Alberta, and Toronto has been working at Mendes. The work of the first two universities, directed by Robert Wenke and Douglas Brewer, has concentrated on periods earlier than the scope of this essay, while the work of the University of Alberta's Department of Anthropology, directed by Nancy Lovell, includes excavations and physical anthropological research dealing with human and animal remains of the Late Period and Ptolemaic era.[82] The University of Toronto's mission, directed by Donald Redford, has been dealing with several monuments relevant to this discussion, among them the Nepherites I sarcophagus. The Toronto excavations have clarified its architectural context and yielded several hundred fragments of limestone relief, including one for a little-known king of the 29th Dynasty. The expedition has also provided data to suggest that the sarcophagus was part of Nepherites I's tomb, that it might have been destroyed by the Persian Artaxerxes III in 343 B.C., and that it was not the only royal funerary monument in this area.[83]

University of Toronto excavations in the area of Mendes's harbor reportedly are finding ceramic and numismatic evidence for trade with various parts of the Mediterranean in the fourth to third centuries B.C.[84] And excavations in the depression long postulated as a sacred lake have confirmed it as such, possibly for a temple (other than that of Banebdjed already investigated) that was in use at least from the Late Period until sometime in the Ptolemaic period.[85] As Redford has noted, "Mendes offers an opportunity to study a royal Egyptian city in its every aspect,"[86] which the expedition wishes to do, comparing the results with those of the Akhenaten Temple Project and, to an extent, other expeditions to the royal cities of Thebes.

Another Egyptian Delta site contains what might be a royal burial. Tell el-Muqdam has long been identified with the city classical writers called Leontopolis (city of the lions), a name befitting the most common guise of its main deity, Mahes. In 1915 a tomb attributed to a queen of the 23d Dynasty was discovered, but its precise location was not recorded. Despite this, it became one of the problematic bits of evidence in the argument about whether Leontopolis was the capital of a Delta 23d Dynasty that included a King Iuput II.[87]

With Carol Redmount and Renée Friedman as codirectors, the University of California, Berkeley, Tell el-Muqdam Project undertook fieldwork in 1992 and 1993, resuming work in 1995. A magnetometer survey of the site has possibly relocated the "lost" tomb, and the expedition hopes to determine if it is, indeed, a royal tomb.[88] The expedition further intends to "investigate the components of a 'typical' Egyptian town over time."[89] The project has begun to produce the first reliable topographic map of the site, to record inscriptions, and to investigate parts of the site via magnetometer, geological coring, and soil augering. It has also made limited excavations, investigating several different structures of the earlier and later Persian periods, when Tell el-Muqdam appears to have been an important site.[90]

A regional survey of endangered sites near Leontopolis by the Berkeley Tell el-Muqdam Project was one of several surveys conducted in the Delta in recent years. Another was part of the Wadi Tumilat Project of the University of Toronto, directed by John Holladay Jr. under the auspices of several institutions, including the Canadian Mediterranean Institute and its affiliate, the Canadian Institute in Egypt, Toronto's Society for the Study of Egyptian Antiquities, the American Schools of Oriental Research, and ARCE. The goals of the project included inter-disciplinary archaeological investigations of issues relating to socioeconomic history, trade, political-military history, and cultural interconnections in a border area and a "gateway" city.[91]

The Wadi Tumilat, in the Eastern Desert, is a valley approximately sixty kilo-meters long that links Egypt and the Sinai and contains a number of sites, among them the large Tell el-Maskhuta. In 1983, following a limited survey in two areas, the project undertook a systematic, stratified, randomized transect survey of the wadi. The codirectors were Holladay and Redmount.[92] The survey determined that between the end of the Second Intermediate Period (Middle Bronze Age) and the 26th Dynasty, there was virtually no settlement in the wadi, even at Tell el-Maskhuta. The only occupied site during this period was Tell el-Rataba.[93] Holladay and Red-mount propose that the revival of occupation was due to King Necho II's decision to build a canal between the Nile and the Bitter Lakes of the Gulf of Suez, thus linking the Mediterranean and the Red Sea through the wadi. This canal was enhanced and completed by Darius I (r. 521–486 B.C.) in the 27th Dynasty.

Since fieldwork ended in 1985, the Wadi Tumilat Project has focused on research and publication. Some articles deal with imported pottery and other material illustrating the trade made possible by the canal,[94] and others concentrate on ceramics of the 26th to 27th Dynasties in general.[95] The Saite and first Persian period ceramic material came from several parts of the site and a variety of structures. Although some of the theories proposed have yet to be confirmed, the work has added significantly to our knowledge of the archaeological history of Tell el-Maskhuta and of the wadi,[96] encompassing chronological periods outside the scope of this essay.

THIS ESSAY COULD NOT INCLUDE every relevant American or American-related archaeological project that has dealt with the Third Intermediate and Late Periods, let alone their study by individual American scholars. Nevertheless, it should help demonstrate that American and American-assisted projects have made important contributions to our knowledge and understanding of the Third Intermediate and Late Periods. This writer hopes that the essay will also help the reader to understand that ARCE has helped facilitate the work of a significant number of the projects mentioned and that it continues to do so.

Notes

1 This essay is largely based on a paper presented at ARCE's annual symposium in New York in 1992. For both, the writer is indebted to the following individuals for information and references on individual projects: Lanny Bell, Peter Dorman, and Emily Teeter for projects of the Oriental Institute, University of Chicago; Donald Redford and Gerald Kadish for the Toronto-Binghamton expedition to the chapel of Osiris Heqa-Djet; Donald Redford for the University of Toronto's work at East Karnak and Mendes; Dorothea Arnold and Marsha Hill for projects of the Metropolitan Museum of Art; Eugene Cruz-Uribe for the Hibis Temple Project; Sharon Herbert for the University of Michigan's work at Coptos; Alan Schulman for the Fisher expedition of the University Museum to Memphis; Donald Hansen and Christine Lilyquist for the New York University excavations at Mendes; Carol Redmount for the Berkeley Tell el-Muqdam project; and John Holladay Jr. and Patricia Paice for the Wadi Tumilat Project.

2 See, e.g., Emil Kraeling, *The Brooklyn Museum Aramaic Papyri: New Documents of the Fifth Century B.C. from the Jewish Colony at Elephantine* (Brooklyn: Brooklyn Museum; New Haven: Yale University Press, 1953); Serge Sauneron, *Le papyrus magique illustré de Brooklyn [Brooklyn Museum 47.218.156]*, Wilbour Monograph 3 (Brooklyn: Brooklyn Museum, 1970); Jean-Claude Goyon, *Confirmation du pouvoir royal au nouvel an [Brooklyn Museum Papyrus 47.218.50]*, text vol., Bibliothèque d'étude 52 (Cairo: IFAO, 1972); idem, *Confirmation du pouvoir royal au nouvel an [Brooklyn Museum Papyrus 47.218.50]*, plate vol., Wilbour Monograph 7 (Brooklyn: Brooklyn Museum, 1974); Serge Sauneron, *Un traité égyptien d'ophiologie: Papyrus du Brooklyn Museum Nos. 47.218.48 et .85*, Bibliothèque générale 11 (Cairo: IFAO, 1989); Richard Jasnow, *A Late Period Hieratic Wisdom Text (P. Brooklyn 47.218.135)*, Studies in Ancient Oriental Civilization 52 (Chicago: Oriental Institute, University of Chicago, 1992).

3 Richard Parker, *A Saite Oracle Papyrus from Thebes in the Brooklyn Museum [Papyrus Brooklyn 47.218.3]*, Brown Egyptological Studies 4 (Providence: Brown University Press, 1962).

4 The Epigraphic Survey, *The Temple of Khonsu*, vol. 1, *Scenes of King Herihor in the Court, with Translations of Texts*, OIP 100 (Chicago: Oriental Institute, University of Chicago, 1979); idem, *The Temple of Khonsu*, vol. 2, *Scenes and Inscriptions in the Court and the First Hypostyle Hall, with Translations of Texts and Glossary for Volumes 1 and 2*, OIP 103 (Chicago: Oriental Institute, University of Chicago, 1981). The Epigraphic Survey field directors at the Khonsu temple were, in order of service, Harold Nelson, Richard Parker, George Hughes, Charles Nims, Edward Wente, and Kent Weeks. For the Khonsu temple in general, see PM, 2d ed., vol. 2, 224–44. For monuments of the 21st–25th Dynasties forming the approach to the Khonsu temple, see Françoise Laroche-Traunecker, "Données nouvelles sur les abords du temple de Khonsou," in *C.F.E.T.K., Cahiers de Karnak VII, 1978–1981* (Cairo: Editions Recherche sur les civilisations, 1982), 313–37; Jean-Claude Goyon, "Aspects thébains de la confirmation du pouvoir royal: Les rites lunaires," *JSSEA* 13 (1983): 2–9.

5 E.g., Edward Wente, in *Scenes of King Herihor*, x–xii, pl. 26.

6 E.g., ibid., xv–xvi; Kent Weeks, in *Scenes and Inscriptions in the Court*, xviii–xix.

7 Karl Jansen-Winkeln, "Das Ende des Neuen Reiches," *ZÄS* 119 (1992): 22–37.

8 Rolf Gundlach, "Das Königtum des Herihor: Zum Umbruch in der ägyptischen Königside-ologie am Beginn der 3. Zwischenzeit," in *Aspekte spätägyptischer Kultur: Festschrift für Erich Winter zum 65. Geburtstag*, ed. Martina Minas and Jürgen Zeidler, Aegyptiaca Treverensia 7 (Mainz: Philipp von Zabern, 1994), 133–38.

9 Wente, in *Scenes of King Herihor*, x.

10 Ann Roth, "Some New Texts of Herihor and Ramesses IV in the Great Hypostyle Hall at Karnak," *JNES* 42 (1983): 43–53. For the Khonsu temple's theological and cultic links to the adjacent temple of Opet in the Ptolemaic period, but possibly beginning in the New Kingdom, see Jean-Claude Degardin, "Correspondances osiriennes entre les temples d'Opet et de Khonsou," *JNES* 44 (1985): 115–31. The Epigraphic Survey publication facilitated Degardin's study of deities in the temple; see Jean-Claude Degardin, "Khonsou et ses compagnes dans son temple de Karnak," in *The Intellectual Heritage of Egypt: Studies Presented to László Kákósy by Friends and Colleagues on the Occasion of His 60th Birthday*, ed. U. Luft, Studia Aegyptiaca 14 (Budapest: Chaire d'Egyptologie, 1992), 101–12.

11 Helen Jacquet-Gordon, "Graffiti at Khonsu," *NARCE*, no. 141 (Spring 1988): 5–6.

12 Helen Jacquet-Gordon, "Deux graffiti de l'époque libyenne sur le toit du temple de Khonsou à Karnak," in *Hommages à la mémoire de Serge Sauneron, 1927–1976*, vol. 1, Bibliothèque d'étude 81 (Cairo: IFAO, 1979), 167–83.

13 Jean Yoyotte, "Pharaon Iny, un roi mystérieux du VIIIe siècle avant J.-C.," *Cahiers de recherches de l'Institut de papyrologie et d'égyptologie de Lille 11* (1989): 113–31, which is a study of Iny and his other monuments or possible monuments. See also David Aston, "Takeloth II—A King of the 'Theban Twenty-Third Dynasty'?" *JEA* 75 (1989): 139–53, esp. 152–53, where the provenance for the graffiti published by Jacquet-Gordon should read "Temple of Khonsu" rather than "Temple of Montu."

14 Klaus Baer, "The Libyan and Nubian Kings of Egypt: Notes on the Chronology of Dynasties XXII to XXVI," *JNES* 32 (1973): 4–25. The origin of this interpretation with Baer is acknowledged on the first page of David Aston and John Taylor, "The Family of Takeloth III and the 'Theban Twenty-third Dynasty,'" in *Libya and Egypt, c. 1300–750 B.C.*, ed. A. Leahy (London: University of London School of Oriental and African Studies, Centre of Near and Middle Eastern Studies, and the Society for Libyan Studies, 1990), 131–54.

15 E.g., Donald Redford, *Pharaonic King-Lists, Annals, and Day Books: A Contribution to the Study of the Egyptian Sense of History*, Society for the Study of Egyptian Antiquities 4 (Mississauga, Ontario: Benben Publications, 1986), 308–10.

16 The Epigraphic Survey, *Reliefs and Inscriptions at Karnak*, vol. 3, *The Bubastite Portal*, OIP 74 (Chicago: University of Chicago Press, 1954).

17 E.g., Kenneth Kitchen, *The Third Intermediate Period in Egypt (1100–650 B.C.)*, 2d ed. with suppl. (Warminster: Aris and Phillips, 1986), pars. 252–58, 398–415, 510.

18 Ricardo Caminos, *The Chronicles of Prince Osorkon*, Analecta Orientalia 37 (Rome: Pontificum Institutum Biblicum, 1958), 1. For more recent commentaries on the chronicle, see, e.g., Kitchen, *Third Intermediate Period*, pars. 148, 291–94, 299, 454–61; and Aston, "Takeloth II," 139–53.

19 E.g., the reference to someone other than a king, in this case a prince, being ritually suckled by a goddess (Caminos, *Chronicles of Prince Osorkon*, 31–32, 175).

20 Richard Parker, Jean Leclant, and Jean-Claude Goyon, *The Edifice of Taharqa by the Sacred Lake of Karnak*, trans. C. Crozier-Brelot, Brown Egyptological Studies 8 (Providence: Brown University Press, 1979). For this building, see also Beatrix Gessler-Löhr, *Die heiligen Seen ägyptischer Tempel: Ein Beitrag zur Deutung sakraler Baukunst im alten Ägypten*, Hildesheimer ägyptologische Beiträge 21 (Hildesheim: Gerstenberg, 1983), 167–74, 454–55.

21 For further comments on relationships between these decorations and New Kingdom monuments, see Jan Assmann, "Das Dekorationsprogramm der königlichen Sonnenheiligtümer des Neuen Reiches nach einer Fassung der Spätzeit," *ZÄS* 110 (1983): 91–98.

22 For a detailed discussion of these ideas and rituals, see Claude Traunecker, in Claude Traunecker, Françoise Le Saout, and Olivier Masson, *La chapelle d'Achôris à Karnak*, vol. 2 (Paris: Editions A.D.P.F., 1981), 115–42. Important references to beliefs concerning Djeme are M. Doresse, "Le dieu violé dans sa châsse et la fête du début de la decade," pts. 1–3, *RdE* 23 (1971): 113–36;

RdE 25 (1973): 92–135; *RdE* 31 (1979): 36–65; and François-René Herbin, "Une liturgie des rites décadaires de Djemê, P. Vienne 3865," *RdE* 35 (1984): 105–26. For 25th Dynasty decorated blocks possibly from a chapel of Osiris at Djeme, see Michel Dewachter, "Deux bas-reliefs perdus du puits 2003 de Deir el-Medineh," *RdE* 37 (1986): 159–63. For an earlier Mound of Djeme at Giza, see Christiane Zivie-Coche, *Giza au deuxième millénaire*, Bibliothèque d'étude 70 (Cairo: IFAO, 1976), 295–97.

23 In Parker, Leclant, and Goyon, *Edifice of Taharqa*, 80–86.

24 Claude Traunecker, in Traunecker, Le Saout, and Masson, *Chapelle d'Achôris*, 133, 140, 142. For another possible substitute cult place for Djeme rituals at Karnak, see Claude Traunecker, "Un exemple de rite de substitution: Une stèle de Nectanebo Ier," in *C.F.E.T.K. Cahiers de Karnak VII*, 339–54. For the images of Djeme rituals in Osiris Heqa-Djet and the Lake Edifice, see Parker, Leclant, and Goyon, *Edifice of Taharqa*, pls. 22, 23, 25.

25 For earlier references to the chapel of Osiris Heqa-Djet, see PM, 2d ed., vol. 2, 204–6, to which add, e.g., Donald Redford, "An Interim Report on the Second Season of Work at the Temple of Osiris, Ruler of Eternity," *JEA* 59 (1973): 16–30; idem, *Pharaonic King-Lists*, 310–17, esp. nn. 110–11, 116, 125. The final publication of the mission's work by Redford, Kadish et al. is expected to appear in early 1995.

26 Donald Redford, "New Light on Temple J at Karnak," *Orientalia* 55 (1986): 9–13. At this time at Thebes it is conceivable that Amun might also have been somehow associated with this mound, just as he was represented in the Isis chapel and in Karnak's Osiris chapels.

27 For a brief history of the Akhenaten Temple Project up to 1979, see Donald Redford, "The Akhenaten Temple Project and Karnak Excavations," *Expedition* 21 (Winter 1979): 54–59.

28 See, e.g., Donald Redford et al., "East Karnak Excavations, 1987–1989," *JARCE* 28 (1991): 75–83. See also Donald Redford et al., "Three Seasons in Egypt: II. Interim Report on the 20th Campaign (17th Season) of the Excavations at East Karnak," *JSSEA* 18 (1988): 33–36, pls. XVIIIb–XIXa.

29 PM, 2d ed., vol. 2, 254–55. Elsewhere at Karnak the project has excavated a late-sixth-to fifth-century B.C. structure, once suggested to be a work of Akhenaten, and the remains of one or two columned structures of the Third Intermediate Period; see Donald Redford, "Excavations at the Kom el-Ahmar, Karnak, 1985," in *Akten des vierten Internationalen Ägyptologen Kongresses, München 1985*, ed. Sylvia Schoske, SAK Beiheft 2 (Hamburg: H. Buske, 1988), 257–63, pls. 30–33.

30 Donald Redford et al., "Three Seasons in Egypt: I. The Excavation of Temple C," *JSSEA* 18 (1988): 1–13, pls. I–XII.

31 For the first of the expedition's soundings yielding pre–New Kingdom remains, see Richard Fazzini and William Peck, "The 1982 Season at Mut," *NARCE*, no. 120 (Winter 1982): 43–44. The remains from the Mut precinct have extended the range of such material south of its former known limits at Karnak; see Barry Kemp, *Ancient Egypt: Anatomy of a Civilization* (London and New York: Routledge, 1989), 160–63, fig. 56. For some of the Ptolemaic and Roman period habitations and inscriptional material from them, see Richard Jasnow, "Demotic Ostraca from the Mut Precinct in Karnak," with preface by Richard Fazzini, *Enchoria* 16 (1988): 23–48, pls. 4–21.

32 Paul Barguet, *Le temple d'Amon-Rê à Karnak: Essai d'exégèse*, Recherches d'archéologie, de philologie et d'histoire 21 (Cairo: IFAO, 1962), 9; Richard Fazzini and William Peck, "The Precinct of Mut during Dynasty XXV and Early Dynasty XXVI: A Growing Picture," *JSSEA* 11 (1981): 121–22. Such a date is possible for some parts of the first court of the temple added to its plan by the expedition; see Richard Fazzini and William Peck, "Introduction" *JARCE* 20 (1983): 65–67.

33 Gerhard Haeny, *Basilikale Anlagen in der ägyptischen Baukunst des Neuen Reiches*, Beiträge zur ägyptischen Bauforschung und Altertumskunde, Heft 9 (Wiesbaden: F. Steiner, 1970), 25; Fazzini and Peck, "Precinct of Mut," 115–19; Richard Fazzini, "Report on the 1983 Season of Excavation at the Precinct of the Goddess Mut," *ASAE* 70 (1985): 294, pl. IVa.

34 Fazzini and Peck, "Precinct of Mut," 122–25; Fazzini, "Report on the 1983 Season," 306. For other comments on whether Temple A was a temple of Khonsu-the-Child or a *mammisi* different in plan from later *mammisi*, see François Daumas, *Les mammisis des temples égyptiens*, Annales de l'Université de Lyon, 3d ser., Lettres, fasc. 32 (Paris:

Belles Lettres, 1958), 52–53; Herman De Meulenaere, "Isis et Mout du mammisi," *Orientalia Lovaniensia Analecta* 13 (1982): 25–29.

35 Richard Fazzini, "A Monument in the Precinct of Mut with the Name of the God's Wife Nitocris I," in *Artibus Aegypti: Studia in Honorem Bernardi V. Bothmer, a Collegis, Amicis, Discipulis Conscripta*, ed. Herman De Meulenaere and Luc Limme (Brussels: Musées royaux d'art et d'histoire, 1983), 51–62. It should be added that the Nitocris block published therein may have been the front lintel of the chapel.

36 Claude Traunecker, "Une chapelle de magie guérisseuse sur le parvis du temple de Mout à Karnak," *JARCE* 20 (1983): 65–92 (including Fazzini and Peck, "Introduction," 65–67), pls. 19–24; idem, "Une pratique de magie populaire dans les temples de Karnak," in *La magia in Egitto al tempi dei faraoni: Atti Convegno Internazionale di Studi, Milano, 29–31 Ottobre 1985*, ed. A. Rocatti and Alberto Siliotti (Milan: Edizioni Panini, 1987), 221–22.

37 See, e.g., Jean Leclant, *Montuemhat, quatrième prophète d'Amon, "prince de la ville,"* Bibliothèque d'étude 35 (Cairo: IFAO, 1961), 65–76, pls. XVI–XVIII (Cairo, Egyptian Museum CG 646), and 193–238, pls. LXVI–LXX (chapel in the Mut temple). For a sculpture from the Mut precinct of a Kushite king (possibly Taharqa) and a ram of Amun that is rare for 25th Dynasty Egypt, although not for Nubia, see Richard Fazzini, "A Sculpture of King Taharqa(?) in the Precinct of the Goddess Mut at South Karnak," *Mélanges Gamal Eddin Mokhtar*, vol. 1, Bibliothèque d'étude 97 (Cairo: IFAO, 1985): 293–306.

38 "Presumed Lost, Recently Recovered Medinet Habu Records Are Boon to Oriental Institute Scholars," *KMT* 4 (Winter 1993–94): 16–18. Hölscher's excavations at Medinet Habu have been described as being "conducted in a far more intensive and thorough manner than anything known in Egyptian archaeology before" (Warren R. Dawson and Eric P. Uphill, *Who Was Who in Egyptology*, 2d rev. ed. [London: Egypt Exploration Society, 1972], 143). For the Medinet Habu excavations by the Architectural Survey, see Uvo Hölscher's articles in OIC vols. 5 (1929), 7 (1930), 10 (1931), 15 (1932), and 18 (1934). Hölscher was also the main

author of *The Excavation of Medinet Habu*, vols. 1–5, OIP 21, 41, 54, 55, 56 (Chicago: University of Chicago Press, 1934–54). *General Plans and Views*, vol. 1, OIP 21 (1934), contains detailed plans of almost all structures of all periods. *The Temples of the Eighteenth Dynasty*, vol. 2, OIP 41 (1939), and *Post-Ramessid Remains*, vol. 5, OIP 56 (1954), are most important for our present purpose. For a useful introduction to the site, see William Murnane, *United with Eternity: A Concise Guide to the Monuments of Medinet Habu* (Chicago: Oriental Institute, University of Chicago; Cairo: American University in Cairo Press, 1980).

39 PM, 2d ed., vol. 2, 460–74. Many of the references are to the treatment of all phases of the Small Temple's history in Hölscher, *Temples of the Eighteenth Dynasty*, 2–62, pls. 2–7, 9–21, 25–34, 36–41. This volume includes contributions by Rudolf Anthes. For the major decoration of the 25th Dynasty on the second pylon, see pp. 464–65. For both definite and possible work here by the 29th Dynasty king Hakoris, see Claude Traunecker, in Traunecker, Le Saout, and Masson, *Chapelle d'Achôris*, 15–16, 104–30, some of which includes material more often ascribed to the 26th and 30th Dynasties (PM, 2d ed., vol. 2, 463–64).

40 PM, 2d ed., vol. 1, pt. 2, 772; Hölscher, *Post-Ramessid Remains*, 8–10. See also Aston, "Takeloth II," 139–40.

41 PM, 2d ed., vol. 2, 476–80; Hölscher, *Post-Ramessid Remains*, 17–70. For other chapels and tombs, see PM, 2d ed., vol. 1, pt. 2, 772–73 (chapels and tombs west of Medinet Habu), and Hölscher, *Post-Ramessid Remains*, 16–17, 30–33 (other tombs at Medinet Habu).

42 For some comments on these structures in the context of the evolution of funerary monuments and the Theban necropolis, see Diethelm Eigner, *Die monumentalen Grabbauten der Spätzeit in der Thebanischen Nekropole*, Untersuchungen der Zweigstelle Kairo des Österreichischen archäologischen Institutes 6 (Vienna: Österreichischen Akademie der Wissenschaften, 1984), 24–27, 91–100. For these tombs and chapels at Medinet Habu being related to developing beliefs concerning the Mound of Djeme, see Claude Traunecker in Traunecker, Le Saout, and Masson, *Chapelle d'Achôris*, 135.

43 Hölscher, *Post-Ramessid Remains*, 3–8, 14–16, 34. These structures have sometimes been referred to briefly in other publications (e.g., Eigner, *Die monumentalen*

Grabbauten der Spätzeit, 100–102) and at greater length in Rachel Campbell, "An Archaeological Study of Egyptian Houses, Particularly Those from the Hellenistic Period" (Ph.D. diss., University of Durham, England, 1984).

44 Herbert E. Winlock, *Excavations at Deir el Bahri, 1911–1931* (New York: Macmillan, 1942), presents a summary of the major works of the Metropolitan Museum of Art at Deir el-Bahri.

45 PM, 2d ed., vol. 1, pt. 2, 628–30, 649, 652–54, and (south of Deir el-Bahri) 668. For some studies utilizing these objects, see Andrzej Niwiński, *21st Dynasty Coffins from Thebes: Chronological and Typological Studies*, Theben 5 (Mainz: Philipp von Zabern, 1988), which includes a brief discussion of the Metropolitan excavations (pp. 27–28) and eleven MMA-excavated coffins (nos. 44, 146, 308–16) as well as five coffins (nos. 175–79) probably from TT 60, excavated by Winlock; idem, *Studies on the Illustrated Theban Funerary Papyri of the 11th and 10th Centuries B.C.*, Orbis Biblicus et Orientalis 86 (Freiburg: Universitätsverlag; Göttingen: Vandenhoeck und Ruprecht, 1989), whose catalogue includes twelve MMA-excavated papyri (Cairo 2–3, New York 4–10, 12–14) and discussions.

46 To cite some recent examples, Andrzej Niwiński, "Three More Remarks in the Discussion of the History of the Twenty-first Dynasty," *BES* 6 (1984): 81–88, and idem, *21st Dynasty Coffins from Thebes*, 44–45, used mainly the decoration of the coffins and a funerary papyrus of a woman named Nauny excavated by Winlock to date her earlier than previously thought and to identify her as a daughter of Herihor, an argument that has not received universal acceptance. See reviews of Niwiński by David Aston (*JARCE* 28 [1991]: 234) and Reijer van Walsem ("The Study of 21st Dynasty Coffins from Thebes," *Bibliotheca Orientalis* 50 [January–May 1993]: cols. 9–90).

47 See PM, 2d ed., vol. 1, pt. 1, 387–88, to which add PM, 2d ed., vol. 1, pt. 2, xxii; Richard Fazzini et al., *Ancient Egyptian Art in the Brooklyn Museum* (Brooklyn: Brooklyn Museum; New York: Thames and Hudson, 1989), no. 73; Eigner, *Die monumentalen Grabbauten der Spätzeit*, 50, 51, 98.

48 See PM, 2d ed., vol. 1, pt. 1, 357–59, to which add Eigner, *Die monumentalen Grabbauten der Spätzeit*, 53, 63, 69, 79, 80, 85–87, 95, 118–19, 126, 138, 188, pl. 18. For the recent restoration of this tomb, see Mohammed A. Nasr, "Report on the Restoration of the Tomb of Pabasa (TT 279),"

MDAIK 41 (1985): 189–96, pls. 26–27. Some American studies of decorated tombs of the 25th–26th Dynasties at Thebes are Nancy Thomas, "A Typological Study of Saite Tombs at Thebes" (Ph.D. diss., University of California, Los Angeles, 1980); Edna Russmann, "Harwa as Precusor of Mentuemhat," in *Artibus Aegypti*, 137–46; idem, "Relief Decoration in the Tomb of Montuemhat," *JARCE* 31 (1994): 1–19. Another American publication deals with the archaizing of this era, including tomb reliefs such as those of Nespeqashuty and, to be sure, Pabasa: Peter Der Manuelian, *Living in the Past: Studies in Archaism of the Egyptian Twenty-sixth Dynasty* (London and New York: Kegan Paul, 1994).

49 PM, vol. 7, 276–89. The restoration work was directed by French architect and archaeologist Emile Baraize of the Egyptian Antiquities Service.

50 It is perhaps worth noting that inscriptional evidence unearthed here by the Metropolitan Museum of Art was one basis for reestablishing the correct order of the 30th Dynasty kings Nectanebo I and II, reversed by Auguste Mariette; see Herbert E. Winlock et al., *The Temple of Hibis in El Khargeh Oasis*, vol. 1, *The Excavations*, MMA Egyptian Expedition 13 (New York: MMA, 1941), 26.

51 H. Evelyn White and James Oliver, *The Temple of Hibis in El Khargeh Oasis*, vol. 2, *Greek Inscriptions*, MMA Egyptian Expedition 14 (New York: MMA, 1938); Winlock et al., *Excavations*; Norman de Garis Davies, *The Temple of Hibis in El Khargeh Oasis*, vol. 3, *The Decoration*, ed. Ludlow Bull and L. Hall, MMA Egyptian Expedition 17 (New York: MMA, 1953).

52 On this sanctuary and its decoration, see, most recently, Eugene Cruz-Uribe, *Hibis Temple Project*, vol. 1, *Translations, Commentary, Discussions, and Sign List* (San Antonio, Texas: Van Siclen Books, 1988), 192–98; Jürgen Osing, "Zur Anlage und Dekoration des Tempels von Hibis," in *Studies in Egyptology Presented to Miriam Lichtheim*, vol. 2, ed. S. Israelit-Groll (Jerusalem: Magness Press, Hebrew University, 1990), 763–67; Heike Sternberg-el Hotabi, "Die 'Götterliste' des Sanktuars im Hibis-Temple von El-Chargeh: Überlegungen zur Tradierung und Kodifizierung religiösen und kultopographischen Gedankengutes," in *Aspekte spätägyptischer Kultur*, 239–54; see also note 54 below.

53 Winlock et al., *Excavations*, 10, 14, 27. On p. 23 Winlock comments on an alternation of capital types prefiguring related usages in Ptolemaic times. For a recent discussion of composite capitals, see Maureen Haneborg-Lühr, "Les chapiteaux composites: Etude typologique, stylistique et statistique," in *Amosiadès: Mélanges offerts au Professeur Claude Vandersleyen par ses anciens étudiants*, ed. Claude Obsomer and A. L. Oosthoek (Louvain-la-Neuve: Université catholique de Louvain, Institut orientaliste, Collège Erasme, 1992), 125–51, esp. 132–34.

54 Osing, "Zur Anlage und Dekoration des Tempels von Hibis," 751–63; idem, "Zum den Osiris-Raümen im Tempel von Hibis," in *Hommage à François Daumas* (Montpellier: Université de Montpellier, 1986), 511–16, for comments on earlier and later related phenomena.

55 Cruz-Uribe, *Translations, Commentary, Discussions, and Sign List*; idem, "The Hibis Temple Project, 1984–85 Field Season, Preliminary Report," *JARCE* 23 (1986): 157–66; idem, "Hibis Temple Project: Preliminary Report, 1985–1986, and Summer 1986 Field Seasons," *Varia Aegyptiaca* 3 (1987): 215–30. Idem, "Oasis of the Spirit," *Archaeology* 42 (September–October 1989): 48–53, is a more popular article dealing

with the mission's work and Cruz-Uribe's interpretation (p. 52) of the decoration of the temple, including the sanctuary, as representing Amun-Re as "not the only god" but as "chief god" who "assumes all the attributes and powers of all the other gods in his many forms."

56 Cruz-Uribe, "Hibis Temple Project: Preliminary Report, 1985–1986 and Summer 1986 Field Seasons," 225–30. Winlock believed the present Hibis temple, which he considered 27th Dynasty and later, replaced a 26th Dynasty shrine and possibly included an image of a deceased king Psamtik II (*Excavations*, 5–6).

57 For a recent description of Memphis, including references to archaeological work there, see David Jeffreys, *The Survey of Memphis*, pt. 1, *The Archaeological Report*, Egypt Exploration Society Occasional Publications 3 (London: Egypt Exploration Society, 1985).

58 PM, 2d ed., vol. 3, pt. 2, fasc. 3, 853–54. See also Kitchen, *The Third Intermediate Period*, 279; Jeffreys, *Archaeological Report*, 24–25, fig. 15.

59 E.g., Kitchen, *The Third Intermediate Period*, 187–89, 560; Alan Schulman, "Two Unrecognized Monuments of Shedsunefertem," *JNES* 39 (1980): 303–11.

60 PM, 2d ed., vol. 3, pt. 2, fasc. 3, 830–31. See also Jeffreys, *Archaeological Report*, 40–42, fig. 10; Anthony Leahy, "The Earliest Dated Monument of Amasis and the End of the Reign of Apries," *JEA* 74 (1988): 196–97.

61 For the most recent study of these reliefs as a whole, see Werner Kaiser, "Die dekorierte Torfassade des spätzeitlichen Palastbezirkes von Memphis," *MDAIK* 43 (1987): 123–54.

62 Clarence Fisher, "The Eckley B. Coxe, Jr., Egyptian Expedition: Memphis," *Museum Journal* 8 (December 1917): 211.

63 See esp. ibid.; see also PM, 2d ed., vol. 3, pt. 2, fasc. 3, 856–61; Jeffreys, *Archaeological Report*, 66–67, fig. 13. On Clarence Fisher and his work, see David O'Connor and David Silverman, "The Museum in the Field," *Expedition* 21 (Winter 1979): 22–26.

64 Alan Schulman, "A Problem of Pedubasts," *JARCE* 5 (1966): 35–41, pl. 13; idem, "Two Unrecognized Monuments of Shedsunefertem"; idem, "Memphis, 1915–1923: The Trivia of an Excavation," in *Memphis et ses nécropoles au Nouvel Empire: Nouvelles données, nouvelles questions*, ed. A.-P. Zivie, Actes du Colloque international Centre national de la recherche scientifique,

Paris, 9 au 11 octobre 1986 (Paris: Centre national de la recherche scientifique, 1988), 81–91. The latter includes a list of Third Intermediate and Late Period stelae (p. 83, n. 13) and statuary (p. 86, nn. 47, 48).

65 PM, 2d ed., vol. 3, pt. 2, fasc. 3, 843–45. See also Jeffreys, *Archaeological Report*, 16, 22, 23, 63, 64, 70, 71, 73.

66 The inscribed objects include parts of two more 21st Dynasty doors of important Memphite priests; see Rudolf Anthes, Hasan S. K. Bakry, and William K. Simpson, "Special Groups of Finds," in Rudolf Anthes et al., *Mit Rahineh 1956* (Philadelphia: University Museum, University of Pennsylvania, 1965), 91–95, pls. 31–33.

67 Jeffreys, *Archaeological Report*, 16. See also O'Connor and Silverman, "The Museum in the Field," 29–32.

68 John Dimick, "The Embalming House of the Apis Bulls," in Anthes, *Mit Rahineh 1955*, 75–79. See also Jeffreys, *Archaeological Report*, 15, 22, 38, 65, 74, figs. 15, 25.

69 Michael Jones and Angela Milward Jones, "The Apis House Project at Mit Rahinah: First Season, 1982," *JARCE* 19 (1982): 51–58; idem, "The Apis House Project at Mit Rahinah: Preliminary Report of the Second

and Third Seasons, 1982–1983," *JARCE* 20 (1983): 33–45; idem, "The Apis Project in Mit Rahinah," *NARCE*, no. 125 (Spring 1984): 14–22; idem, "Apis Expedition at Mit Rahinah: Preliminary Report of the Fourth Season, 1984," *JARCE* 22 (1985): 17–28; idem, "The Apis House Project at Mit Rahinah: Preliminary Report of the Fifth Season, 1984–1985," *JARCE* 24 (1987): 35–46; idem, "The Apis House Project at Mit Rahinah, Preliminary Report of the Sixth Season, 1986," *JARCE* 25 (1988): 105–16; Michael Jones, "The Temple of Apis in Memphis," *JEA* 76 (1990): 141–47.

70 PM, 2d ed., vol. 3, pt. 2, fasc. 3, 841–42.

71 Mustafa el-Amir, "The ΕΗΚΟΣ of Apis at Memphis: A Season of Excavations at Mit Rahinah in 1941," *JEA* 34 (1948): 51–56; John Dimick, "The Embalming house of the Apis Bulls," *Archaeology* 11 (Autumn 1958): 183–89.

72 See esp. Jones, "The Temple of Apis in Memphis," which summarizes the work of the mission and its interpretation of the structure's history and significance.

73 PM, 2d ed., vol. 3, pt. 1, 17–19.

74 Michael Jones and Angela Milward, "Survey of the Temple of Isis, Mistress-of-the-Pyramid, at Giza, 1980 Season: Main Temple Area," *JSSEA* 12 (1982): 139–51.

75 Christiane Zivie-Coche, *Giza au premier millénaire: Autour du temple d'Isis, dame des pyramides* (Boston: MFA, 1991).

76 The two most famous are the temples at Philae and Behbeit el-Hagar. For Philae, see Gerhard Haeny, "A Short Architectural History of Philae," *BIFAO* 85 (1985): 197–233, with references on p. 198 to articles on reused temple remains there of the 25th, 26th, and 30th Dynasties. Eleni Vassilika, *Ptolemaic Philae*, Orientalia Lovaniensia Analecta 34 (Louvain: Peeters Press, 1989), also contains some comments on pre-Ptolemaic structures. For Behbeit el-Hagar, see Christine Favard Meeks, *Le temple de Behbeit el-Hagara: Essai de reconstruction et d'interprétation*, SAK Beiheft 6 (1991). For a very small 22d Dynasty temple of Isis at Karnak, see Donald Redford, "New Light on Temple J at Karnak," *Orientalia* 55 (1986): 1–15. De Meulenaere, "Isis et Mout du mammisi," 25–29, covers inscriptional evidence for a Ramesside *mammisi* of Isis at Abydos, and a statue of Isis of the Mammisi is depicted on the (probably) 26th Dynasty

Inventory Stela from Giza's temple of Isis, Mistress of the Pyramids; see Zivie-Coche, *Giza au premier millénaire*, 232.

77 Zivie-Coche, *Giza au premier millénaire*, 308–9.

78 Donald Hansen, "Mendes 1965 and 1966 I: The Excavations at Tell el Rubʿa," *JARCE* 6 (1967): 5–10; Christine Sogher [Lilyquist], "Mendes 1965 and 1966 II: Inscriptions from Tell el Rubʿa," *JARCE* 6 (1967): 16–32. For a reconstruction drawing of these naoi, see Dieter Arnold, *Die Tempel Ägyptens: Götterwohnungen, Kultstätten, Baudenkmäler* (Zurich: Artemis und Winkler, 1992), 216. Arnold's assignment of specific gods to specific naoi differs somewhat from that proposed in Bernard V. Bothmer, "The Great Naos at Mendes and Its Sculpture," in *The Archaeology of the Nile Delta, Egypt: Problems and Priorities: Proceedings of the Seminar Held in Cairo, 19–22 October 1986, on the Occasion of the Fifteenth Anniversary of the Netherlands Institute of Archaeology and Arabic Studies in Cairo*, ed. E. van den Brink (Amsterdam: Netherlands Foundation for Archaeological Research in Egypt, 1988), 206. Arnold also observes (p. 203) that the room containing the 26th Dynasty shrines was too large to be roofed and, while noting some partial Egyptian prototypes

for shrines being exposed to the sun in this manner, suggests a possible relationship to contemporary Ionian hypaethral temples.

79 Bothmer, "The Great Naos at Mendes." It should be noted that Bothmer, who was most famous for his research on Late Period statuary, together with Emma Swan Hall, functioned as coeditor for two monographs on Mendes: Robert Holz et al., *Mendes*, vol. 1, ed. Emma Swan Hall and Bernard V. Bothmer (Cairo: ARCE, 1980), which includes descriptions of the related sites of Mendes and Thmuis, a history of their cartography, and a discussion of their geography; and Herman De Meulenaere and Pierre MacKay, *Mendes*, vol. 2, ed. Emma Swan Hall and Bernard V. Bothmer (Warminster: Aris and Phillips, 1976), which deals with such subjects as the history of the site and objects at or from the site.

80 Karen Wilson et al., *Mendes: Preliminary Report on the 1979 and 1980 Seasons*, vol. 2 of *Cities of the Delta*, ARCE Reports 5 (Malibu, Calif.: Undena Publications, 1982).

81 Susan Allen and Karen Wilson, "Excavations at Mendes, 1976–1979," in *L'égyptologie en 1979: Axes prioritaires de recherches*, vol. 1 (Paris: Centre national de la recherche scientifique, 1982), 143.

82 Nancy Lovell, "Mendes 1992: Physical Anthropological Research, University of Alberta," *Canadian Mediterranean Institute Bulletin* 13 (April 1993): 5.

83 Donald Redford, "The 1992 Excavations at Mendes, Lower Egypt," *Canadian Mediterranean Institute Bulletin* 13 (April 1993): 4, which includes a plan of the area as excavated. For a photograph of the sarcophagus before excavation, see Holz et al., *Mendes*, pl. 32d.

84 Donald Redford, "Excavations at Mendes," *Canadian Mediterranean Institute Bulletin* 14 (October 1994): 3.

85 Donald Redford, "The 1991 Preliminary Field Season at Tell er-Rubʿa (Mendes)," *NARCE*, no. 155 (Fall 1991): 4; idem in Donald Redford et al., "Three Seasons in Egypt: III. The First Season of Excavations at Mendes (1991)," *JSSEA* 18 (1988): 53–55; Susan Redford, "Mendes: L Trench," *JSSEA* 18 (1988): 64–67; and Steven Shubert and Rexine Hummel, "Preliminary Ceramic Analysis: Mendes L Trench," *JSSEA* 18 (1988): 67–70.

86 Redford, "The 1992 Excavations at Mendes."

87 See above, p. 112 and notes 13, 14. See also Kitchen, *The Third Intermediate Period*, 579–80; Patricia Spencer and Anthony Spencer, "Notes on Late Libyan Period Egypt," *JEA* 72 (1986): 198–201.

88 Carol Redmount and Renée Friedman, "The 1993 Field Season of the Berkeley Tell el-Muqdam Project: Preliminary Report," *NARCE*, no. 164 (Winter 1994): 4.

89 Carol Redmount and Renée Friedman, "Tell el-Muqdam: City of Lions," *Egyptian Archaeology: Bulletin of the Egypt Exploration Society* 3 (1993): 37.

90 See Redmount and Friedman, "1993 Field Season," 10.

91 John S. Holladay Jr. et al., *Tell el-Maskhuta: Preliminary Report on the Wadi Tumilat Project, 1978–1979*, vol. 3 of *Cities of the Delta*, ARCE Reports 6 (Malibu, Calif.: Undena Publications, 1982), 1.

92 Ibid., 5–9; Carol Redmount, "On an Egyptian/Asiatic Frontier: An Archaeological History of the Wadi Tumilat" (Ph.D. diss., University of Chicago, 1989).

93 Redmount, "On an Egyptian/Asiatic Frontier," 15–16. For Tell el-Rataba, see also Manfred Bietak's review of Holladay, *Tell el-Maskhuta*, in *Bibliotheca Orientalis* 61 (September–November 1984): cols. 619–22.

94 Patricia Paice, "A Preliminary Analysis of Some Elements of the Saite and Persian Period Pottery at Tell el-Maskhuta," *BES* 8 (1986–87): 95–107; idem, "The Punt Relief, the Pithom Stele, and the Periplus of the Erythraean Sea," in *Proceedings of the 33d International Congress of Asian and North African Studies* (Toronto: University of Toronto Press, 1990), 1–9.

95 E.g., Holladay, *Tell el-Maskhuta*, 50–55, 80–131, including pls. 2–27; Paice, "Preliminary Analysis."

96 Holladay et al., *Tell el-Maskhuta*, 18–28.

From Dusk to Dawn: The American Discovery of Ptolemaic and Roman Egypt

Robert S. Bianchi

But, hey, how many Journal readers care one way or the other about Greco-Roman Egypt anyway?[1]

An inherent prejudice has dominated and continues to dominate attitudes toward the Ptolemaic and Roman legacy of ancient Egypt. A contributing factor is, no doubt, the cultural complexity of the two periods, whose serious study requires competence not only in Ptolemaic hieroglyphs, which number more than five thousand signs, a sevenfold increase over the seven hundred or so used in classic Middle Egyptian,[2] but also in hieratic, demotic, Greek, some Latin, and Coptic. Few individuals are well versed in all these areas, and consensus on issues often-times emerges only after international symposia are convened and their proceedings published.[3] The results of such symposia and continued research on the material culture of ancient Egypt from these two periods provide a wealth of information unattested in the earlier, pharaonic periods.[4]

Many Americans had their first exposure to Ptolemaic and Roman Egypt in the late eighteenth and early nineteenth centuries, through exhibitions of private collections.[5] Henry Abbott's collection, for example, which contained a number of Ptolemaic and Roman pieces,[6] was exhibited in New York in 1853.

The exhibition and the reassessment of ancient Egyptian antiquities continue to contribute to an understanding of Ptolemaic and Roman Egypt. Some recent shows have drawn almost exclusively on the sponsoring institution's own collections, such as the laudable series mounted by the Kelsey Museum of Archaeology at the University of Michigan, Ann Arbor.[7] Others have been international extravaganzas. Of these, the epic *Egyptian Sculpture of the Late Period, 700 B.C. to A.D. 100* (see fig. 88), mounted by Bernard V. Bothmer at the Brooklyn Museum in 1960, masterfully intercalated the sculptural achievements of the Ptolemaic and Roman periods into the framework of Egyptian art of the Late Period in general.[8]

FIGURE 88
Installation view of
*Egyptian Sculpture of
the Late Period, 700
B.C. to A.D. 100*, at the
Brooklyn Museum,
October 18, 1960 to
January 9, 1961.

FIGURE 89
West half of the façade
of chapel D in the
precinct of Mut, South
Karnak, showing the
lower portion of a scene
of a king before a god-
dess, as excavated in
1977 by the Brooklyn
Museum. The sketch
made by Charles Edwin
Wilbour on January 29,
1886, which shows the
now-missing upper part
of the scene, identifies
the king as Ptolemy VIII
(called IX in the sketch)
and the goddess as Mut.

An American Research Center in Egypt (ARCE) project, again under the able direction of Bothmer, resulted in the publication of catalogues for the Luxor Museum,[9] whose collection includes several monuments from the Ptolemaic and Roman periods. And this author initiated two projects intended to promote a greater understanding of these two periods: the exhibition *Cleopatra's Egypt: Age of the Ptolemies*,[10] which opened at the Brooklyn Museum in 1988, and an ARCE project to catalogue masterpieces of the Graeco-Roman Museum, Alexandria.

The first American to devote himself to Egyptology and to impose the rigors of a scientific method on his work was doubtless Charles Edwin Wilbour.[11] He worked in Egypt each season from December 1880 until May 1891, and he painstakingly recorded his observations in Pitman, an early version of shorthand, in a series of notebooks. These notebooks, and Wilbour's meticulously annotated private library (housed at the Brooklyn Museum), together with his edited letters,[12] contain a wealth of information about the Ptolemaic and Roman periods. At a time when few realized that the Thebaid had indeed seceded from Alexandria during the Ptolemaic period and was being ruled by two counterkings, Wilbour recorded a scarab naming one of these individuals.[13] Moreover, his notebooks contain hand copies of Ptolemaic inscriptions from the precinct of the goddess Mut at southern Karnak, the upper portions of which have long since disappeared (see fig. 89). His copies, therefore, have enabled the mission working this site (under the direction of Richard Fazzini of the Brooklyn Museum) to restore the inscriptions. In addition, Wilbour was an inveterate collector, intrigued more often than not by the unusual and the bizarre object, as demonstrated by his acquisition of a statuette of a falcon-headed crocodile (cat. no. 9).

From the turn of the twentieth century to the 1930s excavators of multiperiod sites largely ignored Ptolemaic and Roman remains. This was perhaps due to the comparatively less glamorous nature of later material in contrast to complex pre-Ptolemaic burial goods or the lack of preexisting contextual information for Ptolemaic or Roman sites. For example, the Metropolitan Museum of Art, New York, conducted major campaigns at Thebes between 1910 and 1936, and save for brief notes in various numbers of the museum's *Bulletin*, no monograph was devoted to the material recovered from the Third Intermediate Period to the Roman era. Nonetheless, the staff of the Metropolitan did conscientiously record what it had cleared on a series of tomb cards keyed to excavation photographs and object lists and locations. Using this data, one can more readily analyze the results of a French mission's recent excavations in a necropolis at Dousch,[14] where the material remains parallel to a remarkable degree the Metropolitan finds at Thebes.

The two complexes taken together throw additional light on material remains being uncovered currently by a Canadian mission in the el-Dakhla Oasis.[15] These three projects confirm the putative relationships between the Thebaid and the Western oases by the similarity of their emerging archaeological record, at least for the Ptolemaic and Roman periods.

Excavations of Ptolemaic and Roman Sites

In the Egyptian Delta, Marsa Matruh (ancient Paraetonium) has been the focus of excavations by Donald White for the University of Pennsylvania Museum of Archaeology and Anthropology between 1986 and 1993.[16] Picking up where Oric Bates (1883–1918) left off in 1915, White's mission, while concentrating on the Bronze Age, has uncovered material dating from the second to fifth centuries A.D.,[17] perhaps to be related to a near-contemporary Byzantine church.[18]

Farther to the east, along the Mediterranean coast, is the site of Taposiris Magna, investigated during the 1975–76 season by Edward Ochsenschlager under the auspices of Brooklyn College. The ridge is dominated by a replica[19] of the pharos, or lighthouse, erected at Alexandria, which doubtless served as a funerary monument, to judge by the one tomb immediately beneath it and adjacent structures. Ochsenschlager's team excavated[20] the neighboring temple of Osiris, the interior of which was so altered during the early Christian period, if not earlier, that virtually none of the ground plan can be reconstructed. Inscribed glass foundation deposits,[21] now in London, discovered by workmen in 1818, suggest the temple was erected during the reign of Ptolemy III Euergetes I (r. 246–221 B.C.).

American archaeological projects at Alexandria have been greatly limited by the urban nature of the site. But Alexandria continues to hold a special place in popular imagination as the location of the as yet undiscovered tomb of Alexander the Great and the home of Cleopatra VII. Birger Pearson of the University of California, Santa Barbara, a zealous protector of archaeological remains in the city, did attempt a survey of the Jewish quarter in 1987–89.[22]

Missions in the Delta proper have included work at Ptolemaic and Roman levels at Mendes,[23] under the auspices first of New York University and then of the University of Toronto. The Brooklyn Museum, the Detroit Institute of Arts, and Brooklyn College shared the one division of objects granted by the Egyptian authorities. Among the finds was an unusual limestone frieze, depicting a feline coursing over the heads of falcons, which might have been dismissed as a forgery had it not come from this controlled excavation (cat. no. 107).

William D. Coulson and Albert Leonard Jr. of the University of Minnesota led a mission to Naukratis, another Delta site, from 1980 to 1986,[24] and John Holladay of the University of Toronto headed the Wadi Tumilat Project from 1978

to 1985.[25] These two sites have yielded little Ptolemaic and Roman material, but the work there has provided a framework within which to regard the development of Alexandria as Egypt's primary port and the Ptolemaic-Roman use of the canal linking the Nile to the Red Sea. The mission to Tell el-Muqdam (Leontopolis), under the auspices of the University of California, Berkeley, may yield valuable information about the site during the Ptolemaic and Roman periods, during which time surviving texts claim an active lion necropolis existed there,[26] similar, perhaps, to the Serapeum for Apis bulls at Saqqara.

Some forty miles northwest of the Giza Plateau lies the site of Kom Abu Billo, or ancient Terenuthis. It was here that a mission dispatched by the University of Michigan, Ann Arbor, uncovered a cemetery of Roman date. Many of its tombs were decorated with stelae (see fig. 90) of such a distinctive style that "Kom Abu Billo stela" has become the descriptive by which others of this typology are labeled (see cat. no. 122). The principal motifs are draped figures, either reclining on *klinai*, or funerary couches, or standing with arms extended in the *orans* gesture. Many are inscribed, often in Greek,[27] yet despite recent attempts to determine the ethnicity of the individuals for whom they were created and the artistic, stylistic antecedents of the stelae themselves,[28] few have been able to improve upon the original suggestions offered by Finley A. Hooper, who saw a strong pharaonic flavor in their style and content.[29]

Work on the Great Sphinx at Giza, sponsored by ARCE, has illuminated the attitude of the Romans toward this icon of ancient Egypt. Roman restorations of the Sphinx were the most ambitious ever undertaken in antiquity (see fig. 91) and included the addition of courses of protective limestone blocks to the paws and flanks of the colossus. Many of these blocks, placed directly over those of Old Kingdom date, were purposefully made smaller than the original ones in order to retain the original proportions and modeling of the beast.

The major Ptolemaic and Roman period site at Karanis[30] was extensively excavated by the University of Michigan, Ann Arbor, between 1924 and 1935 (see figs. 87, 92) and published either singly or jointly by Arthur E. R. Boak and Enoch E. Peterson.[31] Objects recovered from this site and now in the Kelsey Museum of Archaeology have been the subject of several special exhibitions (see cat. nos. 113–19). Boak also led a mission for one season (1931–32) to Dimai when circumstances prevented him from working at Karanis.[32]

The pioneering papyrologists Bernard P. Grenfell (1869–1926) and Arthur S. Hunt (1871–1934) worked in the Ptolemaic-Roman Faiyum at the site of Tebtunis in 1899–1900 as part of the Hearst expedition of the University of California, Berkeley.[33] Four Ptolemaic-Roman items (cat. nos. 109, 120–21) found at the site are representative of the more than seventeen hundred Egyptian objects now in the collections of the university's Phoebe A. Hearst Museum of Anthropology.

American excavations of Ptolemaic and Roman horizons in Middle Egypt sites are limited to Akhmim and the Coptos (Quft)-Quseir corridor. Excavations at Akhmim between 1980 and 1983, under the direction of Sheila McNally of the University of Minnesota, concentrated on Roman pottery[34] and on the development of a computer-assisted database for the analysis of the finds.[35]

Among sites with known Ptolemaic and Roman levels, Coptos has been the objective of three American missions. The earliest was conducted by the University of California, Berkeley, in 1899–1900 near Coptos and at Shurafa. The Museum of Fine Arts, Boston, also worked at Coptos, in 1923, and discovered blocks from

a magnificent gateway inscribed for Ptolemy VIII Euergetes II (cat. no. 111). The best-preserved examples of ancient Egyptian temple architecture in American public collections date from the Ptolemaic and Roman periods and include not only the Coptos gateway but also the temple of Dendur, now reerected in the Metropolitan Museum of Art, New York,[36] and New York City's obelisk, known as Cleopatra's Needle (see fig. 93). Although originally erected at Heliopolis in honor of Tuthmosis III (r. 1479–1425 B.C.), it was admittedly saved from further destruction by P. Rubrius Barbarus, prefect of Egypt, and the architect Pontius, who erected the obelisk in Alexandria in regnal year 18 (13–12 B.C.) of the Roman emperor Augustus. Rededicated at the Metropolitan Museum of Art on February 22, 1881,[37] Cleopatra's Needle now graces Graywacke Knoll in Manhattan's Central Park. Bronze crabs, inscribed in Greek and Latin in commemoration of Barbarus and Pontius, are now in the Metropolitan Museum of Art,[38] where they rank among the first Egyptian antiquities accessioned into the collections.

The University of Pennsylvania Museum of Archaeology and Anthropology did not excavate at Coptos, but it did subscribe to fieldwork conducted there by W. M. Flinders Petrie and shared in the division of the objects recovered.[39] One of these artifacts from the Ptolemaic period, a striding, draped male figure (cat. no. 112), is representative of a statue type first introduced during the fourth century B.C. A series of such statues may have decorated the causeway in front of the Coptos gateway.

Several American missions to the Coptos-Quseir corridor have made tremendous advances toward the understanding of international maritime trade during the Ptolemaic, Roman, and Islamic periods. The University of Michigan, Ann Arbor, in cooperation with the University of Asyut, under the direction of Sharon Herbert and Henry Wright, has been working at Coptos and the Eastern Desert since 1989 but to date has issued only preliminary reports.[40] This project's interest in patterns of trade coincides with that of the Quseir missions under the auspices of the Oriental Institute, the University of Chicago, from 1978 to 1986 under Donald S. Whitcomb and Janet H. Johnson.[41] This work coincides with that conducted by Steven E. Sidebotham, University of Delaware, who began a survey of Roman ports along the Egyptian coast of the Red Sea in 1984–85 before concentrating on Myos Hormos, from 1986 to 1988,[42] and his current site at Abu Sha'ar.[43] David F. Graf of the University of Miami has recently initiated investigations of the Trans-Sinai Roman road between Clysma (Suez) and Aqaba.

The Brooklyn Museum–Detroit Institute of Arts mission to the temple complex of the goddess Mut at southern Karnak, which began its work in 1980, is the longest-running American mission to investigate Ptolemaic and Roman remains at one site. In addition to an intensive investigation of the architectural development of the site, the team is translating[44] and preparing publications of Ptolemaic inscriptional material, which holds the highest relevance for many studies of ancient Egyptian religion.[45]

The western oases are yielding significant results related to the Ptolemaic and Roman periods. The Metropolitan Museum of Art has made a great many small finds from these two periods[46] in the el-Kharga Oasis, at the temple of Hibis and other sites.[47] The Royal Ontario Museum, Toronto, represented by Anthony J. Mills, and the Society for the Study of Egyptian Antiquities, joining forces in a more ambitious el-Dakhla Oasis project, have discovered wall paintings from the Roman period[48] as well as iconography and inscriptions of the Roman temple of Ain Birbiyeh, inscribed for Augustus on a gateway dedicated to the composite deity Amunnakht.[49] The tomb of Kitnes in the hamlet of Ezbet Bashendi is likewise noteworthy for its iconography and the bold quality of its relief sculpting. The dating of this monument is debated, but at least one scholar has placed it within the first century A.D.,[50] thereby making it the most recent of all monumental private tombs from Egypt decorated in relief in purely pharaonic style.

Sites containing Ptolemaic and Roman remains in Nubia are treated elsewhere in this volume, but the work by William Y. Adams, University of Kentucky at Lexington, conducted on behalf of the Egypt Exploration Society from 1980 to 1986 at Qasr Ibrim, or Primis, deserves mention. This site was pivotal in the power struggle between the legions of the Roman emperor Augustus and the candace (reigning queen) who opposed him.[51] It reveals an extensive Ptolemaic occupation antedating these events, particularly in its enclosure walls, and in the discovery of at least one draped, striding male figure of the type commonly dedicated in Egyptian temples of the Ptolemaic period.[52]

THE MATERIAL REMAINS from the Ptolemaic and Roman periods are too often consigned to the gloom of basements, their documentation filed away in dusty archives. And yet, as modern excavation techniques are employed, American missions in the field are painstakingly beginning to break through the darkness. With the perseverance of field excavator and museum curator, and with adequate funding, the Ptolemaic and Roman periods of ancient Egypt will emerge from the shadows.

Notes

1 Rejoinder by G. Chaturachinda, "And a Complaint from Thailand," *KMT* 4 (Winter 1993–94): 3, to [Dennis C. Forbes], "Editor's Report," *KMT* 4 (Summer 1993): 10.

2 Christiane Ziegler, "Les hiéroglyphes et leur disposition," in Galeries nationales du Grand Palais, *Naissance de l'écriture: Cunéiformes et hiéroglyphes* (Paris: Ministère de la culture, Réunion des musées nationaux, 1982), 119. Few realize that the Rosetta Stone, now in the British Museum, London (acc. no. 24: Carol Andrews, *The Rosetta Stone* [London: British Museum Publications, 1981]) is dated to 27 March 196 B.C., in the reign of Ptolemy V Epiphanes. The deciphering of the hieroglyphs by Jean-François Champollion is all the more remarkable, therefore, because the text of this document belongs to this tradition of five thousand signs.

3 Janet H. Johnson, ed., *Life in a Multi-Cultural Society: Egypt from Cambyses to Constantine and Beyond*, Studies in Ancient Oriental Civilization 51 (Chicago: Oriental Institute, University of Chicago, 1992), is a particularly good example of this trend, as was the subject of one of the more recent ARCE-sponsored symposia in New York; see S. Aspropoulos, "Late Egyptian Art:

A Symposium Held in Honour of Professor Bernard V. Bothmer," *Minerva* 3 (1992): 13ff.

4 Serge Sauneron, *Un traité égyptien d'ophiologie: Papyrus du Brooklyn Museum Nos. 47.218.48 et. 85*, Bibliothèque générale 11 (Cairo: IFAO, 1989), and Richard Jasnow, *A Late Period Hieratic Wisdom Text (P. Brooklyn 47.218.135)*, Studies in Ancient Oriental Civilization 52 (Chicago: Oriental Institute, University of Chicago, 1992), represent two such works. The dates of these papyri are not firmly established, but if both were composed in the fourth century B.C., before the beginning of the Ptolemaic period, they nevertheless anticipated the creativity and profundity of intellectual exegesis revealed in the hieroglyphic temple texts of the Ptolemaic and Roman periods (see Serge Sauneron, *Esna*, vol. 8, *L'écriture figurative dans les textes d'Esna* [Cairo: IFAO, 1982]), and provide unprecedented windows for an understanding of the preceding pharaonic periods.

5 See Andrew Oliver Jr., *Beyond the Shores of Tripoli: American Archaeology in the Eastern Mediterranean, 1789–1879*, exh. cat. (Cambridge: Fogg Art Museum, Harvard University; Washington, D.C.: Washington Society of the Archaeological Institute of America, 1979), 7–12.

6 Among the more important Ptolemaic and Roman period objects acquired by the Brooklyn Museum in 1948 from the Abbott collection, via the New-York Historical Society, are no. 37.1345E (a naos stela inscribed in Greek; see G. Lacaze et al., "Deux documents memphites copiés par J. M. Vansleb au XVIIe siècle," *RdE* 35 [1984]: 132ff.), no. 37.1509 (an image of Tutu; see J. Quaegebeur, "Divinités égyptiennes sur des animaux dangereux," in *L'animal, l'homme, le dieu dans le Proche-Orient ancien: Actes du colloque de Cartigny, 1981*, Les cahiers de CEPOA 2 [Leuven: Editions Peeters, 1985] 131–43); and no. 37.1522E (a head of the Serapis-Amun; G. Grimm, "Ein Kopf des Ammon-Serapis aus Elephantine," *MDAIK* 28 (1972): 143.

7 Elaine K. Gazda et al., *Guardians of the Nile: Sculptures from Karanis in the Fayoum (c. 250 B.C.–A.D. 450)*, exh. cat. (Ann Arbor: Kelsey Museum of Archaeology, University of Michigan, 1978); Margaret Cool Root, *Faces of Immortality: Egyptian Mummy Masks, Painted Portraits, and Canopic Jars in the Kelsey Museum of Archaeology*, exh. cat. (Ann Arbor: Kelsey Museum of Archaeology, University of Michigan, 1979); and Elaine K. Gazda et al., *The Art of the Ancient Weaver: Textiles from Egypt (4th–12th century A.D.)*,

exh. cat. (Ann Arbor: Kelsey Museum of Archaeology, University of Michigan, 1980).

8 Bernard V. Bothmer, *Egyptian Sculpture of the Late Period, 700 B.C. to A.D. 100*, exh. cat. (Brooklyn: Brooklyn Museum, 1960), is remarkable as one of the very few exhibition catalogues exploring a rarified topic ever to be reprinted (1973).

9 *The Luxor Museum of Ancient Egyptian Art 1: Catalogue* (Cairo: ARCE, 1979), for which there are smaller, abridged versions in Arabic, English, French, and German.

10 Robert S. Bianchi et al., *Cleopatra's Egypt: Age of the Ptolemies*, exh. cat. (Brooklyn: Brooklyn Museum, 1988).

11 Deborah J. McLeod, "Abu-Dign, Bearing Gifts from Egypt," *Art Gallery* 22 (December–January 1979): 100–101, is a sensitive, albeit brief, biographical sketch of this remarkable individual, whose accomplishments include the translation of Victor Hugo's *Les misérables* into English, as described by Bannon McHenry in a recent letter to the editor of the *New York Times*.

12 Charles Edwin Wilbour, *Travels in Egypt (December 1880 to May 1891): Letters of Charles Edwin Wilbour*, ed. Jean Capart (Brooklyn: Brooklyn Museum, 1936).

Among Wilbour's wide-ranging, perceptive observations were his comments on the so-called Famine Stela on the island of Siheil, dated to the reign of Ptolemy II Philadelphus; see W. Plyte, "Schenkings-oorkonde van Sehéle uit het 18de Jaar van Koning Tosertasis," *Mededeelingen der koninklijke Akademie van Wetenschappen, Afdeeling Letterkunde*, 3d ser., 8 (1891): 1–5.

13 Plyte, "Schenkings-oorkonde," 52, where the name is given as Anch Hor. The readings of the names have been emended, that of Anch Hor now reads Ankh-wen-nefer; see W. Clarysse, in W. Clarysse and Herman De Meulenaere, "Notes de prosopographie thébaine," *Chronique d'Egypte* 106 (1978): 246.

14 Françoise Dunand et al., *La nécropole de Douch (Oasis de Kharga): Exploration archéologique: Structures sociales, économiques, religieuses de l'Egypte romaine* (Cairo: IFAO, 1992).

15 I have been permitted to examine these remains in photographs and slides through the kindness of Ted Brock.

16 Because several of the missions under discussion first began their work in the 1990s, the teams in the field have not had sufficient time to publish extensive excavation reports.

17 Jean Leclant and Gisele Clerc, "Fouilles et travaux en Egypte et au Soudan," *Orientalia* 58 (1989): 337, no. 2.

18 R. G. Goodchild, "A Byzantine Chapel at Marsa Matruh," *JARCE* 28 (1991): 201–11. Supervised archaeological activity in this area is exceedingly important because of recent looting, see *Al-Ahram Weekly* (30 April 1992), as reported in N. Grimal, ed., *Bulletin d'information en archéologie* 5 (January–June 1992): 38–39.

19 F. el-Fakharani, *The Lighthouse of Abusir in Egypt*, Harvard Studies in Classical Philology 78 (Cambridge: Harvard University Press, 1974): 275ff.

20 Edward Ochsenschlager, "Taposiris Magna: 1975 Season," in *Acts: First International Congress of Egyptology, Cairo, 2–10 October 1976*, ed. Walter F. Reineke, Schriften zur Geschichte und Kultur des alten Orients 14 (Berlin: Akademie-Verlag, 1979), 503ff. Ochsenschlager presented a paper on his work at the annual ARCE meeting in Baltimore in 1975, and a brief note was also published by Peter Dorman, "Diary of a Dig," *Science Digest* 80 (September 1976): 38ff.

21 London, The British Museum 1985.10-30.2 and 1985.10-30.3; M. Bimson and I. C. Freestone, "Some Egyptian Glasses Dated by Royal Inscriptions," *Journal of the Glass Society* 30 (1988): 11–15.

22 B. Pearson, "The New Alexandria Library: Promise or Threat?" *NARCE*, no. 158–59 (Summer–Fall 1992): 31, to which add the open letter on the same issue available from Pearson.

23 K. Briggs, "A Season at Mendes," *Institute of Fine Arts News* (New York University) 24 (Winter 1977–78): 5–6; Donald B. Hansen, "Mendes," *JARCE* 4 (1965): 31ff.; idem, *JARCE* 6 (1967): 5ff.; Edward Ochsenschlager, "Excavation of the Graeco-Roman City Thmuis in the Nile Delta," *Annales archéologiques arabes syriennes*, no. 21 (1971): 185 ff.; Robert K. Holz et al., *Mendes I*, ed. Emma Swan Hall and Bernard V. Bothmer (Cairo: ARCE, 1980); Herman De Meulenaere and Pierre MacKay, *Mendes II*, ed. Emma Swan Hall and Bernard V. Bothmer (Warminster, U.K.: Aris and Phillips, 1976); Karen L. Wilson, *Mendes: Preliminary Report on the 1979 and 1980 Seasons*, vol. 2. of *Cities of the Delta*, ARCE Reports 5 (Malibu, Calif.: Undena Publications, 1982); Donald B. Redford, "The 1992 Excavations at Mendes, Lower Egypt," *Canadian Mediterranean Institute* 13, no. 2 (April 1993): 4.

24 William D. Coulson and Albert Leonard, Jr., eds., *Naukratis*, vol. 1 of *Cities of the Delta*, ARCE Reports 4 (Malibu: Undena Publications, 1981); and William D. Coulson, "Ptolemaic and Roman Kilns in the Western Nile Delta," *Bulletin of the American Schools of Oriental Research*, no. 263 (1986): 61–75.

25 John S. Holladay Jr., *Tell el-Maskhuta: Preliminary Report on the Wadi Tumilat Project*, vol. 3 of *Cities of the Delta*, ARCE Reports 6 (Malibu: Undena Publications, 1982); idem, *Tell el-Maskhuta* (Malibu: Undena Publications, 1987).

26 Amsterdam, Allard Pierson Museum no. 7772; see Bianchi et al., *Cleopatra's Egypt*, 212–13, no. 106.

27 G. Wagner, "Inscriptions grecques d'Egypte," *BIFAO* 72 (1972): 139ff.

28 Abd el-Hafeez abd el-Al et al., *Stèles funéraires de Kom Abou Bellou* (Paris: Editions Recherche sur les civilisations, 1985).

29 Finley A. Hooper, *Funerary Stelae from Kom Abou Billou* (Ann Arbor: Kelsey Museum of Archaeology, University of Michigan, 1961).

30 Elaine K. Gazda, ed., *Karanis, an Egyptian Town in Roman Times: Discoveries of the University of Michigan Expedition to Egypt (1924–1935)*, exh. cat. (Ann Arbor: Kelsey Museum of Archaeology, University of Michigan, 1983).

31 Among others Arthur E. R. Boak, ed., *Karanis: The Temples, Coin Hoards, Botanical and Zoological Reports, Seasons 1924–1931* University of Michigan Studies, Humanistic Series 30 (Ann Arbor: University of Michigan Press, 1933); idem, "Selected Papyri from Karanis," *ASAE* 29 (1929): 47ff; Arthur E. R. Boak and Enoch E. Peterson, *Karanis: Topographic and Architectural Report of Excavations during the Seasons 1924–1928*, University of Michigan Studies, Humanistic Series 25 (Ann Arbor: University of Michigan Press, 1931).

32 Arthur E. R. Boak, ed., *Soknopaiou Nesos: The University of Michigan Excavations at Dimê, 1931–32*, University of Michigan Studies, Humanistic Series 39 (Ann Arbor: University of Michigan Press, 1935).

33 Albert B. Elsasser and Vera-Mae Fredrickson, *Ancient Egypt: An Exhibition at the Robert H. Lowie Museum of Anthropology of the University of California, Berkeley*, exh. cat. (Berkeley: Robert H. Lowie Museum of Anthropology, University of California, 1966), 6–7.

34 Sheila McNally, "The Aswan Ware at Akhmim, Egypt," *AJA* 92 (1988): 262.

35 Sheila McNally, "Akhmim Data Base: A Multi-Stage System for Computer-Assisted Analysis of Artifacts," *Journal of Field Archaeology* 11 (1984): 47ff.

36 New York, Metropolitan Museum of Art 68.154: Robert S. Bianchi, *The Temple of Dendur in the Metropolitan Museum of Art*, forthcoming.

37 Martina D'Alton, *The New York Obelisk; or, How Cleopatra's Needle Came to New York and What Happened When It Got Here* (New York: Harry N. Abrams, 1993); *BMMA* 50 (Spring 1994).

38 New York, Metropolitan Museum of Art 81.1–.2; D'Alton, *New York Obelisk*, 22.

39 Sarah Stevenson, "Some Sculptures from Koptos in Philadelphia," *AJA* 10 (1895): 347–50.

40 S. C. Herbert and H. T. Wright, "The University of Michigan/University of Assiut Expedition to Coptos and the Eastern Desert, 1990–1992," *AJA* 97 (1993): 313.

41 R. S. Bagnall, "Papyri and Ostraka from Queseir al-Qadim," *Bulletin of the American Society of Papyrologists* 23 (1986), 1–60; Janet Johnson and Donald Whitcomb, "Qossier el-Qadim und der Rote Meer-Handel," *Das Altertum* 2 (1980): 103ff.; idem, eds., *Quseir al-Qadim 1978: Preliminary Report* (Cairo: ARCE, 1979); idem, *Quseir al-Qadim, 1980*, ARCE Reports 7 (Malibu, Calif.: Undena Publications, 1982).

42 Steven E. Sidebotham, "Archaeological Investigations at Abu Sha'ar," in *ARCE Annual Meeting Abstracts* (Philadelphia: ARCE, 1989), 50–51.

43 Steven E. Sidebotham, "A Roman Fort on the Red Sea Coast," *Minerva* 3 (March–April 1992): 5–8; idem, "University of Delaware Archaeological Project at Abu Sha'ar: The 1990 Season," *NARCE*, no. 153 (Spring 1991): 1–6.

44 Richard A. Fazzini and Richard Jasnow, "Demotic Ostraka from the Mut Precinct in Karnak," *Enchoria* 16 (1986): 23–48.

45 Serge Sauneron, "Les inscriptions ptolémaïque de temple de Mout à Karnak," *Bulletin d'Institut de l'Egypte* 45 (1963–64): 45–52.

46 Herbert E. Winlock, *The Temple of Hibis in El Khargeh Oasis*, vol. 1, *The Excavations*, MMA Egyptian Expedition 13 (New York: MMA, 1941). A number of the finds from el-Kharga are now being studied by Klaus Parlasca with a view toward publication.

47 Norman de Garis Davies, *The Temple of Hibis in El Khargeh Oasis*, vol. 3, *The Decoration*, ed. Ludlow Bull and L. Hall, MMA Egyptian Expedition 17 (New York: MMA, 1953), but see now Eugene Cruz-Uribe, "Hibis Temple Project: Preliminary Report, 1985–1986 and Summer 1986 Field Seasons," *Varia Aegyptiaca* 3 (1987): 215–30, who now redates successive decorative programs.

48 Anthony J. Mills, "Roman Frescoes in the Dakhleh Oasis," *Rotunda* 13, no. 2 (1980): 18ff. with color illustrations.

49 Olaf E. Kaper, "How the God Amon-Nakht Came to Dakhleh Oasis," *JSSEA* 17 (1987): 151–56.

50 Olaf E. Kaper, "Egyptian Toponyms of Dakhla Oasis," *BIFAO* 92 (1992): 120.

51 Robert S. Bianchi, *The Nubians: People of the Ancient Nile* (Brookfield: Millbrook Press, 1994), 48–52.

52 R. D. Anderson and William Y. Adams, "Qasr Ibrim, 1978," *JEA* 65 (1979): 30ff.

The Archaeology of Bronze Age Nubia

Peter Lacovara

The First Archaeological Survey of Nubia

With the exception of a few intrepid explorers, archaeologists largely overlooked Nubia until the beginning of the twentieth century.[1] But with the enlargement of the first dam at Aswan, Nubia became the focus of unprecedented scientific scrutiny. Realizing that archaeological sites would be destroyed, the Egyptian Antiquities Service engaged a young American archaeologist, George Andrew Reisner, to study the area that would soon be covered forever by the floodwaters of the new reservoir.[2] The Antiquities Service could not have made a better choice. Perhaps the most systematic and methodical Egyptologist of his day, Reisner devised the prototypical archaeological survey, which was the forerunner of modern salvage excavation.

The Archaeological Survey of Nubia began in September 1907, with Reisner assisted by English archaeologists Cecil M. Firth (1878–1931) and Aylward M. Blackman (1883–1956). Sailing from one site to the next, Reisner and his staff camped in some of the most barren and forbidding territory imaginable (see fig. 94). Reisner's goals were "the recovery of all the archaeological and [anthropological] material and the reconstruction of the history of the district."[3]

The chronological framework that Reisner devised to order his finds remains the basis for Nubian archaeology today. Working with heretofore unknown cultures, he designated the earliest distinct Nubian culture as the A-Group (Archaic Egypt) and ended his sequence with the X-Group (Byzantine period). His periodization went only as far as the D-Group, equated with the post–New Kingdom occupation of Lower Nubia. The rest of the alphabet was left unused should other cultures be discovered.[4]

Reisner left the survey in 1908 to conduct the Harvard University excavations at Samaria in Palestine and the Harvard-Boston expedition to Giza and elsewhere in Egypt. He left Firth in charge in Nubia and frequently corresponded with him

FIGURE 94
Field camp of the
Archaeological Survey
of Nubia, c. 1907–8.

about the survey and coauthored some of its later reports. Through the courtesy of Firth and the Egypt Antiquities Service, Reisner assembled a type collection of the material he had excavated for the Museum of Fine Arts, Boston.[5] At the end of the survey, in 1911, Firth and Reisner had excavated at 150 sites, from Philae to Dakka, and set the entire framework for the cultural history of Nubia from the Neolithic to Christian periods.

Reisner also advised the American-born Sir Henry Wellcome (1853–1936), who undertook excavations at the site of Gebel Moya, south of Khartoum on the White Nile, from 1910 to 1914.[6] It was a difficult excavation, the site itself consisting of several deflated habitation levels mixed with burials and a number of looter's holes. The occupation appeared to date back at least as early as the Bronze Age and continued into the Meroitic period. The finds consisted of a mix of material familiar from work in Nubia and little-known objects belonging to cultural traditions of more southerly regions.

Wellcome was assisted by Oric Bates, who later excavated at Gamai in Lower Nubia. Bates's excavations for Harvard University at Marsa Matruh,[7] on the Mediterranean coast of Egypt, had been interrupted by the outbreak of World War I. Reisner suggested that he try working at Gamai and later lent him his "right-hand man," Dows Dunham. Gamai was a large cemetery site near Wadi Halfa with burials dating to the A-Group period, the New Kingdom occupation of Nubia, and the late Meroitic period. After Bates's death in the great influenza epidemic of 1918, Dunham published the excavations that he himself had completed.[8]

At this time David Randall-MacIver (1873–1945) and Charles Leonard Woolley (1880–1960), working for the University Museum and the University of Pennsylvania's Eckley B. Coxe Jr. Expedition (see fig. 95), excavated a number of important sites in Nubia, including a small fortified encampment belonging to a late phase of the C-Group culture at Areika.[9] The site covered less than an acre, and within its walls were areas for grain storage, mills, and ovens. Among the artifacts discovered were the typical black incised bowls of the C-Group as well as objects imported from Egypt or strongly influenced by Egyptian wares.[10]

The most impressive site explored by the Coxe expedition was the great fortress of Buhen, one of the largest and most imposing of the mud-brick fortifications built as a chain in the early Middle Kingdom to guard Egypt's Nubian frontier. Its defensive walls, fronted by a deep, dry moat, measured more than a mile in length. Inside were the houses of soldiers as well as temples built of stone

FIGURE 95
The University of Pennsylvania Museum's Coxe expedition to Nubia, c. 1907–11. Field house at Buhen with staff and visitors: Eckley B. Coxe Jr. (seated, center), David Randall-MacIver (standing, third from right), Charles Leonard Woolley (standing, far right).

dating from the New Kingdom reuse of the site. From 1908 to 1910 Randall-MacIver and Woolley uncovered a number of cemeteries dating from the Middle Kingdom through the New Kingdom and recorded the plans of the battlements and the decorated walls of the temples.[11]

FIGURE 96
Tents of the Harvard-Boston expedition beside the Upper Deffufa, Kerma, c. 1913.

The Harvard-Boston Excavations in the Sudan: Kerma

After his preliminary excavations in Egyptian Nubia, Reisner applied to the Sudanese government to survey and excavate the area around Wadi Halfa, particularly the New Kingdom site of Sesebi. Once he was in the Sudan, however, local authorities urged him to work farther south at the site of Kerma, which was threatened by an agricultural irrigation project.[12]

At Kerma, to the east of the Nile above the third cataract, is a wide, lush plain with two massive mud-brick ruins (see fig. 96). These structures, called *deffufa* in the local Nubian dialect, had already been noted by earlier travelers. The Lower Deffufa appears to have been a temple located at the center of a settlement surrounded by workshops and storehouses, where raw materials and imported Egyptian goods were kept and objects for cultic and royal use were manufactured.[13] The Kerma kings imported vast quantities of Egyptian material, including jewelry, stone vessels, and sculpture, to decorate their chapels and outfit their tombs. The other surviving monumental structure, the Upper Deffufa,[14] was situated in an enormous necropolis among great earthen tumuli hundreds of feet in diameter.

Previous to Reisner's work at Kerma, examples of particularly fine, black-topped pottery cups had appeared sporadically in excavations in Egypt, where they were mistakenly attributed to the Pan-Grave culture. Examples also had appeared in some sites discovered in the first Nubian survey, but at Kerma excavators found thousands of samples of the finest possible quality and in myriad forms (see cat. no. 67).[15]

The Kerma artisans were remarkably adept with a variety of materials. They produced large faience tile inlays, glazed quartz jewelry (see cat. no. 70), and sculpture as well as deadly bronze daggers. Through trade and warfare the kingdom of Kerma eventually became powerful enough to invade and control the southernmost portion of Egypt and to enter into an alliance with the Hyksos dynasty against the Theban kings of the Second Intermediate Period.[16]

Reisner was misled by the great quantities of Egyptian imports found at the site, particularly by the beautiful Middle Kingdom statue of the lady Sennuwy

(see fig. 97). He theorized that Sennuwy and her husband, Hepdjefa, had been exiled from Egypt and sent to rule this isolated outpost in Nubia.[17] We now know, however, that the statues were imported into Nubia several hundred years after they had been set up in Egypt and that Kerma was the seat of one of the earliest and grandest of Nubia's own indigenous civilizations.[18]

Excavations at Gebel Barkal

Perhaps Reisner's richest finds of all came from his excavations in the area around the fourth cataract, the great heartland of later Nubian civilization. After defeating the Kerma kingdom at the beginning of the 18th Dynasty, the Egyptians began constructing a series of temples as administrative centers in Nubia. These were first set up in reoccupied Egyptian forts, but by the mid New Kingdom the forts were largely abandoned, and sanctuaries were constructed independently. Ramesses II (r. 1290–1224 B.C.) built many temples in Nubia, the most impressive of which was the great temple at Abu Simbel.

What was to become the most important temple complex in Nubia, however, was that dedicated to Amun at Gebel Barkal.[19] The first temple here seems to have been established by Tuthmosis III (r. 1479–1425 B.C.). Here the illustrious warrior pharaoh set a monumental stela recording his myriad victories in Asia as well as in Nubia. Nearly every pharaoh of the 18th and 19th Dynasties, through Ramesses II, expanded the complex. The temples remained an important cult center long after Nubia had again asserted its independence at the end of the New Kingdom.

The Second Cataract Forts

In addition to excavating the later Kushite royal cemeteries, Reisner also continued work to the north, in the second cataract area, where between 1923 and 1932 the Harvard-Boston mission excavated a number of Egyptian frontier fortresses similar to that at Buhen.[20]

This stretch of the Nile, one of its most inhospitable, is bounded for the most part by trackless desert wastes. Although largely barren agriculturally, the area was rich in gold and valuable as a corridor to the interior of Africa, enabling the trading of ivory, ebony, gold, and animal skins. The Nubian Nile meanders in and out of coarse red sandstone, and in those areas where it cuts into underlying layers of igneous volcanic bedrock, rapids or cataracts are created. The second cataract is known as the Batn el-Hajar, or "belly of rocks," for the numerous rounded granite boulders that appear

there. This dangerous passage filled with eddies and hidden rocks even sank one of the expedition's boats (see fig. 98). The forts built here acted not only as garrisons to maintain order but also as trading posts, not unlike the forts of the American West.

The Harvard-Boston expedition excavated five forts: the twin fortresses of Semna and Kumma, Uronarti, Shalfak, and Mirgissa. Of particular interest were the everyday belongings of soldiers and their families. They possessed not only weapons but mirrors and jewelry of great beauty as well as charming toys and examples of "folk art" produced to make life more pleasurable. Raw ivory along with gold weights and scales attest to the importance of the forts as centers for the transshipment of precious materials.[21]

The objects and inscriptions recovered in the excavations relate that as the fort's residents were cut off from their homeland during the political destabilization of the Second Intermediate Period, they appear to have switched their allegiance to the king of Kush, probably ruling from Kerma.[22] The forts were later restored and enlarged in the 18th Dynasty, when they were reoccupied by the Egyptians.

Later Work in Nubia

Another expansion of the dam at Aswan provided the impetus for the Second Archaeological Survey of Nubia from 1929 to 1934.[23] But no American work was done again in the region until the third and greatest enlargement, the creation of the Aswan High Dam in the 1960s.[24]

The massive scope of the survey was beyond the abilities of the Egyptian and Sudanese governments. They appealed to the United Nations Educational, Scientific, and Cultural Organization (UNESCO) to underwrite and coordinate a worldwide appeal for funds and expertise to salvage those monuments that could be moved and to excavate sites that would be inundated by Lake Nassar, the reservoir created by the High Dam.

More than forty expeditions arrived from all parts of the globe to begin the frantic campaign to wrest what information they could in the face of the advancing floodwaters. A number of American expeditions set to work, including teams from the Oriental Institute of the University of Chicago, which excavated a series of cemeteries around the area of Qustul which held Neolithic, A-Group, C-Group, Kerma culture, New Kingdom Egyptian, and later burials.[25] Another group from the Oriental Institute worked in the forts at Serra, Semna, and Dorginarti.[26] An epigraphic mission from the Oriental Institute recorded the Ramesside temple of Beit el-Wali.[27]

Another survey directed by William Kelly Simpson of Yale University, in conjunction with the University of Pennsylvania, conducted a series of important excavations in the area of Toshka in Lower Nubia (see fig. 99). One of Simpson's most important discoveries was the tomb of a local prince, Hekanefer.[28] In the New Kingdom the C-Group, the remaining Kerma people, and other Nubian groups, particularly the

upper strata of Nubian society, appear to have thoroughly and rapidly taken on Egyptian religious and burial practices. Hekanefer was laid to rest in a typical Egyptian-style tomb with shawabtis (see cat. no. 84) and other standard accoutrements of an Egyptian burial.

The most spectacular efforts of the salvage campaign were the moving of the great temple of Abu Simbel and the temples at Philae. These international efforts were supported by an American society that raised funds for the preservation effort. Chaired by A & P heir Huntington Hartford, the committee included author Pearl S. Buck, actress Joan Crawford, actor Cary Grant, Conrad Hilton, Richard M. Nixon, Senator Claiborne Pell, Marjorie Merriweather Post, journalist Lowell Thomas, and Egyptologists Henry G. Fischer, William Stevenson Smith, and John A. Wilson. The committee raised more than $3.5 million to supplement a $12 million contribution from Congress.

Recent Work on Bronze Age Nubia

Although monumental contributions have been made to the study of the prehistory of the northern Sudan by Fred Wendorf and Anthony Marks,[29] little archaeological work on Bronze Age Nubia has been done by Americans since the close of the UNESCO salvage campaign. As with most archaeological research, however, more important discoveries are made in the analysis and publication of the data recovered than in the actual excavation itself.

William Y. Adams (b. 1927), in *Nubia: Corridor to Africa* (1977) and other publications, has added immeasurably to our knowledge of all phases of Nubian civilization, and Bruce G. Trigger's *History and Settlement in Lower Nubia* (1965) provided a synthesis of Nubian history and settlement patterns.[30] Dunham's publication of the remaining material from Kerma[31] and the work of Brigitte Gratien and the University of Geneva expedition, under the direction of Charles Bonnet, have helped refine the dating and our understanding of the development of the Kerma culture.[32]

Bruce B. Williams (b. 1946) of the University of Chicago has shed important new light on the nature and level of sophistication of the A-Group civilization through his analysis of material from the Oriental Institute's excavations at Qustul.[33] He has been publishing the remainder of the Oriental Institute's excavations at a prodigious pace.[34]

Forthcoming publications of the Old Kingdom Egyptian settlement and the early Nubian material discovered at Buhen by David O'Connor will help to demystify one of the most obscure phases of Nubian history.[35] Analysis of the C-Group finds from Areika by Josef Wegner has amplified our understanding of the Bronze Age in Lower Nubia,[36] as has the study of material from the University of California excavations at the second cataract fortress of Askut.[37]

American Museums and Nubia

In gratitude for the American contributions to the UNESCO campaign, the Egyptian government in 1965 ordered that the temple of Dendur, located in an area below the first cataract which would soon be inundated, be dismantled and given to the United States. This sparked the so-called Dendur Derby, with a number of cities and museums competing for the charming sandstone shrine. William S. Smith of the Museum of Fine Arts, Boston, John D. Cooney of the Cleveland Museum, and Richard Parker of Brown University sat on a confidential panel that advised Washington on the best candidate to receive the temple.[38]

Among the contenders were the Metropolitan Museum of Art, New York; the Smithsonian Institution, Washington D.C.; and the cities of Memphis, Tennessee, and Cairo, Illinois. The Metropolitan eventually was awarded the temple on the strength of its proposal to build a special gallery to house it (see figs. 100, 101).[39]

Beginning with the exhibition *Africa in Antiquity: The Arts of Ancient Nubia and the Sudan*,[40] held at the Brooklyn Museum in 1978, a number of temporary exhibitions and permanent installations have showcased material from Nubia long dismissed as mere provincial versions of Egyptian art. The traveling exhibition from the University Museum in Philadelphia, *Nubia: Egypt's Rival in Africa* (1994),[41] high-lighted the work of the 1907–10 Coxe expedition, and the excavations of the University of Chicago have been the subject of a number of installations at the Oriental Institute Museum. In 1992 the Museum of Fine Arts, Boston, opened a gallery devoted to a small selection of the finds of Reisner and Dunham (see fig. 102), in the same space Dunham had first proposed in 1935.[42]

Notes

I would like to thank Rita E. Freed, curator of the Department of Ancient Egyptian, Nubian, and Near Eastern Art, Museum of Fine Arts, Boston, for permission to use the accompanying photos and illustrations. I am grateful to Joseph Wegner of the University of Pennsylvania for sharing his work on the C-Group settlement at Areika. I would also like to thank Maureen Melton, archivist for the Museum of Fine Arts, for her help in locating unpublished material on the UNESCO committee and the temple of Dendur.

1 William Y. Adams, *Nubia: Corridor to Africa* (Princeton, N.J.: Allen Lane, 1977), 71–90.

2 On the history of the archaeological surveys of Nubia, see ibid. See also *Archaeological Survey of Nubia*, Bulletins 1–7 (Cairo: National Printing Department, 1908–11), and the field reports for 1907 to 1911, published in George A. Reisner et al., *The Archaeological Survey of Nubia*, 8 vols. (Cairo: National Printing Department, 1910–27).

3 George A. Reisner, "Archaeological Survey of Nubia," in *Archaeological Survey of Nubia*, Bulletin 1 (1908), 9.

4 Reisner encountered his groups A through C in the first cemeteries he excavated. He noted that they were three distinct phases of the same cultural type. He equated the A-Group with the period of the first dynasties in Egypt and identified the B-Group as an impoverished descendant of the A-Group. While it has been suggested that the evidence for the B-Group is not compelling (see Harry S. Smith, "The Nubian B-Group," *Kush* 14 [1966]: 69–124), scholars more recently have wondered whether in fact Reisner was correct and that some post–A-Group culture did survive in Lower Nubia. Whether or not this group was ancestral to the C-Group or Kerma cultures remains a matter of speculation (Brigitte Gratien, personal communication).

5 Peter Lacovara and Lisa Heidorn, *The First Archaeological Survey of Nubia: Catalog of Objects and Records in the Museum of Fine Arts, Boston* (Boston: MFA, forthcoming).

6 Frank Addison, *The Wellcome Excavations in the Sudan*, vols. 1–2, *Jebel Moya* (London: Oxford University Press, 1949).

7 Oric Bates, "Excavations at Marsa Matruh," in *Varia Africana*, vol. 4, Harvard African Studies 8 (Cambridge: Peabody Museum, Harvard University, 1927), 123–97.

8 Oric Bates and Dows Dunham, "Excavations at Gammai," in ibid., 1–122.

9 David Randall-MacIver and Charles Leonard Woolley, *Areika*, Eckley B. Coxe Junior Expedition to Nubia 1 (Oxford: Oxford University Press, 1909).

10 David O'Connor, *Nubia: Egypt's Rival in Africa*, exh. cat. (Philadelphia: University Museum, University of Pennsylvania, 1994), 48–50.

11 David Randall-MacIver and Charles Leonard Woolley, *Buhen* (Philadelphia: University Museum, University of Pennsylvania, 1911).

12 George A. Reisner, *Excavations at Kerma, Parts I–III*, Harvard African Studies 5 (Cambridge: Peabody Museum, Harvard University, 1923), 3.

13 Ibid., 21–34; Charles Bonnet, *Kerma, territoire et métropole: Quatre leçons au College de France* (Cairo: IFAO, 1986).

14 Peter Lacovara, "The Funerary Chapels at Kerma," *Cahiers de recherches de l'Institut de papyrologie et d'égyptologie de Lille* 8 (1986): 49–58.

15 George A. Reisner, *Excavations at Kerma, Parts IV–V*, Harvard African Studies 6 (Cambridge: Peabody Museum, Harvard University, 1923), 320–504; Peter Lacovara, "The Internal Chronology of Kerma," *Beiträge zur Sudanforschung* 2 (1987): 51–74.

16 Bruce G. Trigger, *Nubia under the Pharaohs* (Boulder, Colo.: Westview Press, 1976), 103–4.

17 Reisner, influenced by the prejudices of his day, rather fancifully postulated that Sennuwy and her husband, Hepdjefa, were sent to administer an Egyptian trading post at Kerma, and upon his death Hepdjefa "went native" and was buried in local Nubian style; see Reisner, *Kerma I–III*, 556–58.

18 William Y. Adams, "Reflections on the Archaeology of Kerma," in *Ägypten und Kusch*, ed. Steffen Wenig et al., Schriften zur Geschichte und Kultur des alten Orients 13 (Berlin: Akademie-Verlag, 1977), 41–53.

19 Dows Dunham, *The Barkal Temples* (Boston: MFA, 1970).

20 Dows Dunham and Jozef A. Janssen, *The Second Cataract Forts*, vol. 1, *Semna-Kumma* (Boston: MFA, 1960); Dows Dunham, *The Second Cataract Forts*, vol. 2, *Uronarti, Shalfak, and Mirgissa* (Boston: MFA, 1967).

21 Bruce G. Trigger, "The Function of the Second Cataract Forts," *JSSEA* 12, no. 1 (1982): 1–6.

22 Harry S. Smith, *The Fortress of Buhen: The Inscriptions* (London: Egypt Exploration Society, 1976), 66–85.

23 Walter B. Emery and Laurence Kirwan, *Survey between Wadi es-Sebua and Adindan* (Cairo: Cairo Government Press, 1935).

24 Adams, *Nubia*, 81–88; for a popular account of the project, see Leslie Greener, *High Dam over Nubia* (New York: Viking, 1962).

25 Keith C. Seele, "University of Chicago Oriental Institute Nubian Expedition: Excavations between Abu Simbel and the Sudan Border: Preliminary Report," *JNES* 33 (1974): 1–43.

26 George R. Hughes, "Serra East: The University of Chicago Excavations, 1961–62," *Kush* 11 (1963): 112–30.

27 Herbert Ricke, George R. Hughes, and Edward Wente, *The Beit el-Wali Temple of Ramesses II*, OINE 1 (Chicago: Oriental Institute, University of Chicago, 1967).

28 William Kelly Simpson, *Heka-nefer and the Dynastic Material from Toshka and Arminna*, Pennsylvania-Yale Expedition 1 (New Haven: Peabody Museum of Natural History, Yale University, 1963).

29 Fred Wendorf, ed., *Contributions to the Prehistory of Nubia* (Taos, N.M.: Fort Burgwin Research Center; distributed by Southern Methodist University Press, 1965).

30 Adams, *Nubia*; Bruce G. Trigger, *History and Settlement in Lower Nubia* (New Haven: Yale University Press, 1965).

31 Dows Dunham, *Excavations at Kerma, Part VI* (Boston: MFA, 1982).

32 Brigitte Gratien, *Les cultures Kerma: Essai de classification* (Lille: Université de Lille, 1978); Charles Bonnet, "Fouilles archéologiques à Kerma (Soudan): Rapport préliminaire de la campagne 1977–1978, 1978–1979 et 1979–1980," *Genava*, n.s., 26 (1978): 107–43; 28 (1980): 31–62; idem, *Les fouilles archéologiques de Kerma (Soudan): Rapport préliminaire de campagnes de 1980–1981 et 1981–1982* (1982); idem, "La Deffufa occidentale à Kerma: Essai d'interprétation," *BIFAO* 81 (1981): 205–12.

33 Bruce B. Williams, *Excavations between Abu Simbel and the Sudan Frontier*, pt. 1, *The A-Group Royal Cemetery at Qustul, Cemetery L*, OINE 3 (Chicago: Oriental Institute, University of Chicago, 1986).

34 Bruce B. Williams, *Excavations between Abu Simbel and the Sudan Frontier*, pts. 2–4, *Neolithic, A-Group, and Post–A-Group Remains from Cemeteries W, V, S, Q, T, and a Cave East of Cemetery K*, OINE 4 (Chicago: Oriental Institute, University of Chicago, 1989); idem, *Excavations between Abu Simbel and the Sudan Frontier*, pt. 5, *C-Group, Pan Grave, and Kerma Remains at Adindan Cemeteries T, K, U, and J*, OINE 5 (1983); idem, *Excavations between Abu Simbel and the Sudan Frontier*, pt. 7, *Twenty-fifth Dynasty and Napatan Remains at Qustul: Cemeteries W and V*, OINE 7 (1990); idem, *Excavations between Abu Simbel and the Sudan Frontier*, pt. 8, *Meroitic Remains from Qustul Cemetery Q, Ballana Cemetery B, and a Ballana Settlement*, OINE 8 (1991); idem, *Excavations between the Abu Simbel and the Sudan Frontier*, pt. 9, *Noubadian X-Group Remains from Royal Complexes in Cemeteries Q and 219 and Private Cemeteries Q, R, V, W, B, J, and M at Qustul and Ballana*, OINE 9 (1991).

35 David O'Connor, *Buhen: The Old Kingdom Town* (London: Egypt Exploration Society, forthcoming).

36 Josef Wegner, "The History and Function of the Settlement at Arieka" (M.S. thesis, University of Pennsylvania, 1992).

37 Stuart Tyson Smith, "The First Imperialists," *KMT* 3, no. 3 (1992): 40ff.

38 Cyril Aldred, "The Temple of Dendur," *BMMA* 36, no. 1 (1978).

39 For an entertaining popular account of the reconstruction, see Thomas Hoving, *Making the Mummies Dance* (New York: Simon and Schuster, 1993), 51–53, 58–63, 129, 162.

40 Steffen Wenig, ed., *Africa in Antiquity: The Arts of Ancient Nubia and the Sudan*, exh. cat., vol. 2, *The Catalogue* (Brooklyn: Brooklyn Museum, 1978).

41 O'Connor, *Nubia*.

42 See Joyce L. Haynes, *Nubia: Ancient Kingdoms of Africa* (Boston: MFA, 1992).

The American Discovery of Meroitic Nubia and the Sudan

Timothy Kendall

Although a few intrepid Europeans had glimpsed the temples of Lower Nubia by 1814, the Upper Nubian cities of fabled Kush—or "Ethiopia" as the Greeks and Romans called it—remained as mysterious to the nineteenth-century savants as they had been to the classical historians. Among the highly competitive adventurers of the period, they became an eagerly sought prize.[1]

The Swiss explorer John L. Burkhardt traveled in Upper Nubia in 1813, disguised as an Arab. In his book, published posthumously in 1819, he established two important facts that excited the cupidity of Egypt's new ruler, Mohammed Ali.[2] Not only was Upper Nubia prosperous, but the firearm was virtually unknown there. Thus, in 1820, keen to expand his empire, grasp new tax revenues, and seize control of the profitable slave trade, the viceroy invaded with a well-armed force of four thousand men under the command of his twenty-five-year-old son Ismail Pasha.[3] While this war and the ensuing decades of Turkish rule would prove disastrous for what would come to be called the Sudan, it would, ironically, prove a boon to archaeology.

Traveling with the Egyptian army were several foreigners eager to be the first to find and record the legendary cities of Napata and Meroe for the glory of self and nation. A British pair, George Waddington and Barnard Hanbury, who dressed and behaved like Englishmen, were forced by the pasha to turn back at the fourth cataract and thus, in 1822, became the first to get a book into print.[4] A French duo, Frédéric Cailliaud (1787–1869) and Pierre Letorzec, who dressed and behaved like Turks, had better luck and were allowed to continue to Sennar. Cailliaud published a set of glorious plates and maps in 1823, which were followed in 1826–27 by his detailed commentaries.[5] Although it was primarily these works that would drive the next wave of explorers, there was yet a third writer on this expedition with publishing aspirations, who happened to be American.

George Bethune English (1787–1828), a native of Boston and a Protestant by birth, had wandered to Egypt by means unknown. By 1821 he had converted to

151

Islam, taken a Turkish name, and was attached to the army as an artillery officer. With him as common soldiers were two young sailors from New York who evidently had jumped ship in Alexandria, and under his influence they too had become Muslims. Although no scholar, English apparently picked up his knowledge of ancient "Ethiopia" from Cailliaud, with whom he had been friendly, and he and his companions had not only eagerly sought out ancient ruins but even excavated what they thought was an ancient Egyptian tomb. When English's own book appeared in Boston in early 1823, it was the second publication by months to provide descriptions of the antiquities of the Upper Nile, and the first to correctly identify the sites of the ancient capitals of Kush.[6]

Between 1822 and 1845 few others would repeat this journey. One was yet another Bostonian, John Lowell Jr. (1799–1836) (see fig. 104).[7] Lowell, heir to the inventor of the power loom, was a young man whose great intellect was matched by his wealth. In 1831 he set out on a circuit of the world, overland via the Near East, India, Central Asia, and China.[8] After a year spent in England and France, reading, studying exotic languages, and ordering the finest scientific instruments money could buy, he traveled on to Rome, where he hired a young Swiss academic painter named Charles Gleyre (1806–74) to accompany him and make sketches and aquarelles. December of 1834 found them in Egypt, where, after a private audience with Mohammed Ali, Lowell was persuaded to venture into the Sudan. This he did, thoroughly versing himself in the works of his predecessors, including Jean-François Champollion, and learning to speak Arabic fluently.

In June of 1835 Lowell and Gleyre, with another American named Mutchett, were at Philae, from which, in the furnace of the Nubian summer, they headed for Khartoum. Plagued by severe physical ailments as well as by heat, sandstorms, and untrustworthy servants, Lowell visited every site and doggedly wrote descriptions of the monuments, sometimes sleeping with a gun under his pillow. At Gebel Barkal, while Gleyre sketched, he and Mutchett excavated in the Great Temple of Amun, exposing the hawk statue taken nine years later by Karl Richard Lepsius and, "in the interests of science," dismantled one of the minuscule pyramids on the edge of the necropolis to try to determine the location of its burial chamber. To their disappointment, they found it of solid masonry and the tomb elusive.[9]

As the trio continued across the Bayuda and Butana deserts, Gleyre became morose and ceased sketching altogether. At Khartoum the three parted company, Lowell and Gleyre[10] on very bad terms. Lowell eventually backtracked down the Nile to Berber, visiting Meroe, and crossed the desert to Suakin on the Red Sea. After surviving a shipwreck in an Arab dhow with most of his records intact, he secured passage to Bombay on an English ship but died soon after arriving in India.

Lowell's account of the pyramids of Meroe is of special interest since he was evidently the first interested party to visit them after the destructive "excavations" of the Italian adventurer Giuseppe Ferlini, who pulled down or truncated a number of the pyramids in his search for treasure.[11] Lowell's diary offers several pages of outraged commentary.[12] Lowell did not realize that Ferlini had found a fabulous gold hoard in a hidden chamber near the top of one of the largest pyramids or that he had managed to secret it from his workmen and smuggle it out of the country. Later he would sell it in halves to the kings of Prussia and Bavaria.[13] Only in 1992, with the fall of the Berlin Wall, would the Ferlini Treasure be reunited again in an exhibition at the Ägyptisches Museum, Berlin.[14]

A third early American writer-traveler in the Sudan was the Pennsylvanian Bayard Taylor (1825–78), a noted journalist, poet, novelist, world traveler, and diplomat. Taylor's travels of 1852 were published in a highly readable account seven years later.[15] Believing himself the first American to venture into the Sudan, he named his boat the *America* and flew the Stars and Stripes from the masthead. His account, extremely valuable for its ethnographic data, is of peculiar interest in that it reflects what must have been a typical, though by no means universal, nineteenth-century reaction to the monuments of the Sudan. This same attitude for almost another full century would retard and confuse the discipline of Meroitic studies and the study of African civilization in general. To Taylor, and many of his contemporaries, it was inconceivable that the great stone cities of Kush had been built by peoples of the "black race," whom they regarded as incapable of high cultural achievement. Rather, he asserted, they must have been built by Egyptians or by immigrants from India or Arabia, or, in any case, "by an offshoot... of the race to which we belong."[16]

Despite such racist speculations, the ancient history of the Sudan began to come into sharper focus following the chance discovery at Gebel Barkal in 1862, by an Egyptian army officer, of a series of four Kushite royal stelae, written in Egyptian.[17] Sent to Cairo, the largest of these was that of a king named Piankhy (or Piye, as his name is now read), which described his conquest of Egypt around 726 B.C.[18] Translated by Théodule Devéria and Auguste Mariette, the text was an immediate sensation, not only corroborating the classical accounts of the 25th Dynasty but also inspiring the production of Egypt's great national opera *Aïda*

(1871), which opened in Cairo in 1874. The score was by Giuseppe Verdi, and the story, libretto, and costume designs were produced anonymously by Mariette.[19] It was the first and, until recently, the last time that the "pious Ethiopians" would enter modern popular consciousness.

Although Americans—former officers of the Union and Confederate armies—would be employed to survey and map much of the Sudan during the 1870s,[20] the Mahdist revolt and the ensuing Nile War of 1885–98 brought further archaeological exploration in the Sudan to an abrupt halt. To transport troops and weapons, British forces constructed a railway across the Nubian desert. Following the cataclysmic Battle of Omdurman on September 2, 1898, and the passage of the Sudan into British control, the railway made the region accessible to archaeologists as never before.[21] The new British governors general, sympathetic to scientific research, offered their encouragement and in 1903 established an antiquities department.[22]

Apart from the unsystematic search for portable monuments conducted in the Sudan by E. A. Wallis Budge between 1897 and 1905 for the British Museum,[23] the first archaeological expedition to arrive in the Sudan after the Nile War was the Epigraphic Survey of the University of Chicago, led by James H. Breasted. His mission was the modern equivalent of that conducted sixty years previously by Lepsius and his royal Prussian expedition. Rather than make precise drawings and plans of monuments, as Lepsius's team had done, Breasted would record them for the first time by camera (see fig. 103).[24]

During the 1905–6 season the Chicago team photographed all the temples and visible inscriptions between Aswan and Wadi Halfa. The following season, with Norman de Garis Davies and the German photographer Horst Schliephack, Breasted moved south to record the monuments between Wadi Halfa and Khartoum. Starting at the capital and traveling northward alternately by boat and camel, they photographed the temples at Naqa and Musawwarat el-Sufra, the pyramids and their chapels at Meroe, surveyed the fourth cataract, photographed and excavated for inscriptions at the Gebel Barkal temples and surrounding sites, and thus passed on down to the third cataract. Ultimately they arrived back again at Wadi Halfa, from which the photographic plates were transported to Egypt and thence to Chicago, where to this day they comprise the finest photographic archive of Nubian monuments in existence.

Scientific exploration of Lower Nubia was initially called for by the Egyptian government following its decision to raise the Aswan Dam. Thus the Archaeological Survey of Nubia was inaugurated during 1906–7, led by George A. Reisner and his team, which was lent for the purpose by his new sponsors, the Museum of Fine Arts, Boston, and Harvard University.[25] At the same time the University of Pennsylvania launched an important Nubian expedition to excavate the sites of Areika, Buhen, and Karanog, directed by British archaeologists David Randall-MacIver and Charles Leonard Woolley.[26] These excavations revealed the first large Meroitic cemeteries, which produced a trove of magnificent pottery, rather startling *ba* sculptures (see cat. no. 123), and a large corpus of inscriptions in the mysterious Meroitic script. Almost immediately the latter provided the key to the remarkable decipherment of the phonetic values of the letters by the British Egyptologist Francis Llewellyn Griffith, who published his results in 1911, also for the University of Pennsylvania.[27] The bright hope, however, that the Meroitic language might be as quickly deciphered, or that a bilingual key would soon be found, was not realized.

The first major field excavations in the Sudan, conducted by British teams, were suspended with the outbreak of World War I. They were almost immediately continued by Reisner and his Boston juggernaut in 1916, when the Anglo-Egyptian authorities of the Sudan issued him the license to excavate at Napata, which included the Gebel Barkal temples and pyramids, and the pyramids of Nuri and el-Kurru.[28] Now, while his British colleagues became preoccupied by the war, Reisner continued digging without interruption.

Commencing excavations at the Barkal pyramids in the fall of 1916, Reisner, "before noon of the first day," would determine the means by which the tombs were entered, a problem that had baffled all previous comers.[29] This discovery gave him the key that would ultimately enable him to excavate all the Kushite royal tombs in the Sudan, from the ninth century B.C. to the fourth century A.D.

In the Barkal temples Reisner was rewarded the same season by an equally lucky find. While searching for a place to site his dumps, by pure accident he came upon a cache of ten fragmentary royal statues, some of them colossal, which represented the Kushite pharaoh Taharqa (r. 690–664 B.C.), four of his five successors (occasionally in multiple image), and one contemporary queen.[30]

It was at Nuri, the site of the largest pyramids in the Sudan, that Reisner expected to find the tombs of the 25th Dynasty rulers of Egypt (see fig. 105), but he found the tomb of only one, Taharqa, and those of nineteen of his shadowy successors and fifty-four queens.[31] Not until the 1919 season would he discover his missing kings—Piye (r. 750–712 B.C.), Shabako (r. 712–698 B.C.), Shebitku (r. 698–690 B.C.), and Tanwetamani (r. 664–656 B.C.)—among the small ruined pyramids at nearby el-Kurru, together with fourteen of their wives, fourteen nameless ancestors, and even a cemetery of horses, all of which had been buried standing up (see cat. nos. 97–99).[32]

By the 1919–20 season Reisner had excavated seven temples at Gebel Barkal and two palaces—about half the extent of the sanctuary—and had established the site's essential history from the New Kingdom to the Christian era.[33] He had also

recovered more statues as well as several extremely important historical inscriptions, including the famous Barkal stela of Tuthmosis III (r. 1490–1468 B.C.),
another of Piye, and that of the Meroitic king Tanyidamani, one of the two longest
inscriptions in the mysterious Kushite language.[34]

At the conclusion of his work at Barkal, Reisner received the concession for
Meroe and, for the next three seasons, continued his operations in the pyramid
fields east of the city. There he discovered not only remarkable evidence of the
material wealth of the Kushite royalty but also many objects of contemporary Greek
and Roman manufacture, evidence of Meroe's close ties with the Mediterranean
world. By applying Griffith's phonetic values of the Meroitic alphabet to the
inscriptions he found, and by arranging the pyramids in chronological order
according to their apparent evolutionary features, he was able to reconstruct the
names and approximate order of most of the seventy-odd Meroitic rulers from the
25th Dynasty to the late Roman period, thus laying the foundation for the reconstruction of the entire history of the Kushite state, which until then had been
completely obscure. Reisner's contract provided for a fifty-fifty split of excavated
objects with the Sudan Antiquities Service. His finds not only formed the nucleus
of the Sudan National Collections but also furnished the Boston Museum of
Fine Arts with a collection of Nubian royal treasures unique in this hemisphere
(see cat. nos. 124–25).[35]

In the Sudan Reisner worked with a core group of Egyptians from Coptos and
hired locally sometimes up to two hundred diggers and basket carriers, who were
also taught to use Decauville railcars for earth moving. He employed two Egyptian
photographers, Mohammedani and Mohammed Shadduf, and often sent his
much-esteemed *reis*, Said Ahmed, to a site to direct preliminary clearing of it in his
absence, teaching him how to keep his own diaries in Arabic. It was Said Ahmed,

in fact, who discovered the first shawabtis of Piye and Shabako at el-Kurru, which convinced Reisner to move his operations there in February 1919.[36]

Among Reisner's many assistants who made significant contributions to the study of Meroitic civilization, two can be singled out for special mention. Oric Bates was a Bostonian and Harvard graduate (1905) who in 1906 served as acting curator in the Egyptian department of the Museum of Fine Arts, Boston (before Reisner's official appointment), and who went on to work with Reisner at Giza and Samaria in Palestine. In 1910 he was "lent" by Reisner to Sir Henry Wellcome (1853–1936) to direct the excavations at Gebel Moya in the Sudanese *gezira*. Wellcome was also an American, of great wealth, who had transferred his citizenship to Great Britain, established the Wellcome Medical Research Laboratories in Khartoum, and between 1901 and 1914, under the influence of another "pseudo-American," the African explorer Henry M. Stanley, sponsored the earliest archaeological expeditions in central Sudan. In 1915, after becoming curator of African archaeology and ethnology at the Peabody Museum at Harvard University, Bates excavated the important late Meroitic site at Gamai, near Wadi Halfa (see fig. 106), together with Dows Dunham and a crew lent by Reisner;[37] two years later he founded the Harvard African Studies series.[38]

While Bates's interests were clearly African, those of Dunham (see fig. 107) were primarily Egyptological. Dunham, a native New Yorker, was the rare individual who had actually studied with Reisner at Harvard, in 1913, his senior year. At Reisner's urging, Dunham embarked on a career with the Harvard-Boston team, serving first as an assistant in Boston, then with Reisner at Giza, and then with Bates at Gamai. In 1916 he was with Reisner at Gebel Barkal, and he spent the following year studying Egyptian language with Breasted in Chicago. After a stint in the army in 1917–18 he returned to work with Reisner at Meroe and actually directed the excavations there during much of the final season in 1923.[39]

Dunham returned to Boston in 1927 and remained Reisner's liaison at the museum until the latter's death in 1942, when Dunham became curator. Since Reisner had never fully published the results of his Sudan work, Dunham now dedicated himself to this task. Incredibly, until about 1960 he remained the only American scholar working in Meroitic studies. Over twenty-eight years, apart from publishing a stream of articles on Meroitic subjects,[40] he completed his monumental five-volume opus *Royal Cemeteries of Kush* (1950–63), his two-volume *Second Cataract Forts* (1960–67), and *The Barkal Temples* (1970), always working in collaboration with his devoted assistant, artist Suzanne E. Chapman (1903–90).[41]

From the 1930s to the early 1950s virtually all archaeological fieldwork in Nubia focused on prehistoric, pharaonic, and Christian sites. The primary exceptions were the British-run Second Archaeological Survey, which exposed the massive X-Group tombs at Ballana and Qustul, and the Oxford University excavations at the temples at Kawa, both of which took place between 1929 and 1936.[42] The latter produced a trove of new historical documents of the Napatan period, which were published in 1949 by M. F. L. Macadam, who, together with Dunham, attempted to unravel the names and relationships of the Napatan royal family.[43] This work did much to revive interest in Meroitic civilization, and by 1960 Humboldt University of Berlin had surveyed the Butana region (the classical "Island of Meroe"), and the Sudan Antiquities Service had excavated the Meroitic royal seat at Wad Ben Naqa.[44]

The renaissance of American Nubian studies began only in 1960 with the advent of the Nubian Salvage Campaign, an international effort to promote archaeological exploration of Lower Nubia and parts of northern Sudan, the area to be flooded as a result of building the Aswan High Dam. This emergency, with its generous terms for division of objects, brought a number of American teams into the picture.

Of the twenty-five expeditions that took part in the campaign in Egyptian Nubia, seven were American, three of which worked on Meroitic or post-Meroitic sites.[45] A joint expedition of the University of Pennsylvania and Yale University, under the direction of William Kelly Simpson, worked three seasons between Toshka and Arminna, revealing settlement remains and cemeteries.[46] The young field directors, Bruce G. Trigger (b. 1937) and Nicholas B. Millet (b. 1934), would both become prominent North American Meroitic scholars. Millet, who had worked summers in the 1950s as a college student with Dunham in Boston, went on to serve as the Cairo director of the American Research Center in Egypt (ARCE). Between 1962 and 1966, following the Penn-Yale expedition, he organized ARCE's own Nubian expedition at the Meroitic site of Gebel Adda.[47]

Beginning in 1960 the Oriental Institute of the University of Chicago worked six seasons at sites ranging from Beit el-Wali in the north to Semna in the south, and at a cluster of 25th Dynasty, Napatan, Meroitic, and post-Meroitic sites in the vicinity of Ballana and Qustul. The wide-ranging expedition was led alternately by Keith C. Seele (1889–1971), George R. Hughes (1907–92), and Louis V. Zabkar (1914–94), with Trigger again serving as staff archaeologist. The mobile headquarters of the expedition was the venerable Nile steamer *Fostat*, which ultimately became the permanently berthed Cairo field office of ARCE (see fig. 108).[48]

There was little or no coordination between the Egyptian and Sudanese governments in the Nubian campaign. Each country affected by the dam organized its own solutions. In the Sudan, which had achieved independence in 1956, the antiquities service had undertaken an aerial survey and requested a UNESCO expert to interpret the photographs. The job was offered to an American, William Y. Adams, who was then directing archaeological salvage work on the San Juan and Colorado Rivers for the Museum of Northern Arizona. Adams, without any previous experience reading aerial photographs or in working with Nubian antiquities, arrived in Khartoum, and what was to be a four-month appointment lasted seven years.[49] Adams became not only the director of the Sudan's salvage campaign but ultimately the outstanding American excavator in Nubia since Reisner himself (see fig. 109).

Adams had not come from the old Boston school. He was a Californian who had been raised on the Navajo Indian reservation. He spoke fluent Navajo and operated a Navajo trading post as part of his graduate work.[50] Trained at the University of Arizona, he was a product of the school of "new archaeology," which strongly advocated the excavation of habitation and factory sites rather than temples and cemeteries. He placed greater value on the acquisition of general cultural data than of texts and museum objects.

For the Sudan emergency, assisted by his wife, Nettie Adams (b. 1934), also an archaeologist, Adams organized a survey of vast scope with limited resources and time. Working with nineteen international teams in twenty-eight areas, he and his small staff personally recorded nearly three hundred sites and excavated thirty. He excavated stratified pottery kilns and rapidly published chronologies of pottery types so that other excavators could quickly identify surface remains. Because he knew that other expeditions were interested primarily in pharaonic material, he dedicated himself only to sites that were not likely to be excavated and thus became a specialist in medieval Nubia. Following the campaign, he spent seven seasons with the Egypt Exploration Society's team at Qasr Ibrim, three as director, and became chairman of the anthropology department at the University of

FIGURE 109
William Y. Adams paying workmen at Kulubnarti in 1962, during the Nubian Salvage Campaign.

Kentucky. Of the tremendous bibliography generated by this outstanding scholar, the crowning achievement is his great cultural history of the Middle Nile, *Nubia: Corridor to Africa* (1977).[51] Nettie Adams became the leading specialist in the field of ancient Nubian textiles.[52]

Another American who became involved in Nubian studies during the salvage campaign was Helen Jacquet-Gordon (b. 1915). A native of New York City, she studied ancient Egyptian and Coptic philology in Paris and in 1955 went to Egypt. There she met and assisted her future husband, Jean Jacquet, an architect, who had been delegated by the Swiss government to record the temples at Gerf Hussein, Derr, Kalabsha, and Abu Simbel. She participated in the University of Pennsylvania–Yale excavations at Arminna (1961), worked with Adolf Klasens of the University of Leiden at Meroitic and Christian sites north of Abu Simbel (1963–64), and with Millet at Gebel Adda (1965). Between 1966 and 1976 she was a chief archaeologist on the University of Geneva mission at Tabo, Sudan, under the direction of Charles Maystre, before becoming a permanent fixture of the French team, with her husband, at Karnak North. With Maystre's passing in 1993, Jacquet-Gordon, in collaboration with her husband and Charles Bonnet, is preparing the final reports for Tabo, one of the most important temple sites of the Napatan and Meroitic periods.[53]

In the 1970s Canada took a strong step in Meroitic studies. In 1970 the University of Calgary appointed Peter Shinnie to head its department of archaeology. Bruce Trigger became chairman of the anthropology department at McGill University in Montreal, and Nicholas Millet became curator of the Egyptian department at the Royal Ontario Museum in 1974. Three years later Millet hosted the first International Meroitic Studies Conference in North America.[54]

Shinnie (b. 1915), a British native turned Canadian, arrived in Calgary as one of the premier figures in African archaeology. Between 1948 and 1955 he had served as the last of the British commissioners for archaeology at Khartoum. He returned to the Sudan from 1966 to 1970 to head the department of archaeology, University of Khartoum. There he excavated the post-Meroitic burial mounds at Tanqasi and the Christian sites of Ghazali, Soba, and Debeira West and was engaged in excavations at Meroe city. In 1953 he founded *Kush*, the journal of the Sudan Antiquities Service, and in 1967 he authored the most popular primer on Meroitic civilization, *Meroë: A Civilization of the Sudan*.[55]

At Calgary, Shinnie became the mentor of many students who went on to achievement in Meroitic studies. Rebecca Bradley (b. 1952), for example, became his assistant at Meroe and collaborated with him in writing final reports.[56] Krzysztof A. Grzymski (b. 1951), a Pole turned Canadian, in 1984 became both Millet's assistant curator at the Royal Ontario Museum and director of that museum's ongoing archaeological expedition to the Sudan.[57] In 1992 Grzymski became associate professor at the University of Toronto, offering, upon Shinnie's retirement, the only graduate courses in Meroitic studies in North America.

By the 1970s the torrent of new data and artifacts generated by the Nubian Salvage Campaign inevitably inspired the first great exhibition of Nubian art in the United States, *Africa in Antiquity: The Arts of Ancient Nubia and the Sudan* (1978), organized by Bernard V. Bothmer, curator of the Brooklyn Museum's Egyptian department, and his staff. With the support of Dominique de Menil, Bothmer and his team traveled to every museum in the world possessing Nubian objects, compiling the first and finest photographic archive of Nubian art ever produced, which is now shared in duplicate by the Brooklyn Museum, New York University, the de Menil Foundation, and Humboldt University, Berlin.[58]

The magnificent two-volume catalogue of the exhibition, which drew together the best Nubian scholars on both sides of the Atlantic, still remains the best resource on the art and material culture of ancient Nubia.[59] The opening of the exhibition was followed by the first international Nubian studies conference held in the United States.[60] The exhibition at once clearly defined Nubia as a cultural area distinct from Egypt and introduced to a resistant American consciousness the idea that the Middle Nile had been part of a civilized community of nations.

Bothmer's career is singular. Born and educated in Germany, he fled his country in 1941 and offered his services to the U.S. Army. In 1946 he was hired by Dunham, whom he assisted in Boston for eight years. His earliest exposure to Meroitic art had been in Berlin, where as a junior staff member at the Ägyptisches Museum he had entirely reinstalled the Ferlini Treasure. Later in Boston he assisted Dunham in the preparation of the earliest volumes of *Royal Cemeteries of Kush*.[61] Once, when a visitor to the museum brought a jewel from the Ferlini Treasure into the Egyptian department for identification, Bothmer immediately recognized it as something "liberated" from the Ägyptisches Museum during the war. Dunham, as curator, "retained it for study" and soon saw that it was repatriated.[62]

In 1955 Bothmer left the Museum of Fine Arts, Boston, on a Fulbright scholarship in Egypt, later joining the staff of the Brooklyn Museum and assuming the curatorship of the Egyptian department in 1964. Long before it was fashionable among museums in this country, both John D. Cooney (1905–82), curator at Brooklyn from 1938 to 1963, and Bothmer had taken a keen interest in late Egyptian and Nubian art and had tried to collect it for Brooklyn.[63] In fact, Cooney accompanied Dunham on his last trip to the Sudan, in 1946, having then in mind the idea of organizing a Brooklyn Museum expedition there.[64]

The 1978 Brooklyn exhibition was only the most obvious manifestation of the American groundswell of interest in Meroitic studies. In 1974 Edna R. Russmann

(b. 1936), a student of Bothmer's, wrote a landmark study of 25th Dynasty royal portraiture and made Kushite art in Egypt one of her specialties.[65] In 1975 Louis V. Zabkar, then professor of Egyptology at Brandeis University, produced the single most important study of Meroitic religion, *Apedemak: Lion God of Meroë*.[66] Two of his students, Susan K. Doll (b. 1949) and Janice Yellin (b. 1950), were to pursue his interests and, on his recommendation, study in Paris with Jean Leclant, one of the greatest of the French Nubiologists. After a sojourn in the Sudan, Doll completed her doctoral dissertation on the texts of the Napatan sarcophagi from Nuri.[67] Yellin wrote hers on the role of Anubis in Meroitic religion. Ultimately Yellin became a professor at Babson College and a specialist in Meroitic religion.[68] In 1994 she received a Getty Senior Research Grant to publish the royal pyramid chapels at Meroe in collaboration with Friedrich W. Hinkel, the distinguished German architect who, almost annually from the time of the Salvage Campaign to 1989, worked with the Sudan Antiquities Service to restore and record the pyramids.

At Chicago, Bruce B. Williams, a young assistant of Keith Seele's, assumed responsibility for publishing the results of the Oriental Institute's Nubian expedition.[69] At the same time two outstanding classical scholars made Meroitic studies a particular focus: Frank M. Snowden Jr. (b. 1911), of Howard University, who produced numerous studies tracking Africans in classical art and literature,[70] and Stanley M. Burstein (b. 1941), California State University at Los Angeles, a specialist in the classical sources pertaining to Meroe, the Upper Nile, and East Africa.[71] Yale-trained Anthony J. Spalinger (b. 1947), who became a senior lecturer in Egyptology at the University of Auckland, New Zealand, has published numerous important articles on the history of the 25th Dynasty, his area of specialty.[72]

It is at this point that history intersects with the personal experience of this writer (b. 1945). I knew nothing of Nubia when I began working at the Museum of Fine Arts, Boston, in 1974. I had been trained as an Assyriologist and was hired to tend the Ancient Near Eastern collection, then an adjunct to the Egyptian. But I had met the Brooklyn team when they came to photograph the museum's Nubian holdings and acquired some familiarity with the material. In those days Dows Dunham still came daily to the office to work, always enthralling the junior staff with stories of the "old days." In 1978 I attended the opening of the Brooklyn exhibition and Meroitic conference. The following year the Brockton (Mass.) Art Museum requested a loan exhibition from Boston, and I was asked to mount it. I proposed a Meroitic show from the museum's storage holdings, which led to the exhibition and catalogue *Kush: Lost Kingdom of the Nile* (1981–82).[73] This show had been planned to serve as the nucleus of the first exclusively Nubian gallery at the Boston museum, but funding and space problems would delay this plan for another eight years.

FIGURE 110
David A. Goodman, veteran surveyor for the California Transportation Department and for American expeditions to Egypt and the Sudan, taking sightings from the cliff of Gebel Barkal, February 1989, for the expedition of the Museum of Fine Arts, Boston.

In 1982 I received a sabbatical to travel to the Sudan to revisit all of Reisner's sites and was touched when Dows Dunham handed me a check for five hundred dollars as a contribution. Peter Lacovara, who was on his way to Egypt, asked to join, and we went together. At Nuri we not only met an old man who had worked with Reisner as a boy, but we also found the ruins of Reisner's camp, recognizable in the old photographs. When I returned to Boston and reported to Mr. Dunham, I put into his hands an old thermos lid that I had found there, and he wept. He died several months later at the age of ninety-two.

Four years later I received a permit from the Sudan Antiquities Service to reopen excavations at Gebel Barkal in the Reisner concession area, and in three seasons (1986–89) my new Boston team surveyed and mapped the site (see fig. 110), revealed reliefs of Piye, illustrating his conquest of Egypt, found remains of a once-gilded monument of Taharqa atop the seventy-five-meter pinnacle on Gebel Barkal, and discovered that this statuelike rock had been conceptualized in ancient times as a rearing uraeus. The symbolic implications of the latter seemed to explain not only why Gebel Barkal had such strong religious associations but also why it had become the birthplace of a Nubian monarchy with outwardly pharaonic appearances and aspirations.[74]

If the Gebel Barkal finds shed light on the origin of the Egyptianized Kushite state, another, made almost simultaneously by another American, dramatically illuminated its end. Boyce N. Driskell (b. 1948), one of Adams's students at the University of Kentucky and a specialist in prehistoric Native American cultures of the Southeast, was a site archaeologist at Qasr Ibrim for the Egypt Exploration Society between 1980 and 1986. While directing the American contingent in 1986, he discovered the ruins of the latest Meroitic temple on the site, which had clearly been desecrated and destroyed in a single violent episode by the earliest Christians in the sixth century A.D. Here were smashed Egyptian statues, overthrown altars, fragments of magnificent textiles that had obviously adorned the sanctuary, all of which had been torn to shreds, and painted wooden panels, reminiscent of Christian icons but portraying Egyptian deities or symbolic animals, which had been scattered about wildly. It was the decisive and vivid terminus of Egyptian antiquity.[75]

THE SUDAN STILL REMAINS UNDEREXPLORED ARCHAEOLOGICALLY and offers bright promise for major research, although historically the number of foreign archaeologists working there has been small. Unfortunately the pressures of over-population and the need for ever more arable land threaten the ancient sites with destruction far faster than they can be recorded. Equally ominous for the natural and archaeological environment is the government's announced plan to construct a new giant dam at the fourth cataract, and representatives of the Sudan Antiquities Service have been speaking about launching a new international archaeological salvage campaign.[76] How the world will respond to this call remains to be seen.

Notes

1 For a brief account of the earliest non-Arab travelers in Nubia, see Jean Leclant, "Le voyage en Nubie 1813–1913," chap. 3 of *D'un orient l'autre: Les métamorphoses successives des perceptions et connaissances*, vol. 1, *Configurations* (Paris: Centre national de la recherche scientifique, 1991), 405–15. See also Thomas Legh, *Narrative of a Journey in Egypt and the Country beyond the Cataracts* (Philadelphia: M. Thomas, 1817), 146.

2 John L. Burkhardt, *Travels in Nubia* (London: John Murray, 1819), esp. 286–88.

3 A. Moorehead, *The Blue Nile* (Middlesex, U.K.: Penguin Books, 1984), 139–208.

4 George Waddington and Barnard Hanbury, *Journal of a Visit to Some Parts of Ethiopia* (London: John Murray, 1822).

5 Frédéric Cailliaud, *Voyage à Meroë, au fleuve blanc, au delà de Fazoql…*, 4 vols. (Paris: Imprimerie Royale, 1826–27; reprint, Farnborough, Hants.: Greg International, 1972).

6 George B. English, *A Narrative of the Expedition to Dongola and Sennar* (Boston: Wells and Lilly, 1823), esp. 56–58, 104–5. Among these first observers of the monuments of the Sudan, one should not fail to mention Louis M. A. Linant de Bellefonds and his companion Alessandro Ricci, whose notes and superb drawings are published in Margaret Shinnie, *Linant de Bellefonds: Journal d'un voyage à Méroë dans les années 1821 et 1822* (Khartoum: Sudan Antiquities Service, 1958); see also Warren R. Dawson and Eric P. Uphill, *Who Was Who in Egyptology*, 2d rev. ed. (London: Egypt Exploration Society, 1972), 179–80, 248.

7 On the early travelers to the Sudan in this period, see Leclant, "D'exploration." For Lowell, see E. Everett, *A Memoir of John Lowell, Jun., Delivered as the Introduction to the Lectures on His Foundation in the Odeon, 31st Dec., 1839* (Boston: Charles C. Little and James Brown, 1840); N. S. Newhouse, "From Rome to Khartoum: Gleyre, Lowell, and the Evidence of the Boston Watercolors and Drawings," in *Charles Gleyre: 1806–1874*, exh. cat. (New York: Grey Art Gallery and Study Center, New York University, 1980), 78–111; J. MacDonald, "The Egyptian Trip of John Lowell, Jr.," *BES* 6 (1985): 69–79.

8 The primary source for Lowell's travels in the Sudan is his voluminous unpublished diary, which is preserved at the Boston Athenaeum, and in a slightly edited copy at the Museum of Fine Arts, Boston.

9 Lowell, "Diary," 20–28 September 1835.

10 In time Gleyre would become one of the founders of the orientalist school of painting; see O. W. Hauptman, "Charles Gleyre: Tradition and Innovation," in *Charles Gleyre*, 13. See also C. Clement, *Gleyre: Etude biographique et critique* (Paris: Librairie académique Didier, [1880]), esp. 82–128.

11 Joseph Ferlini, *Relation historique des fouilles operées dans la Nubie* (Rome: Imprimerie de Salviucci, 1838).

12 Lowell, "Diary," 20 November 1835.

13 E. A. Wallis Budge, *The Egyptian Sudan: Its History and Monuments*, vol. 1 (London: Kegan Paul, 1907), 285–320.

14 Karl-Heinz Priese, *The Gold of Meroë*, exh. cat. (New York: MMA; Mainz: Philipp von Zabern, 1993). The exhibition traveled to New York and Toronto in 1993–94.

15 Bayard Taylor, *A Journey to Central Africa, or Life and Landscapes from Egypt to the Negro Kingdoms of the White Nile* (New York: E. P. Putnam, 1859).

16 Ibid., 236–37. See also the similar opinion expressed by Karl Richard Lepsius, *Letters from Egypt, Ethiopia, and the Peninsula of Sinai*, 2d ed. (London: Richard Bentley, 1853), 208–9. Legh left open the possibility that the ancient Egyptians might have been "negroes" (*Narrative of a Journey in Egypt*, 137–39).

17 E. A. Wallis Budge, *Egyptian Religion*, vol. 2, *Annals of Nubian Kings, with a Sketch of the History of the Kingdom of Napata*, Books on Egypt and Chaldaea 33 (London: Kegan Paul, 1909).

18 N.-C. Grimal, *La stèle de Pi('ankh)y au Musée du Caire JE 48862 et 47086–47089, Etudes sur la propagande royale égyptienne* 1, Mémoires publiés par les membres de l'Institut français d'archéologie orientale du Caire 105 (Cairo: IFAO, 1981), xi–xiii.

19 William K. Simpson, "Mariette and Verdi's Aida," *BES* 2 (1980): 111–19.

20 See, e.g., William B. Hesseltine and Hazel C. Wolf, *The Blue and the Gray on the Nile* (Chicago: University of Chicago Press, 1961), 120ff.

21 Winston S. Churchill, *The River War* (1899, reprint; London: New English Library, 1985), esp. 156–76; Budge, *The Egyptian Sudan*, vol. 2, 463–80 (on railroads); Philip Ziegler, *Omdurman* (New York: Dorset Press, 1987).

22 For the early history of the Sudan Antiquities Service, see J. W. Crowfoot and F. Addison, "Early Days, 1903–31," *Kush* 1 (1953): 54–59.

23 Budge, *The Egyptian Sudan*, vol. 1, 146–49, 169–76, 240ff., 321ff., 436ff.

24 Charles Breasted, *Pioneer to the Past: The Story of James Henry Breasted, Archeologist* (New York: C. Scribner's Sons, 1943), 173–214; James H. Breasted, "Second Preliminary Report on the Egyptian Expedition," *American Journal of Semitic Languages and Literatures* 24 (October 1908). See also Karl Richard Lepsius, *Denkmäler aus Ägypten und Äthiopien* (Berlin: Nicolaische Buchhandlung, 1849–56); idem, *Discoveries in Egypt, Ethiopia, and the Peninsula of Sinai in the Years 1842–1845* (London: Richard Bentley, 1853).

25 George A. Reisner, *The Archaeological Survey of Nubia: Report for 1907–1908*, vol. 1, *Archaeological Report* (Cairo: National Printing Department, 1910).

26 Charles Leonard Woolley and David Randall-MacIver, *Karanog: The Romano-Nubian Cemetery* (Philadelphia: University Museum, University of Pennsylvania, 1910).

27 Francis L. Griffith, *Karanog: The Meroitic Inscriptions of Shablul and Karanog* (Philadelphia: University Museum, University of Pennsylvania, 1911).

28 George A. Reisner, autobiographical ms. (hereafter "Ms."), Department of Ancient Egyptian, Nubian, and Near Eastern Art, MFA, Boston, p. 9; Francis L. Griffith, "Oxford Excavations in Nubia," *University of Liverpool Annals of Archaeology* 9 (1922): 67.

29 George A. Reisner, unpublished field diaries (hereafter "Diaries"), Department of Ancient Egyptian, Nubian, and Near Eastern Art, MFA, 24 January 1916; idem, "Ms.," 9.

30 *Boston Daily Advertiser*, 7 October 1916; *Boston Transcript*, 27 June 1917; *Boston Globe*, 28 August 1923 (MFA clipping file); George A. Reisner, "The Barkal Temples in 1916," *JEA* 6 (1920): 251–53; Dows Dunham, *The Barkal Temples* (Boston: MFA, 1970), 17–20, pls. 1, 7–22.

31 George A. Reisner, "Preliminary Report on the Harvard-Boston Excavations at Nuri: The Kings of Ethiopia after Taharqa," in *Varia Africana*, vol. 2, Harvard African Studies 2 (Cambridge: Peabody Museum, Harvard University, 1918), 1–64, figs. 1–54, pls. I–XVII; idem, "Known and Unknown Kings of Ethiopia," *BMFA* 16 (1918): 67–81; Dows Dunham, *Royal Cemeteries of Kush*, vol. 2, *Nuri* (Cambridge: Harvard University Press, 1955).

32 George A. Reisner, "Discovery of the Tombs of the Egyptian XXVth Dynasty at El-

Kurruw in Dongola Province," *Sudan Notes and Records* 2 (1919): 35–67; idem, "Notes of the Harvard-Boston Excavations at El-Kurruw and Barkal in 1918–19," *JEA* 6 (1920): 61–64; Dows Dunham, *Royal Cemeteries of Kush*, vol. 1, *El-Kurru* (Cambridge: Harvard University Press, 1950). See also Timothy Kendall, *The Origin of the Napatan State: El-Kurru and the Evidence for the Royal Ancestors*, Meroitica 16 (in press).

33 George A. Reisner, "The Barkal Temples in 1916," pts 1, 2, *JEA* 4, 6 (1917–20): 213–27, 247–64; Dunham, *El-Kurru*; Timothy Kendall, "The Napatan Palace at Gebel Barkal: A First Look at B 1200," in *Egypt and Africa: Nubia from Prehistory to Islam*, ed. W. V. Davies (London: British Museum, 1991), 302–13.

34 George A. Reisner, "Inscribed Monuments from Gebel Barkal," pts. 1–4, *ZÄS* 66, 68, 69, 70 (1931–34): 76–100, 24–39, 73–78, 35–46; Fritz Hintze, "Die meroitische Stele des Königs Tanyidamani aus Napata (Boston MFA 23.736)," *Kush* 8 (1960): 125–62.

35 George A. Reisner, "The Royal Family of Ethiopia," *BMFA* 19 (1921): 112–27; idem, "The Pyramids of Meroë and the Candaces of Ethiopia," *BMFA* 21 (1923): 11–27; idem, "The Meroitic Kingdom of Ethiopia: A Chronological Outline," *JEA* 9 (1923): 34–77;

Dows Dunham, *Royal Cemeteries of Kush*, vol. 4, *Royal Tombs of Meroe and Barkal* (Cambridge: Harvard University Press, 1957).

36 Reisner, "Diaries," 16–20 March 1918 and 3–4 February 1919; Dows Dunham, *Recollections of an Egyptologist* (Boston: MFA, 1972) 16, 19–20; idem, *El-Kurru*, 8.

37 Oric Bates and Dows Dunham, "Excavations at Gamai," in *Varia Africana*, vol. 4, Harvard African Studies 8 (Cambridge: Peabody Museum, Harvard University, 1927), 1–121, pls. 1–72, maps 1–2.

38 C. Coolidge, "Oric Bates," foreword to *Varia Africana*, vol. 2; Mark De Wolfe Howe, *Memoirs of the Harvard Dead in the War against Germany*, vol. 4 (Cambridge: Harvard University Press, 1924), 547–66; Reisner, "Ms.," 8–9.

39 Dunham, *Recollections*, 27; see also William K. Simpson and Whitney M. Davis, eds., *Studies in Ancient Egypt, the Aegean, and the Sudan: Essays in Honor of Dows Dunham* (Boston: MFA, 1981), esp. 214–18.

40 For Dows Dunham's bibliography, see Simpson and Davis, *Studies in Ancient Egypt*, iv–viii.

41 Dows Dunham and Suzanne E. Chapman, *Royal Cemeteries of Kush*, vol. 3, *The Decorated Chapels of Meroë and Barkal* (Cambridge: Harvard University Press, 1952); Museum of Fine Arts, *In Tribute to Suzanne E. Chapman* (Boston: MFA, 1970).

42 William Y. Adams, *Nubia: Corridor to Africa* (Princeton: Princeton University Press, 1977), 72–80.

43 Dows Dunham and M. Macadam, "Names and Relationships of the Napatan Royal Family," *JEA* 35 (1949): 139–49.

44 Fritz Hintze, "Preliminary Report of the Butana Expedition 1958," *Kush* 7 (1959): 171–96; Jean Vercoutter, "Un palais de 'Candaces,' contemporain d'Auguste (fouilles de Wad-ban-Naga 1958–1960)," *Syria* 39 (1962): 263–99.

45 Adams, *Nubia*, 81–90.

46 William K. Simpson, "Nubia: 1962 Excavations at Toshka and Arminna," *Expedition* 4, no. 2 (1962): 37–46; idem, "The Pennsylvania-Yale Expedition to Egypt Preliminary Report for 1963: Toshka and Arminna (Nubia)," *JARCE* 3 (1964): 15–23; idem, "The Archaeological Expedition to Egyptian Nubia," *Discovery: Magazine of the Peabody Museum of Natural History, Yale University* 1, no. 1 (1967): 4–11.

47 Nicholas B. Millet, "Gebel Adda Preliminary Report," *JARCE* 2 (1963): 147–65; idem, "Gebel Adda Expedition Preliminary Report, 1963–1964," *JARCE* 3 (1964): 7–14; idem, "Gebel Adda Progress Report, Third Season," *NARCE* 58 (June 1966): 10–14; idem, "Gebel Adda Preliminary Report, 1965–1966," *JARCE* 4 (1967): 53–63; idem, "The Gebel Adda Archaeological Project, Nubia, 1963–1965," in *1964 Projects*, National Geographic Society Research Reports (Washington, D.C., 1969), 153–57.

48 Keith C. Seele, "University of Chicago Oriental Institute Nubian Expedition: Excavations between Abu Simbel and the Sudan Border, Preliminary Report," *JNES* 33 (1974): 1–43.

49 William Y. Adams, "The Nubian Archaeological Campaigns of 1959–1969: Myths and Realities, Successes and Failures," in *Seventh International Conference for Nubian Studies: Prepublication of Main Papers*, ed. Charles Bonnet (Geneva: University of Geneva, 1990), 1–37.

50 William Y. Adams, personal communication.

51 For a select bibliography of Adams prior to 1977, see Steffen Wenig, *Africa in Antiquity: The Arts of Ancient Nubia and the Sudan*, exh. cat., vol. 2 (Brooklyn: Brooklyn Museum, 1977), 333.

52 E.g., Nettie Adams, "Meroitic High Fashion: Examples from Art and Archaeology," in *Studia Meroitica 1984*, ed. Sergio Donadoni and Steffen Wenig, Meroitica 10 (Berlin: Akademie-Verlag, 1989), 747–55; idem, "Textiles from Qasr Ibrim," *Nyame Akuma* (Calgary: University of Calgary Press, 1981), and see n. 75; idem, "Late Medieval Textiles from Kulubnarti, Sudan. Pts. 1 and 2," *Archaeological Textiles Newsletter* 8, 9 (1989).

53 Helen Jacquet-Gordon, personal communication. See, e.g., Helen Jacquet-Gordon, "Tombs of the Tanqasi Culture at Tabo," *JARCE* 9 (1971–72): 77–83; idem, "Pnubs and the Temple of Tabo on Argo Island," *JEA* 55 (1969): 103–11; Charles Maystre, *Tabo I*, Mission archéologique de la Fondation Henry M. Blackmer et du Centre d'études orientales de l'Université de Genève 2 (Geneva: Georg, 1986).

54 Nicholas B. Millet and Allyn L. Kelley, eds., *Meroitic Studies: Proceedings of the Third International Meroitic Conference, Toronto, 1977*, Meroitica 6 (Berlin: Akademie-Verlag, 1982). For a select Nubian bibliography of both Trigger and Millet prior to 1977, see Wenig, *Africa in Antiquity*, vol. 2, 341, 344–45. See also, e.g., Bruce G. Trigger, "Reisner to Adams: Paradigms of Nubian Cultural History," in

Nubian Studies: Proceedings of the Society for Nubian Studies, Selwyn College, Cambridge, 1978, ed. J. Martin Plumley (Warminster, U.K.: Aris and Phillips, 1978), 223–26; idem, "History and Settlement in Lower Nubia in the Perspective of Fifteen Years," in *Meroitische Forschungen 1980*, ed. Fritz Hintze, Meroitica 7 (Berlin: Akademie-Verlag, 1984), 367–80; idem, "Land and Trade Patterns in Sudanese History," in *Studi di paleontologia in onore di Salvatore M. Puglisi*, ed. M. Liverani et al. (Rome: Università di Roma "La Sapienza," 1985), 465–75; Nicholas B. Millet, "Writing and Literacy in the Ancient Sudan," in *Studies in Ancient Languages of the Sudan*, ed. A. M. Abdalla (Khartoum: Khartoum University Press, 1975); "Social and Political Organization in Meroë," *ZÄS* 108 (1981): 124–41; idem, "Meroitic Religion," in *Meroitische Forschungen 1980*, 111–21.

55 See Krzystof A. Grzymski and Ronald Leprohon, eds., "Nubian Studies in Canada: Papers Presented to Peter L. Shinnie on His 75th Birthday," *JSSEA* 17 (January–April 1987), [vii]; N. David, "Peter Lewis Shinnie: An Appreciation," in *An African Commitment: Papers in Honor of Peter Lewis Shinnie*, ed. J. Sterner and N. David (Calgary: University of Calgary Press, 1992), xiii–xxxii.

56 Peter L. Shinnie and Rebecca J. Bradley, *The Capital of Kush*, vol. 1, *Meroë Excavations, 1965–1972*, Meroitica 4 (Berlin: Akademie-Verlag, 1980).

57 See, e.g., Krzystof A. Grzymski and J. R. Anderson, "Three Excavation Seasons at Hambukol (Dongola Reach): 1989, 1990, and 1991–92," *Archéologie du Nil moyen* 6 (1992).

58 Bernard V. Bothmer, personal communication.

59 Brooklyn Museum, *Africa in Antiquity: The Arts of Ancient Nubia and the Sudan*, exh. cat., 2 vols. (Brooklyn: Brooklyn Museum, 1978), with essays by William Y. Adams, Bruce G. Trigger, A. M. Ali Hakem, David O'Connor, Jean Leclant, Karl-Heinz Priese, and Fritz Hintze, and catalogue by Steffen Wenig.

60 Fritz Hintze, ed., *Africa in Antiquity: The Arts of Ancient Nubia and the Sudan, Proceedings of the Symposium Held in Conjunction with the Exhibition, Brooklyn, Sept. 29–Oct. 1, 1978*, Meroitica 5 (Berlin: Akademie-Verlag, 1979).

61 Bernard V. Bothmer, personal communication.

62 Bernard V. Bothmer and Dows Dunham, personal communication.

63 Bernard V. Bothmer, *Egyptian Sculpture of the Late Period, 700 B.C. to A.D. 100*, exh. cat. (Brooklyn: Brooklyn Museum, 1960); see Sherman E. Lee, "To John D. Cooney," preface in *Ancient Art: The Norbert Schimmel Collection*, ed. Oscar W. Muscarella (Mainz: Philipp von Zabern, 1974); idem, "In Honor of John D. Cooney," *BES* 5 (1983).

64 Dunham, *Recollections*, 39–44.

65 Edna R. Russmann, *The Representation of the King in the XXVth Dynasty*, Monographies reine Elisabeth 3 (Brussels: Fondation égyptologique reine Elisabeth; Brooklyn: Brooklyn Museum, 1974); idem, "Further Aspects of Kushite Art in Brooklyn," *Brooklyn Museum Journal* 11 (1969–70): 145–59; idem, "An Egyptian Royal Statuette of the Eighth Century B.C.," in Simpson and Davis, *Studies in Ancient Egypt*, 149–56; idem, "Harwa as Precursor of Mentuemhat," *Artibus Aegypti: Studia in Honorem Bernardi V. Bothmer, a Collegis, Amicis, Discipulis Conscripta*, ed. Herman De Meulenaere and Luc Limme (Brussels: Musées royaux d'art et d'histoire, 1983), 137–43; idem, "Relief Decoration in Theban Private Tombs of the 25th and 26th Dynasties" (Ph.D. diss., New York University, 1993).

66 Louis V. Zabkar, *Apedemak, Lion God of Meroë: A Study in Egyptian-Meroitic Syncretism* (Warminster, U.K.: Aris and Phillips, 1975).

67 Susan K. Doll, "Texts and Decoration on the Napatan Sarcophagi of Anlamani and Aspelta" (Ph.D. diss., Brandeis University, 1978); and Timothy Kendall, with Susan K. Doll, *Kush: Lost Kingdom of the Nile*, exh. cat. (Brockton, Mass.: Brockton Art Museum/Fuller Memorial, 1982).

68 E.g., Janice Yellin, "The Role of Anubis in Meroitic Religion," in *Nubian Studies*, 227–34; idem, "The Use of Abaton Style Milk Libations at Meroë," in *Meroitic Studies*, 151–55; idem, "The Iconography of an Astronomical Text from Begrawiya South," in *Meroitische Forschungen 1980*, 577–82; idem, "The Decorated Pyramid Chapels of Meroë and Meroitic Funerary Religion," in *Studia in Honorem F. Hintze*, Meroitica 12 (Berlin: Akademie-Verlag, 1991), 361–74.

69 Williams deals with Meroitic remains in *Excavations between Abu Simbel and the Sudan Frontier* (Chicago: University of Chicago Press): pt. 7, *Twenty-fifth Dynasty and Napatan Remains at Qustul: Cemeteries W and V*, OINE 7 (1990); and pt. 8, *Meroitic Remains from Qustul, Cemetery Q, Ballana, Cemetery B, and Ballana Settlement*, OINE 8 (1991).

70 E.g., Frank M. Snowden, Jr., *Blacks in Antiquity: Ethiopians in the Greco-Roman Experience* (Cambridge: Harvard University Press, 1970); idem, "Ethiopians and the Greco-Roman World," in *The African Diaspora: Interpretive Essays*, ed. R. I. Rotberg and M. L. Kilson (Cambridge: Harvard University Press, 1976), 11–36; idem, "Iconographical Evidence on the Black Populations in Greco-Roman Antiquity," in *The Image of the Black in Western Art*, vol. 1, *From the Pharaohs to the Fall of the Roman Empire*, by Jean Vercoutter et al. (Cambridge: Harvard University Press, 1976), 133–245; idem, *Before Color Prejudice: The Ancient View of Blacks* (Cambridge: Harvard University Press, 1983).

71 E.g., Stanley M. Burstein, "Herodotus and the Emergence of Meroë," *JSSEA* 11 (1981): 1–5; idem, "The Nubian Campaigns of C. Petronius and G. Reisner's Second Meroitic Kingdom of Napata," *ZÄS* 106 (1979): 95–105; idem, "Cornelius Gallus and Aethiopia," *The Ancient History Bulletin* 2 (1988); idem, "Axum and the Fall of Meroë," *JARCE* 18 (1981), 47–50; idem,

"The Hellenistic Fringe: The Case of Meroë," in *Hellenistic History and Culture*, ed. Peter Green (Berkeley: University of California Press, 1993), 38–54.

72 Anthony J. Spalinger, "The Year 712 B.C. and Its Importance for Egyptian History," *JARCE* 10 (1973): 95–101; idem, "Assurbanipal and Egypt: A Source Study," *Journal of the American Oriental Society* 94 (1974): 316–28; idem, "Esarhaddon and Egypt: An Analysis of the First Invasion of Egypt," *Orientalia* 43 (1974): 295–326; idem, "Psammetichus, King of Egypt," pts. 1, 2, *JARCE* 13, 15 (1976–78): 133–47, 49–57; idem, "The Military Background of the Campaign of Piye (Piankhy)," *SAK* 7 (1979): 273–301.

73 Kendall and Doll, *Kush*.

74 Timothy Kendall, *Gebel Barkal Epigraphic Survey, 1986: Preliminary Report on First Season's Activity* (Boston: MFA, 1986); idem, "Gebel Barkal Epigraphic Survey, 1987: Summary of Second Season's Activities of the Boston Museum of Fine Arts Sudan Mission," *Nubian Letters* 9 (1987): 7–10; idem, "Gebel Barkal Temples, Karima, Sudan, 1987 Season, Museum of Fine Arts, Boston," *Newsletter of the Institute of Art and Archaeology* (Memphis), (1988); idem, "Le Djebel Barkal: Le Karnak de Koush," in *La Nubie: L'archéologie au Soudan*, Histoire et archéologie 196 (Dijon: Archéologie, 1994), 46–53.

75 Boyce N. Driskell, Nettie Adams, and P. G. French, "A Newly Discovered Temple at Qasr Ibrim," *Archéologie du Nil moyen* 3 (1989): 11–54.

76 Report presented to the Seventh International Conference for Meroitic Studies by Ahmed A. M. Hakem, director, Sudan Antiquities Service, Berlin, 17 September 1992. See also Jacques Montluçon, "Une rapide aperçu de la region de la IVᵉ cataracte du Nil," in *La Nubie*, 70–71.

Archaeological and Research Expeditions to Egypt and Nubia

Sponsored by North American Institutions

American Museum of Natural History

Archaeological Research at Hierakonpolis (Nekhen)
1967–94
DIRECTORS: Walter A. Fairservis (1967–70, 1978–82); Michael A. Hoffman, University of South Carolina (1982–90); Jay Mills, University of South Carolina, and Walter A. Fairservis, Vassar College (1990–94)

American Research Center in Egypt

Gebel Adda
1962–66
DIRECTOR: Nicholas B. Millet

Catalog of the Luxor Museum Project
1973–76
DIRECTOR: Bernard V. Bothmer

Remains of a Temple of Tutankhamen and Ay, Karnak
1977–78, 1985–86
DIRECTOR: Otto Schaden

Isis Temple Project
1978
DIRECTOR: Mark Lehner

Sphinx Project
1980–84
DIRECTORS: James P. Allen and Mark Lehner

Archaeological Survey of the Southern Fayyum
1980–86
DIRECTORS: Mary Ellen Lane and Robert J. Wenke, University of Washington

Archaeological Survey of the Western Desert of Egypt
1982–83
DIRECTOR: Alan H. Simmons

Giza Plateau Mapping Project
1983–90
DIRECTOR: Mark Lehner
See also Oriental Institute, University of Chicago

Royal Mummies of the Egyptian Museum
1985, 1987, 1992
DIRECTORS: James E. Harris and Fawzia Hussein

Watetkhethor Copying Project
1986
DIRECTOR: Ann Macy Roth

Urban Archaeology Project
1989–90
DIRECTOR: Michael Jones

A Catalog of the Masterpieces of the Graeco-Roman Museum in Alexandria
1991–present
DIRECTOR: Robert S. Bianchi

Theban Tomb Publications Project
1992–present
DIRECTOR: Peter Piccione

American Schools of Oriental Research

Wadi Abu Had-Wadi Dib, Eastern Desert Project
1995–
DIRECTOR: Ann Bomann

American University in Cairo

Old Kingdom Mastabas in the Great Western Cemetery of Giza Necropolis
1972–74
DIRECTOR: Kent R. Weeks

Theban Mapping Project: To Prepare a New Archaeological Map of the Theban Necropolis
1989–present
DIRECTOR: Kent R. Weeks
See also University of California, Berkeley

Boston University

The Predynastic Site of Hu
1991
DIRECTOR: Kathryn Bard

Brigham Young University

Egypt Archaeology—Fayyum
1980–present
DIRECTOR: C. Wilfred Griggs

Brooklyn College

Taposiris Magna
1975–76
DIRECTOR: Edward Ochsenschlager

The Brooklyn Museum

Excavations between Esna and Edfu at el-Mamariya, el-Adaima, Kom el-Ahmar, el-Qara, and el-Kilabiya (East)
1906–7
DIRECTOR: Henri de Morgan

Excavations between Esna and Gebel el-Silsila at el-Mamariya, el-Adaima, Kom el-Ahmar, Abu Zaidan, el-Masaid, and el-Sibaiya (East)
1907–8
DIRECTOR: Henri de Morgan

Expedition to the Precinct of the Goddess Mut (South Karnak)
1976–79
FIELD DIRECTOR: Richard A. Fazzini
1980–present (in association with the Detroit Institute of Arts)
PROJECT DIRECTOR AND CO–FIELD DIRECTOR: Richard A. Fazzini
CO–FIELD DIRECTOR: William H. Peck, Detroit Institute of Arts

The Brooklyn Museum Theban Expedition (Mut Expedition and Theban Royal Tomb Project)
1977–79
PROJECT DIRECTORS: Richard A. Fazzini and James B. Manning
FIELD DIRECTOR: John Romer

Beni Hasan Photographic Project
1994–present
DIRECTOR: Donald B. Spanel

Brown University
Hibis Temple, Kharga Oasis
1985–86
DIRECTOR: Eugene Cruz-Uribe

The Canadian Museum of Civilization (The National Museum of Man)
Canadian Prehistoric Expedition to Nubia at Kom Ombo
1962–63
DIRECTOR: Philip E. L. Smith

Claremont Graduate School (Institute for Antiquity and Christianity)
Excavations at Gebel el-Tarif
1975
DIRECTOR: James M. Robinson
ARCHAEOLOGICAL DIRECTOR: Torgny Säve-Söderbergh, University of Uppsala

Columbia University
Nubian Expedition in Sudan
1961–62
DIRECTORS: Rhodes W. Fairbridge and Ralph S. Solecki

Cranbrook Institute of Science
Prehistoric Egyptian Socioeconomic Structure Project
1987–89
DIRECTORS: Richard Redding and Robert J. Wenke, University of Washington

Detroit Institute of Arts
Expedition to the Precinct of the Goddess Mut (South Karnak)
See The Brooklyn Museum

Egypt Exploration Society/ Brown University
Epigraphic Recording at Semna East (Kumma) and Semna West
1962–64
DIRECTOR: Ricardo Caminos

Getty Conservation Institute/ Egyptian Antiquities Organization
Conservation of Wall Paintings of the Tomb of Nefertari
1986–92
DIRECTOR: Luis Monreal and Miguel Angel Corzo
FIELD DIRECTORS: Paolo Mora and Laura Mora

Harvard University
(*see also* Museum of Fine Arts, Boston)
Excavations at Marsa Matruh
1913–14, 1915
DIRECTOR: Oric Bates

Excavations at Gamai
1915
DIRECTORS: Oric Bates and Dows Dunham

Excavations at Serabit el-Khadem (Sinai)
1927, 1930
DIRECTOR: Kirsopp Lake

The Johns Hopkins University
First Cataract Epigraphic Survey
1964, 1967
DIRECTOR: Hans Goedicke

Excavations at Giza
1972, 1974
PROJECT DIRECTOR: Hans Goedicke

Tell el-Rataba Survey
1977–80
DIRECTOR: Hans Goedicke

The Johns Hopkins University Expedition to Thebes
1993–present
DIRECTOR: Betsy M. Bryan

The Metropolitan Museum of Art
Excavations at Lisht
1906–9, 1912–14, 1916–18, 1920–25, 1931–34
DIRECTORS: Albert M. Lythgoe, Arthur C. Mace, and Ambrose Lansing

Excavations at el-Kharga Oasis
1907–13, 1924–31
DIRECTORS: Albert M. Lythgoe, Herbert E. Winlock, H. G. Evelyn White, and Walter Hauser

Graphic Section of the Museum's Egyptian Expedition
1907–17, 1919–37 (Thebes, el-Kharga Oasis, Beni Hasan, Amarna, Maidum, Lisht, Wadi Natrun)
DIRECTOR: Norman de Garis Davies

Excavations at Wadi Natrun
1909–11, 1919–21
DIRECTORS: Walter J. Palmer-Jones and H. G. Evelyn White

Excavations at Thebes
1910–31, 1934–36
DIRECTORS: Herbert E. Winlock, Ambrose Lansing, and Arthur C. Mace

Excavations at Hierakonpolis
1934–35
DIRECTOR: Ambrose Lansing

Memphis
1971
DIRECTORS: Christine Lilyquist and Donald P. Hansen, New York University

Senenmut Tombs Project
1981–87
DIRECTOR: Peter F. Dorman

Lisht Project
1984–89, 1991–present
DIRECTOR: Dieter Arnold

Tomb of the Three Wives of Thutmosis III Project
1988–89
DIRECTOR: Christine Lilyquist

Excavations at Dahshur (Senwosret III)
1990–present
DIRECTOR: Dieter Arnold

**Museum of Fine Arts, Boston/
Harvard University**

Excavations at Giza
1905–10, 1912–16, 1923–37
DIRECTOR: George A. Reisner

Archeological Survey of Nubia
1906–11
DIRECTORS: George A. Reisner
(1906–8) and Cecil Firth
(1908–11)

Excavations at Zawiyet el-Aryan
1910–11
DIRECTOR: George A. Reisner

Excavations at Mesa'eed
1910, 1913
DIRECTOR: George A. Reisner

Excavations at Mesheikh
1912
DIRECTOR: George A. Reisner

Excavations at Naga el-Deir
1912, 1923–24
DIRECTOR: George A. Reisner

Excavations at Naga el-Hai
1913
DIRECTOR: George A. Reisner

Excavations at Kerma
1913–16
DIRECTOR: George A. Reisner

Excavations at Sheikh Farag
1913, 1923–24
DIRECTOR: George A. Reisner

Excavations at Deir el-Bersha
1915
DIRECTOR: George A. Reisner

*Excavations at Gebel Barkal
(el-Kurru)*
1916, 1918–20
DIRECTOR: George A. Reisner

Excavations at Nuri
1916–18, 1920
DIRECTOR: George A. Reisner

*Excavations at Begrawiya
(Meroe)*
1920–23
DIRECTOR: George A. Reisner

Excavations at Coptos
1923
DIRECTOR: George A. Reisner

Excavations at Kafr Ghattati
1924
DIRECTOR: George A. Reisner

Excavations at Kumma
1924
DIRECTOR: George A. Reisner

Excavations at Semna
1924, 1927–28
DIRECTOR: George A. Reisner

Excavations at Uronarti
1924, 1928–30
DIRECTOR: George A. Reisner

Excavations at Shalfak
1931
DIRECTOR: George A. Reisner

Excavations at Mirgissa
1931–32
DIRECTOR: George A. Reisner

Museum of Fine Arts, Boston

*Yale University/Museum of
Fine Arts, Boston, Giza Pyramids
Mastabas Project*
1970–present
DIRECTORS: Edward Brovarski
and William Kelly Simpson,
Yale University

*University of Pennsylvania
Museum/Yale University/
Museum of Fine Arts Giza
Mastabas Project*
1972–75, 1977, 1981–82
DIRECTOR: William Kelly Simpson

Deir el-Ballas Project
1980, 1982–83, 1985, 1986
DIRECTOR: Peter Lacovara

Excavations at Gebel Barkal
1986–89
DIRECTOR: Timothy Kendall

*Giza Pyramids Mastabas Project
(Western Cemetery)*
1989–90, 1994
DIRECTOR: Ann Macy Roth

*Museum of Fine Arts, Boston/
University of Pennsylvania
Museum/State University of
Leiden Expedition to Bersheh*
1989–present
DIRECTORS: Edward Brovarski,
Rita E. Freed, and David Silver-
man, University of Pennsylvania
Museum

Giza Mastabas Project
1993–present
DIRECTOR: Peter Der Manuelian

*Museum of Fine Arts, Boston/
University of Pennsylvania
Museum Expedition to Sakkara*
1993–present
DIRECTORS: Edward Brovarski,
Rita Freed, and David Silver-
man, University of Pennsylvania
Museum

New York University

Excavations at Mendes
1964–66, 1976–80
DIRECTOR: Bernard V. Bothmer
FIELD DIRECTORS: Donald P.
Hansen (1964–78) and Karen L.
Wilson (1979–80)

Memphis
1971
DIRECTORS: Donald P. Hansen
and Christine Lilyquist,
Metropolitan Museum of Art

Embalming House of the Apis Bulls
1982–88
DIRECTORS: John Dimick and
Bernard V. Bothmer
FIELD DIRECTORS: Michael Jones
and Angela Milward Jones

Northern Arizona University

Hibis Temple Project
1984–86, 1988, 1990, 1992–93,
1995
DIRECTOR: Eugene Cruz-Uribe

**The Oriental Institute,
University of Chicago**

*Epigraphic Survey of the
Oriental Institute of the
University of Chicago, Luxor*
1924–present
FIELD DIRECTORS:
Harold H. Nelson (1924–47),
Richard Parker (1948–49),
George Hughes (1949–58),
John A. Wilson (acting, 1958–59),
George Hughes (1959–64),
Charles Nims (1964–72),
Edward Wente (1972–73),
Kent R. Weeks (1973–76),
Charles Van Siclen, III
(acting, 1976–77),
Lanny Bell (1977–89), and
Peter F. Dorman (1989–present)

*Architectural Survey of the
Oriental Institute of the
University of Chicago, Luxor*
1926–32
FIELD DIRECTOR: Uvo Hölscher

*Prehistoric Survey in Egypt and
the Sudan*
1926–38
DIRECTORS: Kenneth S. Sandford
(1926–38) and William J. Arkell
(1926–30)

*Sakkarah Expedition
(Mastaba of Mereruka)*
1930–36
FIELD DIRECTOR: Prentice Duell

*Excavations at Qasr el-Wizz,
Serra East, and the Qustul-
Adindan Area*
1961–64
DIRECTORS: George Hughes
(1961), Herbert Ricke (1961),
and Keith C. Seele (1962–64)

*Excavations of Serra East and
Dorgainarti*
1963–64
DIRECTOR: James Knudstad

Qasr el-Wizz
1965
DIRECTOR: George T. Scanlon

Quseir el-Qadim Project
1978–86
DIRECTORS: Donald S.
Whitcomb (1978–86) and Janet
H. Johnson (1985–86)

Giza Plateau Mapping Project
1990–present
DIRECTOR: Mark Lehner
See also American Research
Center in Egypt

Bir Umm Fawakhir Survey Project
1991–present
DIRECTOR: Carol Meyer

*Luxor-Farshut Desert Road
Survey*
1992–present
FIELD DIRECTOR: John Darnell

Pacific Lutheran University
Valley of the Kings Project
1989, 1990, 1991
DIRECTOR: Donald Ryan

*Valley of the Kings
Preservation Project*
1993
DIRECTOR: Donald Ryan

**Royal Ontario Museum/
The Society for the Study of
Egyptian Antiquities**
*Royal Ontario Museum Survey
Expedition to Dongola Reach*
1976–86
DIRECTORS: Nicholas B. Millet
(1976–82) and Krzysztof
Grzymski (1984–86)

*Dakhleh Oasis Project:
An Archaeological Study*
1978–83, 1988–present
DIRECTOR: Anthony Mills

*Royal Ontario Museum
Expedition to Illahun*
1988–present
DIRECTOR: Nicholas B. Millet

Southern Methodist University
Initial Survey of West Bank
1962
DIRECTOR: Fred Wendorf

Excavation at Ballana and Tushka
1963–65
DIRECTOR: Fred Wendorf

Excavations at Wadi Tushka
1966
DIRECTOR: Fred Wendorf

Survey of Aswan-Dishna Area
1967
DIRECTOR: Fred Wendorf

Survey of Dendera-Luxor Area
1968
DIRECTOR: Fred Wendorf

*Excavations at Dishna and
Mucadema*
1968
DIRECTOR: Fred Wendorf

Excavations at Fayyum
1969
DIRECTOR: Fred Wendorf

*Excavations at Bir Sahara and
Bir Tarfawi*
1972–74, 1985–89
DIRECTOR: Fred Wendorf

*Combined Prehistoric
Expedition*
1972–74, 1986–present
DIRECTOR: Fred Wendorf

Excavations at Nabta
1975, 1977
DIRECTOR: Fred Wendorf

Excavations at Kharga Qasim
1976
DIRECTOR: Fred Wendorf

Excavations at Wadi Kubbaniya
1978, 1981–84
DIRECTOR: Fred Wendorf

*Excavations at Bir Kiseiba and
Bir Eyde Areas*
1979, 1980
DIRECTOR: Fred Wendorf

*Excavations at Nabta Playa
and Isna Areas*
1990–94
DIRECTOR: Fred Wendorf

**Southwest Missouri State
University**
*Archaeological Investigation of
Pastoral Nomadism in Egypt*
1982–86

Eastern Desert Project
1983–84, 1989
DIRECTOR: Juris Zarins

**State University of New York at
Binghamton/The Society for
the Study of Egyptian Antiquities**
*Chapel of Osiris Heqa-Djet
Project*
1971–72
CODIRECTORS: Gerald Kadish,
Donald B. Redford

Texas A & M University
*Institute of Nautical Archaeology
Red Sea Expedition*
1994–present
DIRECTORS: Cheryl Haldane and
Douglas Haldane

*The Underwater Archaeological
Survey between Sidi Abd
al-Rahman and Ras Hawala*
1995–
DIRECTOR: Douglas Haldane

University of Arizona
Western Valley of the Kings Project
1990–93
FIELD DIRECTOR: Otto Schaden

Amenmesse Project (KV–10)
1992–94
FIELD DIRECTOR: Otto Schaden

Valley of the Kings Motif Alignment Project
1992–present
FIELD DIRECTOR: Richard Wilkinson

University of California, Berkeley

Excavations near Coptos and Surafa
1899–1900
DIRECTOR: George A. Reisner

Expedition to Tebtunis
1899–1900
DIRECTORS: Bernard P. Grenfell and Arthur S. Hunt

Excavations at el-Ahaiwah
1900
DIRECTOR: George A. Reisner

Excavations at Deir el-Ballas
1900–1901
DIRECTOR: George A. Reisner

Excavations at Naga el-Deir
1901–4
DIRECTOR: George A. Reisner

Excavations at Giza
1903–5
DIRECTOR: George A. Reisner

Sociological Analysis of Village at Deir el-Medina
1975–76
DIRECTOR: Cathleen A. Keller

Theban Mapping Project: To Prepare a New Archaeological Map of the Theban Necropolis
1980–88
DIRECTOR: Kent R. Weeks
See also The American University in Cairo

Seila (Faiyum) Project
1981
DIRECTOR: Leonard Lesko

Craftsmen of Deir el-Medina Project
1986–88
DIRECTOR: Cathleen A. Keller

Tell el-Muqdam Leontopolis Project
1992–present
DIRECTORS: Carol Redmount and Renee Friedman

University of California, Los Angeles

Excavations at Askut
1962–64
DIRECTOR: Alexander Badawy

Excavations at Dabinarti
1963–64
DIRECTOR: Jay Ruby

UCLA Expedition to Giza: Tombs of Iteti, Sekhemankhptah, and Kaemnofert
1973
DIRECTOR: Alexander Badawy

UCLA Expedition to Giza and Saqqara: Tombs of Nyhetepptah and Ankhmahor
1974
DIRECTOR: Alexander Badawy

UCLA Expedition to Saqqara: Tomb of Kagemni
1975–78
DIRECTOR: Alexander Badawy

UCLA Expedition to Saqqara: Tombs of Meriteti and Watetkhethor
1978–79
DIRECTOR: Alexander Badawy

UCLA/Christ College Cambridge Theban Tombs Expedition (TT 253, 254, 294)
1988
DIRECTOR: Nigel P. Strudwick

UCLA/Universität Göttingen Ma'abda Project
1990
DIRECTORS: Antonio Loprieno and Ursula Rößler Köller, Universität Göttingen

UCLA/Deutsches Archäologisches Institut Dra' Abu el-Naga Project
1994–present
DIRECTOR: Daniel C. Polz
FIELD DIRECTOR: Stuart T. Smith

University of Chicago
(*see also* The Oriental Institute, University of Chicago)
Photographic Survey of Nubia (Aswan to Meroe)
1905–7
DIRECTOR: James H. Breasted

University of Colorado
Nubian Expedition
1962–66
DIRECTORS: Gordon W. Hewes (1962–63, 1964–66), Joe Ben Wheat, and Henry Irwin (1963–64)

University of Delaware
Red Sea Roman Ports Survey
1984–85
DIRECTOR: Steven E. Sidebotham

Red Sea Project, Myos Hormos Project
1986–88
DIRECTOR: Steven E. Sidebotham

Abu Sha'ar Roman/Byzantine Fort Red Sea Project
1988–present
DIRECTOR: Steven E. Sidebotham

Excavations at Bernice on the Red Sea Coast (in conjunction with Leiden University)
1994
DIRECTOR: Steven E. Sidebotham

University of Illinois
Wadi Feiran Project
1982–86
DIRECTOR: James L. Phillips

Ecological Survey of the Egyptian Eastern Desert
1987–89
DIRECTORS: Douglas Brewer and Steven Goodman, University of Michigan

Early Pharaonic Socioeconomic Structure of the Nile Delta
1989–94
DIRECTORS: Douglas J. Brewer and Robert J. Wenke, University of Washington

University of Kentucky
Egypt Exploration Society Archaeological Investigations at Qasr Ibrim
1972, 1974, 1976, 1978, 1980, 1982, 1984
DIRECTOR: William Y. Adams

University of Memphis (Memphis State University)
Amarna Project
1983–86
DIRECTORS: William Murnane and Charles Van Siclen, III

Amarna Boundary Stele Project
1988–91
DIRECTORS: William Murnane
and Charles Van Siclen, III

*Great Hypostyle Hall Project
Joint Centre franco-égyptien
d'étude des temples de Karnak
and the Institute of Egyptian Art
and Archaeology, University of
Memphis*
1991–present
DIRECTOR: William Murnane

University of Miami
*Trans-Sinai Roman Road
Between Clysma (Suez) and
Aqaba*
1992–94
DIRECTOR: David F. Graf

**University of Michigan,
Ann Arbor**
*Excavations at Karanis
(Kom Aushim)*
1924–35
DIRECTORS: J. L. Starkey
(1924–26) and Enoch E.
Peterson (1926–35)

*Excavations at Dimai
(Soknopaiou Nesos)*
1931–32
DIRECTOR: Arthur E. R. Boak

*Excavations at Terenouthis
(Kom Abu Billo)*
1934–35
DIRECTOR: Enoch E. Peterson

*Cemetery Populations of Gebel
Adda*
1965
DIRECTOR: James E. Harris

*Royal Mummies of the Egyptian
Museum*
1966–68, 1970–71, 1982–83,
1985, 1987, 1992
DIRECTOR: James E. Harris

*Skeletal Material from Giza
Necropolis*
1968
DIRECTOR: James E. Harris

*Mummies of the Nobles in the
Valley of the Kings*
1970
DIRECTOR: James E. Harris

*Mummies in the Tomb of
Amenhotep II*
1974
DIRECTOR: James E. Harris

*Mummies of the Old Kingdom
Nobles at Aswan*
1974
DIRECTOR: James E. Harris

Mummy of Tutankhamun
1978
DIRECTOR: James E. Harris

*Greek-Roman Mummies of the
Alexandria Museum*
1982–83
DIRECTOR: James E. Harris

*Ecological Survey of the
Egyptian Eastern Desert*
1987–89
DIRECTORS: Steven Goodman
and Douglas Brewer, University
of Illinois at Champaign-Urbana

*University of Michigan/
University of Asyut Joint Project
at Coptos and the Eastern Desert*
1989–94
DIRECTORS: Sharon Herbert and
Henry Wright

University of Minnesota
Western Valley of the Kings Project
1972
DIRECTOR: Otto Schaden
See also University of Arizona

Excavations at Akhmim
1980–1983
DIRECTOR: Sheila McNally

Naukratis Project
1980–86
DIRECTORS: William D. E.
Coulson and Albert Leonard Jr.

**University of Pennsylvania
Museum of Archaeology and
Anthropology**
*Excavations at Areika, Aniba,
Karanog, Shablul, and Buhen*
1907–11
DIRECTOR: David Randall-
MacIver

Excavations at Giza
1915
DIRECTOR: Clarence S. Fisher

Excavations at Dendera
1915–18
DIRECTOR: Clarence S. Fisher

Excavations at Memphis
1915–19, 1921–23
DIRECTOR: Clarence S. Fisher

*Excavations at Dra Abu
el-Naga, Thebes*
1921–23
DIRECTOR: Clarence S. Fisher

Excavations at Maidum
1929–32
DIRECTOR: Alan Rowe

*University of Pennsylvania
Museum/Egyptian Antiquities
Organization Excavations at
Memphis*
1955, 1956
DIRECTOR: Rudolf Anthes

*University of Pennsylvania
Museum/Yale University
Expedition to Nubia*
1960–63
DIRECTOR: William Kelly
Simpson, Yale University

Expedition to Dra Abu el-Naga
1967
DIRECTOR: Lanny Bell

*University of Pennsylvania
Museum/Yale University Abydos
Expedition*
1967–present
DIRECTORS: David O'Connor
and William Kelly Simpson,
Yale University
FIELD DIRECTORS: David Silver-
man (1978, Ramesses II Portal
Epigraphy), Janet Richards
(1986, Abydos North Cemetery
Project), Matthew Adams (1991,
Abydos Settlement Site: Kom el-
Sultan), Stephen Harvey (1993,
Ahmose Complex Project) and
Josef Wegner (1994, Senwosret
III Mortuary Temple)

Museum Excavations at Malqata
1971–77
DIRECTORS: David O'Connor
and Barry Kemp, Cambridge
University

*University of Pennsylvania/Yale
University/Museum of Fine Arts,
Boston, Giza Mastabas Project*
1972–75, 1977, 1981–82
DIRECTOR: William Kelly Simpson

Archaeological Survey of Abydos
1982–86
DIRECTOR: David O'Connor
FIELD DIRECTOR: Diana Craig
Patch (1982–83)

*The University of Pennsylvania
Late Bronze Age Project at
Marsa Matruh*
1985–90, 1995–96
DIRECTOR: Donald White

*Archaeological Survey of Marsa
Matruh (Western Egypt)*
1986–93
DIRECTOR: Donald White

*Agricultural Scenes in the
Private Tombs at Thebes*
1989–90
DIRECTOR: Patricia A. Bochi

*Museum of Fine Arts,
Boston/University of Pennsylvania Museum/State University of
Leiden Expedition to Bersheh*
1989–92
DIRECTORS: David Silverman;
Edward Brovarski, Museum of
Fine Arts, Boston; Rita E. Freed,
Museum of Fine Arts, Boston;
and Harco Willems, State University of Leiden

*Museum of Fine Arts, Boston/
University of Pennsylvania
Museum Expedition to Sakkara*
1993–94
DIRECTORS: David Silverman;
Edward Brovarski, Museum of
Fine Arts, Boston; and Rita Freed,
Museum of Fine Arts, Boston

See also University of Toronto

University of South Carolina
*Archaeological Research at
Hierakonpolis (Nekhen)*
1994–present
DIRECTOR: Jay Mills
See also American Museum of
Natural History

Excavations at HK64
1986–94
DIRECTOR: Renee Friedman

University of Toledo
*Topographical and Petrological
Survey of Ancient Egyptian
Quarries*
1989–present
DIRECTOR: James A. Harrell

University of Toronto
*University of Toronto/University
of Pennsylvania Akhenaten
Temple Project*
1965–present
DIRECTORS: Ray Winfield Smith
(1965–71) and Donald B.
Redford (1972–present)

*The Akhenaten Temple Project
(Field Operations)*
1976–present
DIRECTOR: Donald B. Redford

East Karnak Excavations
1976–present
FIELD DIRECTOR: Donald B.
Redford

Wadi Tumilat Project
1978–85
DIRECTOR: John Holladay

Epigraphic Tomb Survey
1988–present
FIELD DIRECTOR: Susan Redford

*Mendes Expedition
(Tell el-Rub'a)*
1990–present
FIELD DIRECTOR: Donald B.
Redford

*Tel Kedwa Excavations (Joint
Sinai Expedition with the Egyptian Antiquities Organization)*
1993–present
DIRECTOR: Donald B. Redford

University of Washington
Old Kingdom Delta Project
1984–88
DIRECTORS: Robert J. Wenke
and Richard Redding

Prehistoric Egyptian Socioeconomic Structure Project
1987–89
DIRECTORS: Robert J. Wenke
and Richard Redding, Cranbrook Institute of Science

*Early Pharaonic Socioeconomic
Structure of the Nile Delta*
1989–present
DIRECTORS: Robert J. Wenke;
Douglas J. Brewer, University of
Illinois at Champaign; and
Donald B. Redford, University
of Toronto

Mendes Archaeological Project
1989–present
DIRECTORS: Robert J. Wenke
and Douglas Brewer

Vassar College
*Archaeological Research at
Hierakonpolis (Nekhen)*
1990–94
DIRECTOR: Walter A. Fairservis
See also American Museum of
Natural History

Yale University
*University of Pennsylvania
Museum/Yale University
Expedition to Nubia*
1960–63
DIRECTOR: William Kelly Simpson

*Yale University Prehistoric
Expedition to Egypt and Nubia*
1962–64
DIRECTOR: Charles Reed

*University of Pennsylvania
Museum/Yale University
Abydos Expedition*
See University of Pennsylvania
Museum of Archaeology and
Anthropology

*University of Pennsylvania/Yale
University/Museum of Fine Arts,
Boston, Giza Mastabas Project*
See University of Pennsylvania
Museum of Archaeology and
Anthropology

*Yale University/Museum of
Fine Arts, Boston, Giza
Pyramids Mastabas Project*
See Museum of Fine Arts,
Boston

Index

Photo Credits

Unless an acknowledgment appears below, the photographs in this volume have been provided by their owners or by the Los Angeles County Museum of Art. We are grateful to all those who supplied photographs for this book.

The Akhenaten Temple Project: fig. 80.
Peter Brenner, Los Angeles County Museum of Art: figs. 56, 62–63, 68; p. 176.
The Brooklyn Museum: figs. 81–82, 84–86, 88–89.
Edward Brovarski: fig. 19.
Anne Gauldin, Gauldin/Farrington Design: pp. 10–11; figs. 11, 26, 52.
The Hierakonpolis Project: fig. 8.
Gerald E. Kadish: fig. 79.
The Kelsey Museum Archives: figs. 87, 90, 92.
Timothy Kendall: fig. 109.
Mark Lehner: figs. 20–21, 91.
The Metropolitan Museum of Art: figs. 29–30, 34–35, 38, 49–50, 67, 83, 93, 100–101.
The Metropolitan Museum of Art, Egyptian Exhibition: figs. 33, 36-37, 39–48, 55.
The Oriental Institute of the University of Chicago: cover, title page, figs. 7, 23, 25, 27–28, 64–66, 69–70, 75, 78, 103, 108.

The Oriental Institute of the University of Chicago, Epigraphic Survey: figs. 71–74.
Museum of Fine Arts, Boston: figs. 6, 10, 12, 14, 22, 32, 60, 94, 96–99, 102, 104-7, 110; pp. 168, 188.
Private collection: fig. 76.
John G. Ross: p. 2, fig. 77.
The University of Pennsylvania Museum, Philadelphia: figs. 51 (neg.# G6-33944), 57–59, 61 (neg# S4-140198), 95 (neg#: S4-141695).
Kent R. Weeks: figs. 53–54.
Fred Wendorf, Southern Methodist University: figs. 1, 5.

ABOVE "Reserve heads" excavated from 4th Dynasty tombs at Giza by the Museum of Fine Arts, Boston–Harvard University Expedition, photographed on December 17, 1913.

EDITORS
Suzanne Kotz and Karen Jacobson

DESIGNER
Pamela Patrusky

PHOTOGRAPHIC SUPERVISION
Peter Brenner

PRODUCTION ASSISTANCE
Theresa Velázquez

MAPS
Anne Gauldin,
Gauldin/Farrington Design